Foundations of Educational Research

ALSO AVAILABLE FROM BLOOMSBURY

Educational Research, *Gert Biesta*
Building Research Design in Education, edited by *Lorna Hamilton and John Ravenscroft*
Philosophy of Educational Research, *Richard Pring*
Narrative Inquiry, *Vera Caine, D. Jean Clandinin and Sean Lessard*
Research Methods for Early Childhood Education, *Rosie Flewitt and Lynn Ang*
Research Methods for Educational Dialogue, *Ruth Kershner, Sara Hennessy, Rupert Wegerif and Ayesha Ahmed*
Research Methods for Classroom Discourse, *Jenni Ingram and Victoria Elliott*
Research Methods for Social Justice and Equity in Education, *Liz Atkins and Vicky Duckworth*
Higher Education Research, *Malcolm Tight*
Educational Research, *Jerry Wellington*

Foundations of Educational Research

Victoria Elliott

BLOOMSBURY ACADEMIC
LONDON • NEW YORK • OXFORD • NEW DELHI • SYDNEY

BLOOMSBURY ACADEMIC
Bloomsbury Publishing Plc
50 Bedford Square, London, WC1B 3DP, UK
1385 Broadway, New York, NY 10018, USA
29 Earlsfort Terrace, Dublin 2, Ireland

BLOOMSBURY, BLOOMSBURY ACADEMIC and the Diana logo are trademarks of Bloomsbury Publishing Plc

First published in Great Britain 2023

Copyright © Victoria Elliott, 2023

Victoria Elliott has asserted her right under the Copyright, Designs and Patents Act, 1988, to be identified as Author of this work.

For legal purposes the Acknowledgements on p. ix constitute an extension of this copyright page.

Cover design: Toby Way
Cover image © Getty Images / Yevgen Romanenko

All rights reserved. No part of this publication may be reproduced or transmitted in any form or by any means, electronic or mechanical, including photocopying, recording, or any information storage or retrieval system, without prior permission in writing from the publishers.

Bloomsbury Publishing Plc does not have any control over, or responsibility for, any third-party websites referred to or in this book. All internet addresses given in this book were correct at the time of going to press. The author and publisher regret any inconvenience caused if addresses have changed or sites have ceased to exist, but can accept no responsibility for any such changes.

A catalogue record for this book is available from the British Library.

A catalog record for this book is available from the Library of Congress.

ISBN: HB: 978-1-3501-6117-7
PB: 978-1-3501-6116-0
ePDF: 978-1-3501-6118-4
eBook: 978-1-3501-6119-1

Typeset by Newgen KnowledgeWorks Pvt. Ltd., Chennai, India

To find out more about our authors and books visit www.bloomsbury.com and sign up for our newsletters.

Contents

List of Theorist Textboxes vii
Acknowledgements ix

1 **Outlining the Field** 1

2 **Ontology and Epistemology** 13

3 **Fundamental Concepts of Design** 31

4 **What Counts as Evidence?** 53

5 **Theory as the Beginning and End of Research** 69

6 **The Body of the Researcher** 87

7 **Data Analysis** 103

8 **Research as an Ethical Practice** 121

9 **Research as a Political Practice** 143

References 161
Index 185

Theorist Textboxes

1.1 John Dewey 10

2.1 W. E. B. Du Bois 20

2.2 Antonio Gramsci 28

3.1 Jean Piaget 39

3.2 Lev Vygotsky 44

3.3 B. F. Skinner 50

4.1 Abraham Maslow 58

4.2 Jerome Bruner 66

5.1 Urie Bronfenbrenner 75

5.2 Paulo Freire 80

5.3 Frantz Fanon 85

6.1 Michel Foucault 98

6.2 Pierre Bourdieu 101

7.1 Jean Lave and Etienne Wenger 108

7.2 Gayatri Chakravorty Spivak 113

7.3 Howard Gardner 119

8.1 Linda Tuhiwai Smith 129

8.2 bell hooks 142

9.1 Judith Butler 147

9.2 Kimberlé Williams Crenshaw 154

Acknowledgements

This book has been formed over a long period of time working with students and colleagues at the Department of Education, as Director of Doctoral Research, as a lecturer on the *Foundations of Educational Research* module and as convenor of the Qualitative Methods Hub and the Race and Education reading group. David Mills and Sarah-Jane Cooper-Knock both introduced me to important theorists to whom I have referred in these pages. I am indebted to conversations with my students Jessy McCabe and Lesley Nelson-Addy which provoked thinking about points I have raised in the book. I am very grateful for the unending supportiveness of Nicole Dingwall, Susan James Relly and Ashmita Randhawa.

I need to acknowledge an intellectual debt to the many many people with whom I interact on Twitter and who are generous with their knowledge and time. I am indebted to a point made on Twitter by Kirsty Rolfe which led to Ruth Harley introducing us to Karen Guth's article on moral injury and expanding my thoughts on citational politics, and I am grateful for many interactions with Zara Bain which have expanded my knowledge of the world and particularly of disability and philosophy which have filtered into various thoughts in this book. I am also grateful for some discussions between Darren Chetty and Guilaine Kinouani, which led me to some useful sources on standpoint epistemology; and a timely tweet from Kelly Wickham Hurst that reminded me to give the Blackfeet Nation the credit that Maslow did not.

I am very grateful to those who have kindly read pieces of this, including Nicole Dingwall, Mohan Ganesalingam, Beth Borne, Jenni Ingram and Jonah Stewart (to whom I am particularly grateful for introducing me to Dan-el Padilla Peralta's term 'smash and grab citation'). All mistakes remain my own.

It turns out that writing a book during a pandemic with two small children is not an ideal working practice. I am extremely grateful, as always, to my husband Chris who looked after me, Harry and George while I wrote this.

This book is for Lila and Stephanie, my original *Foundations of Educational Research* course-mates. It is also for Professor Ingrid Lunt, without whom I would not be where I am today.

1

Outlining the Field

Truth rests with God; for us remains research.
Translated inscription from Whitley Stokes's memorial cross
in Sutton graveyard, North Dublin

Educational research is a broad field in which we can find studies from applied linguistics to pedagogy, from child development to higher education, from international and comparative education to learning and technology. It brings together researchers from disciplinary backgrounds as varied as psychology, sociology, anthropology, economics, history, linguistics and psychometrics. This book provides an introduction to the foundations of this broad field. It is not a methodology book. Rather, what it does is provide an introduction to what you need to know to flourish as a consumer, reader and beginning producer of educational research. Throughout the book you will find textboxes on different theorists and their theories that are utilized in education research. These are the people that you might not ever meet explicitly in a lecture but whose work and names you might be assumed to know, or will come across in passing references. When you have read the book you will know the principles on which you should be judging research, and you will have enough broad knowledge of the field to be able to make informed choices about where and what you want to research, if research is your aim. The range of references does not only include the historical foundations of the field but also the emerging twenty-first-century contexts and concerns of educational research.

We begin in the next chapter with the underlying questions of ontology and epistemology, reflecting on how our own backgrounds inform our ontological and epistemological beliefs. Then the book moves on to research design and the essential concepts that need to be taken into consideration, as well as outlining some of the dominant designs in the field. In Chapter 4 we consider further the epistemological question of evidence and what ways of demonstrating claims are accepted and why. Chapter 5 returns us to theory and its role in the process of educational research, as a foundation, a tool and an outcome of the process. Then we turn to the role of the researcher themselves in the process and how the embodied person affects data. In Chapter 7 we explore principles of design analysis, before considering research as an ethical process (Chapter 8) and research as a political process (Chapter 9). Rather than espousing a particular approach, the book explores concepts in terms of how they play out in different types of research, whether that variation is by name or by application. Throughout the book real-life research examples are drawn on, with reference to the many different branches of educational research, taken from all over the world, and considering many different methodologies and contexts.

First though, this chapter will outline the current state of the field in educational research, moving from classic studies, such as the behaviourist approaches of Skinner, to current movements, such as the Global Educational Reform Movement, evidence-based practice and control via educational metrics. It will also consider the status of educational research as a discipline – or not.

What Makes Up Education?

It is inevitably hard to trace the absolute beginning of anything, but a beginning could be said to be the publication of *Education as a Science* (1879) by Alexander Bain, professor of logic at Aberdeen University and a polymath who produced works in philosophy, linguistics and psychology. In the United States the origin of the discipline is often traced to Joseph Mayer Rice, who published a number of articles in *The Forum*, a monthly magazine, on educational topics. He conducted one of the earliest large-scale educational studies, carrying out a sixteen-month survey of over thirty thousand children. One outcome was his rejection of spelling drills as being unrelated to test scores, which led to *The Rational Spelling Book* (1898). Such were the concerns of early educational researchers.

Germany led the field of psychology in the late nineteenth century, developing experimental work in various areas to gain access to the workings of the mind and measuring what could be measured. Ebbinghaus applied these methods to the study of aspects of learning from 1885 onwards, for example, inventing the use of nonsense syllables to measure memory (Nisbet, 2005) – almost 150 years later in England nonsense syllables are used to test whether five- and six-year-olds have learned to read using systematic synthetic phonics. Psychological work in Germany in the late nineteenth century created the field of *Didaktiks* – or what we would refer to as 'pedagogy' in English.[1] Many American researchers travelled to Germany for their doctoral studies before returning to shape the field in the United States (Nisbet, 2005).

Educational research in the nineteenth century was primarily experimental and primarily psychological in nature (Furlong, 2013; Nisbet, 2005), a state of affairs which dominated into the twentieth century. We might note particularly the development of intelligence testing in the early 1900s and the dark history it created when used to justify racism and eugenics. In the United States an infamous Supreme Court ruling in *Buck vs Bell* in 1927 legalized forced sterilization for persons of low IQ (Reilly, 1987). It is of no surprise to discover that the majority of those sterilized under such a law were poor people and people of colour. Doubt has been cast on IQ tests since their inception, with a strong argument that they largely measure socio-economic advantage (Richardson, 2002). We might consider how far similar critiques could be made of standardized testing in the twenty-first century.

In the first half of the twentieth century, educational research continued to establish itself but largely separate from the practice of education in schools.

> Until about the 1960s, research was essentially a small-back-room activity. Researchers may have dreamed about reforming the world of education, but it was a long-term aspiration, to be achieved by patient scholarship. There was little expectation that policy-makers, administrators or teachers would be much influenced by, or even interested in, research. (Nisbet, 1984, p. 3)

In the 1960s, however, in the UK, recommendations on teacher education made by the Robbins Report (1963) brought education as a field of study firmly into the mainstream, and debate arose as to what this subject should actually look like as a university discipline. In the manner of the early church fathers convening to decide orthodoxy, in 1964 the Department of Education gathered together a group of professors of education from across England in

---

[1] For a complete history of the field of educational research, including many delightful quotations from nineteenth- and early-twentieth-century writings on education, see Nisbet (2005), including correlations between bread-eating and intelligence in children (Binet, 1908) and an experiment in spraying children with a mild nerve toxin towards the end of the day to counter fatigue (Claparede, 1911).

Hull in a closed session (Richardson, 2002). They agreed that the foundation disciplines of education as a university subject would be: philosophy, psychology, sociology and history. Economics was considered but rejected. With the addition of anthropology and linguistics, these four remain the core of education as a field today. Economics does appear in some education departments, but economists of education are as likely to work in economics departments. Indeed, educational topics are investigated by researchers working in departments of social policy, history, psychology and sociology. Education is both a field of its own and a topic for those working in many other disciplines.

The field of psychology continued to burgeon in the 1960s, and the work of Skinner, the behaviourist (see *B. F. Skinner* textbox), developed concepts that remain key to our understanding of animal behaviour – and educational behaviour management – today. Rats pressing levers to receive food treats might seem an odd foundation for educational practice, but it is not too far removed from the sticker system for potty training, or the focus which students train onto the grades attached to their work today. The 1960s and 1970s produced a number of classic studies for social sciences as a whole, some of which would not be allowed under current ethics rules, and are discussed in Chapter 8.

Today's educational playing field sits in a globalized world in which countries compete via international large-scale assessments run by the OECD (the Organisation for Economic Co-operation and Development) to demonstrate who has the best value for money education system. The prevailing neoliberal discourses in the United States, UK, Australia and elsewhere demand the governance of education systems via metrics:

> Quantification brings the power of numbers, in all its forms: numbers can be more persuasive to certain audiences; through aggregation metrics are used to represent large-scale systems in an apparently coherent manner; calculations can be carried out upon them; and they can be compared. Assigning numbers to qualitative features of education gives these benefits, but the richness of life is lost in the process. ... Governing volume and complexity in any system is devastatingly difficult and can lead to system failure. Therefore simplifying the world to deal with large-scale systems is a logical response to the situation that governments and their agents find themselves in. (Baird and Elliott, 2019, pp. 533–4)

Educational research sits in a world in which quantification rules; teachers, schools and students all find themselves reduced to numbers and held to certain norms across the globe. 'I'll be a nothing' says one of the students in Reay and Wiliam's (1999) exploration of the effects of national assessments on eleven-year-olds in England. The internalization of high-stakes metrics across the globe has powerful knock-on effects on identity, belonging and mental health. But numbers also enable educational researchers to see problems, like the 'gap' in attainment between the rich and poor. They are not the only story, however: Gloria Ladson-Billings, former president of the American Educational Research Association, has suggested that we should reframe the gap – a neutral object that exists – as the 'education debt', with the linguistic implications of 'historical, economic, sociopolitical and moral' elements to that debt (2006, p. 3). In doing so she illustrates not only the richer understanding that educational research can bring, beyond numbers, but also the concerns of educational research in the round.

A Discipline?

Sociology is the study of humans organized into groups (and societies) and how social factors create human behaviour. Anthropology is the study of human cultures. Psychology is the study of the individual, of their mind and behaviour. Philosophy is the theorization of the nature of knowledge, of existence, of thinking and of how people should live. History is the study of the past. Linguistics is the study of language, the principal means by which humans communicate. Each discipline has commonalities with the other, but each has its own particular focus and characteristic methods. There is an advantage in bringing all of them together under one roof, allowing for the multiplicity of dimensions to the massive human endeavour that is education.

John Furlong sums up the complexities of education in his book *Education – An Anatomy of the Discipline*:

> Using the term *discipline* to refer to the university-based study of education will be seen by some readers as inappropriate. The most common term used to characterise education is a 'field'. Because the study of education covers so many different educational contexts (from early years to lifelong learning), so many different topics (from the teaching of reading to the management of higher education), because it draws on so many other disciplinary perspectives (from neuroscience to economics and philosophy) and because it is studied by using so many different approaches to research and scholarship (from history or literary studies to ethnography or randomised

> control trials), because of all this diversity, how could it be anything else but a 'field'? (Furlong, 2013, p. 6)

He chooses to argue for education as a discipline, but I have preferred the term 'field' in this book, partly because I think it is important to remain aware of the constituent disciplines that make up the field, and how they respond differently to some of the questions raised in this book. The discipline you favour may have implications for your ontological and epistemological beliefs and your methodological actions.

In any case, this debate reflects some of the anxiety in the pursuit of education as a university-based topic of study and research. Some of this anxiety is drawn from the subject's origins in teacher training, in both the United States and the UK; as a training ground it was rooted in professional practice, not academic study. Some of it is due to the relatively recent status of education as a doctoral discipline: ten or twenty years ago the vast majority of professors and lecturers in education departments (who were not working in teacher education) would have done their doctorates in one of the disciplines on which education draws: psychology, anthropology, sociology and so on. Now it is more common to find lecturers who did their doctoral work in education themselves, who are trained in a synthesis of these disciplines. This anxiety can express itself in various ways; one is a concern with differentiating academic writing in education from 'journalism', which can result in a bias against clear communication; another is a suspicion of some of the less traditional forms of research. However, the composite nature of education also provides strength to the field.

> Over the past 130 years, dominant discourses of educational research have certainly changed but rather than one approach being succeeded by another with old traditions withering away, the reality is that new ones have simply added to previous traditions. As a result, today educational research is multivariate, embracing a range of different traditions each of which might claim different historical roots. (Furlong, 2013, pp. 21–2)

We are able as educationalists to approach problems from the most appropriate angle for the particular context. We can draw on theory from a range of disciplines, constructing the most robust explanations for what we see in the field. The practice of education also has the potential to create real and lasting change in society: the impetus in educational research is not just to critique but to change. One element of the history of the field that is particularly relevant to this is the teacher-researcher movement. Stemming from the concerns of Lawrence Stenhouse, who

> was greatly concerned that behaviorism was an ideology that saturated school curricula of the 1960s and, as such, it was essential for teachers to be researchers in their own classrooms in order to identify oppression of students due to an ideology of empiricism. His stance launched the teacher as researcher movement in England and drew attention to the potential danger of the ideology of behaviorism as a source of hegemony. (Kincheloe and Tobin, 2009, p. 516)

Teacher or practitioner-researchers have been a core part of education research ever since. The importance of practitioner research to the field of education demonstrates why it is not always the generalizable, the large-scale, the 'gold standard' research which has the most potential for change. Small-scale research, carried out on the ground, utilizing creative methods as well as conventional ones, has the potential to change lives by altering the educational experiences of those involved in the research process. Education is concerned with the individual as well as the group.

The Topics of Educational Research

Departments and faculties of education gather together not just researchers from different disciplines but also researchers with widely differing interests. 'Education' as a topic takes in all stages of development and learning from birth to higher education, including adult, vocational and skills learning and informal learning. It incorporates almost all elements of children's lives, and those of teachers too. It moves from classroom to home, from playground to sports field, from workplace to examination centre.

In a room of educational researchers you might find yourself sitting with applied linguists, who are interested in how people learn language(s), or those who study education internationally via comparative means, or those who are interested in pedagogy and learning at the school level, or those who focus on higher education, or those who are interested in learning and technology. This section showcases a small number of studies to show the breadth and diversity of what educational research is and does.

A classic text of educational research is Paul Willis's *Learning to Labour* (1978), an ethnography of twelve white working-class boys from Birmingham, in which he asked why working-class children get working-class jobs.

Following the children for eighteen months in school and then a further six months into the world of work, it is a study of class reproduction. Willis examined the interaction of masculinity with class standards, and how both the institution of school and the boys' own positioning of themselves in relation to the macho world of work contributed to their resistance to education. The book represented a step change in the understanding of cultural contributions to social reproduction (Gordon, 1984). Here we have an example of an anthropological (ethnographic) approach to educational research, which focuses on the role of the school, the educational institution, in society and the part it plays in maintaining inequality. Over forty years later the same kinds of questions are still relevant in education, as we ask why and how inequality between classes, genders and races is reproduced despite – or because of – education.

Another extremely well-known study, this time in the discipline of psychology, which touches on education is Ericsson's 10,000 hour rule, which has been popularized by Malcolm Gladwell. Ericsson, Krampe and Tesch-Römer (1993) presented a theoretical framework drawing on studies of expertise in a number of domains to show the role of deliberate practice over innate talent in the development of expertise. They actually argued that this deliberate practice started in childhood and seemed to take ten years to come to fruition (see, e.g. professional tennis players, chess players or musicians), which equates roughly to 10,000 hours of deliberate practice. The characteristics of deliberate practice include immediate feedback, working on tasks pitched at the right level to be achievable but stretching, and the repeated practice at the same or similar tasks to create improvement. These characteristics are far more important than the catchier number of hours, and are also remarkably reminiscent of good instructional practice. Many studies have shown the importance of timely feedback for learning; the pitch of the activity is theorized by Vygotsky as the Zone of Proximal Development (see *Lev Vygotsky* textbox). The emphasis on deliberate practice as being the key, as opposed to natural talent, also recalls Carol Dweck's work on mindset which is discussed further in Chapter 4.

Educational research also responds in the moment to crises: in 2020 the Covid-19 pandemic caused a massive shift to 'emergency remote teaching' (Hodges, Moore, Lockee, Trust and Bond, 2020), which drew on but also confounded all previous research into online learning. Bacher-Hicks, Goodman and Mulhern (2021) take an economics-based approach and utilize high-frequency internet search data in the United States to examine real-time demand for online learning resources as schools closed. Higher income, better internet access and fewer rural schools were all characteristics of areas that saw greater increases in searches for online learning resources. Such analysis demonstrates the very real inequality in educational resource in even a wealthy country like the United States, and the researchers predict a widening of the achievement gap on the basis of income. It also shows the increasing importance of online resources in education, not only in terms of online teaching but also in terms of the supplementing of formal schooling with internet-based resources.

One of my personal favourite areas of research in online learning is the use of virtual worlds, particularly MMORPG's (Massively Multiplayer Online Role-Playing Game) as online educational environments. Snelson, Wertz, Onstott and Bader (2017), for example, report their experiences using World of Warcraft as an environment to teach research methods in online doctoral education. They utilized a number of innovative methods and approaches, including recording all meetings as unlisted YouTube videos (i.e. not accessible by anyone outside the research team). The researchers argue that 'the World of Warcraft game offered ample opportunity for students to practice the types of activities qualitative researchers engage in such as participant observation, data collection, and application of research design' (Snelson, Wertz, Onstott and Bader, 2017, p. 1452). However, they also noted that learning to use the online game overshadowed the actual intended learning programme for some of the participants who were less familiar with online gaming.

One of the joys of educational research is the vast range of methods and data which the field draws on. Corpus linguistics, the analysis of large corpora of linguistic data, utilizing software to identify collocations (words that are found next to each other), frequencies and other patterns in word use, for example, has a long history in applied linguistics and is now being used to study other modes of education. It enables the comparison of real language input versus that given by English as a foreign language learning materials (Römer, 2004); it can also be used to show the role of a single word ('just') in inviting or suppressing dialogue in the mathematics classroom (Wagner and Herbel-Eisenmann, 2008). But equally we might see educational research that draws on 'sandboxing' – a technique which asks participants to create three-dimensional scenes in sand as a stimulus for discussing their experiences, and which stimulates not just cognitive but also affective responses in the participants (Mannay and Turney, 2020).

These are just a handful of examples to illustrate the range of possibilities. Whatever your particular topic of interest you will find a wide range of research to speak to it, and likely a wide range of research designs and methods used to address those topics.

Conclusion

The major concerns of educational research – learning and how to improve it – remain constant, but the contexts change with the times. Educational research is now a fully grown field, bringing together in a unique way different disciplines and subjects of interest, and covering one of the major endeavours of the human condition. Social research in the twenty-first century is undergoing major changes as the decolonization of knowledge and the university gathers momentum, and the disciplines engage with the work of the Global South. Globalization, climate change, increasing economic inequality, pandemic – all these contribute to the challenging international context of educational research in the present day. What I hope these pages offer is the foundations upon which you can build to engage in this complex field and its global context.

1.1 John Dewey

John Dewey (1859–1952) was an American philosopher of education and political thought. He was also an educational reformer who founded a Laboratory School while a professor at the University of Chicago, where he applied and tested his educational theories and pedagogical beliefs. He published widely across topics. Although best known for his educational writings, he also wrote about art and aesthetics, something he has in common with Lev Vygotsky. Two themes run through his work: a commitment to democracy and an emphasis on the importance of experience as a source of knowledge. Of particular importance are Dewey's books *Democracy and Education* (1916) and *Experience and Education* (1938). For Dewey 'the purpose of education was the intellectual, moral, and emotional growth of the individual and, consequently, the evolution of a democratic society' (Rodgers, 2002, p. 845).

Dewey's philosophy is a constructivist one. Knowledge is constituted through action: learning is experiential and knowing is transactional – it is developed through the interaction of individuals with each other and with their environment. This means that educators should build educational experiences for students, rather than expecting to fill them with factual knowledge. Dewey also emphasized the importance of reflective thought for learning from action, a concept which has become influential on teacher education (Rodgers, 2002). English (2016) uses Dewey's own example of a child sticking their finger into a flame to explain how reflection figures in experiential learning:

> *The undergoing side of experience is the feeling of a pain of a burn … Without connecting the pain of the burn to the act of touching the flame, the child does not learn; however, if the child reflects and considers why his finger was in pain after touching the flame, then the child is beginning a process of learning from the interaction with the world. (English, 2016, p. 1049)*

Dewey's work remains influential on both educational practice and research, particularly in a North American context. His work emphasized the fulfilment of individual potential, and the consequent ability to contribute to democratic society.

2

Ontology and Epistemology

Ontology and epistemology are key terms in social science research which can intimidate and confuse those starting out as readers or creators. In this chapter we will consider what these terms mean, and what the range of 'options' is in each category. We will also consider ways of thinking about your own position in these categories.

As we have noted in the first chapter, education is made up of many disciplines. Furlong warns us that 'there are also major debates between different research traditions in education with fundamental differences in theory and in method. Epistemologically, education therefore lacks the consensus and indeed the coherence of some of the more established disciplines' (Furlong, 2013, p. 4). Beyond this, many entrants to educational research come via teaching, and will have internalized norms based on their own subject disciplines: I can see clearly, for example, how my background as a teacher of English literature has influenced how I think about what knowledge is and how it can be justified, and has contributed to my own identity as a mainly qualitative researcher. As we move forward to considering what ontology and epistemology are, it is worth taking a moment to reflect explicitly on what your background has taught you about knowledge and what it is. Such awareness enables you to see that it is not necessarily a question of *choosing* an ontological and epistemological position, and also to ensure that you are clear about where you stand so as to avoid making judgements or choices based on opaque criteria. As you read consider which of the positions described under ontology and epistemology most closely reflects your existing position. In doing so we are considering the question 'In what ways do our own educational and life experiences shape our research trajectory and the academic we become?' (Menter, 2020, p. vi). Both ontological and epistemological positions sit on a wide continuum.

Defining Ontology

Ontology is effectively what we can know – what is out there to know about. Peim (2018) frames this as the 'first philosophy' – the classic 'what is a table?' question. He points out that while it seems odd to ask this question of a mundane object like a table, there are gains to be achieved from asking about more complex things – what is education?, for example.

Ontological claims are 'claims and assumptions that are made about the nature of social reality, claims about what exists, what it looks like, what units make it up and how these units interact with each other. In short, ontological assumptions are concerned with what we believe constitutes social reality' (Blaikie, 2000, p. 8). An objectivist approach to ontology considers that there is a single objective reality which can be known, in which the social world, like the physical one, is governed by general laws and in which 'social phenomena and their meanings have an existence that is independent of social actors' (Bryman, 2001, p. 16). In contrast a constructivist approach considers that there are multiple, constructed realities, generated by individuals and groups.

Various approaches are used to bridge the gap between objectivist and constructivist ontologies. One is critical realism, based on the work of Roy Bhaskar (see Collier (1994) for an accessible introduction). Critical realists argue for an underlying 'real' world that exists whether or not it is observed; what exists can be visible (like the physical world) or invisible (like relationships between humans), and the methods used to study each are therefore different. (Naïve realism, on the other hand, is a belief that we see the world as it actually is, objectively, but that those who do not see the world in the same way are therefore wrong or mistaken.) Knowledge in critical realism is transitive – our knowledge of the world can shift, but the underlying reality remains (moving into epistemological concerns). Critical realism is a useful midpoint between positivism and constructivism that allows us to believe that there is a 'real world' which we may or may not know but also that social reality is constructed by individuals, groups and societies.

Relational ontology provides another way of conceptualizing social reality, prominent in Indigenous thinking, which considers people as part of a network of relations and connections. 'They have connections with the living and the nonliving, with land, with the earth, with animals, and with other beings. There is an emphasis on an I/we relationship as opposed to the Western I/you relationship with its emphasis on the individual' (Chilisa, 2020, p. 24). This ontology is at the base of different ways of thinking about education, land and people. Chilisa links relational ontology (and relational epistemology) to the Bantu philosophy of *Ubuntu*, a term which has been translated in varying ways but which encapsulates a collective vision of humanity, and which has been used as an ethical and theoretical framework in some research (e.g. Sharra, 2009) as well as entering the popular imagination, sometimes rendered in English as 'I am because We are'.

Biesta (2015, 2020) raises an important question of ontology in relation to education and the classic 'what works' agenda in educational research. He notes that the 'magic bullet' version of causality where 'interventions are causes and results effects, and that, under optimal conditions, the causes will *necessarily* generate the effects' only works in a particular set of conditions, that is, 'in closed systems that operate in a linear deterministic way' (2020, p. 55, italics in original). He argues instead,

> This is precisely what education is not; education is an open, semiotic and recursive system. It functions through meaning and interpretation rather than in a deterministic way, and it functions recursively rather than in a linear manner. (Biesta, 2020, p. 55)

This is a claim about the nature of social reality – an ontological claim, which highlights that an objectivist ontology might lead us to 'what works' but that educational reality is based on constructed meanings. For Biesta, then, questions of ontology sit at the very heart of the endeavour of educational research, and he emphasizes this in order to highlight that connections which might in another accounting be called cause and effect are not so certain in educational research.

Defining Epistemology

If ontology is 'what is there to be known' then epistemology is 'how can we know it?' As a field epistemology is the study of the origins and nature of knowledge, sometimes known as the theory of knowledge. The 'epistemological dimensions of disciplines focus on questions of theory, of method, debates about the nature of evidence and how it should be represented and defended' (Furlong, 2013, p. 11). No longer is the question 'what is a table?' The questions are, 'How can we measure a table? How can we describe a table? How can we define a table?'

The parallel epistemologies to objectivist and constructivist ontologies are positivism and interpretivism, respectively. Positivism expects the application of the methods of the natural sciences in relation to social science research: experiments, hypothesis testing and so on. In practical terms it can be seen in the tendency to report research in the passive voice, taking the 'I' out of the equation. Interpretivism, meanwhile, relies on the interpretation and understanding of the meanings ascribed by humans to their world(s); we can know things by engaging with the social actors who create reality. These two epistemologies are generally held in opposition, with the former represented by quantitative methods and the latter by qualitative methods. You may hear this referred to as 'the paradigm wars'. Post-positivism meanwhile takes a pluralist approach, adopting aspects of both positivism and interpretivism, allowing for greater effect of both researcher and researched on data generation but still seeking a wider generalizable truth.

Critical realist epistemologies look for what can be known about the world via whatever means are available, via a pragmatic approach which understands that our perceptions (both the researchers' and the participants') are influenced by who we are and what we have experienced (see also Standpoint Epistemology section).

Epistemology works both on a particular and a general level:

> It is important to distinguish between epistemological beliefs and epistemological world views. Epistemological beliefs consist of specific beliefs about a particular dimension of knowledge such as its **certainty, simplicity, origin, or justification**. In contrast, epistemological world views consist of a set of beliefs that collectively define one's attitudes about the nature and acquisition of knowledge. An epistemological world view includes all of one's explicit and implicit beliefs, attitudes, and assumptions about the acquisition, structure, representation, development, and application of knowledge. (Schraw, Olafson and VanderVeldt, 2012, p. 1165, emphasis author's)

It is easiest to establish your own epistemological *world view*, as based on the reflections suggested in the introduction to this chapter; it is likely to have been shaped by the discipline which you first trained in, and the ontology and epistemologies which were emphasized within it. I recently wrote the following about knowledge in English literature in the secondary school:

> These two characteristic pedagogies, the communal reading of a text, and the later discussion of that text, tell us things about how we construct knowledge in English. The first is that the text is intrinsically important: we

draw on detail, on a close reading, to construct our knowledge. An encounter with the text itself is a key component of knowledge in English Literature; while we might argue about whether that textual encounter needs to be committed to memory or merely held in the pages of the text, we all agree that textual detail, plot points, structure, language, imagery and quotations are what provide the raw material for the construction of knowledge. … The second characteristic pedagogy, of discussion, moves us further on: we construct knowledge through discursive means, as a community. Even scholars of English Literature in the ivory tower of the academy work through interaction with others, whether that is in person or through reading and responding to their critical works. Knowledge within the academic discipline of English Literature is not produced in isolation: it is produced through argument with others whether real or imagined, as we work through possible interpretations and make the case for our own particular take on a text. (Elliott, 2020, p. 13)

I quote it here because within it I can see echoes of how I understand knowledge to work within educational research also: I see the construction of argument through detailed drawing on data to be key to generating what I would consider to be knowledge. I also see that knowledge as an interaction with what has been produced by others, including participants and other researchers or 'the literature' as we often term it. This speaks to a somewhat interpretivist epistemology, and as an ex-English teacher who knows that 'The Author is Dead' I am prepared to acknowledge a constructivist ontology for much of what can be known in relation to literature – interpretations and close reading are hugely varied dependent on the person creating the interpretation and the sum of their existence to date. However, I also acknowledge that there are some 'real' facts – dates, information about authors, real geographical locations, truly identifiable literary techniques and so on – which impinge on the study of literature. This too echoes my understanding of social sciences – in other words I am a critical realist and although the methodologies I employ tend towards the qualitative and interpretivist traditions, I am largely a pragmatist in terms of the ways in which I engage with research questions (of which more in Chapter 4). Had I been a science teacher I might have come to educational research with a completely different epistemological world view. This is not direct cause and effect, however: it is possible to be an ex-English teacher who views knowledge in a completely different way in educational research; it is possible to be trained in the hard sciences but approach social science completely differently.

The question of where knowledge is located and created – in the individual or between individuals in the social – is key to the epistemology that accompanies a relational ontology. Wilson argues,

> Dominant paradigms are built on the fundamental belief that knowledge is an individual entity: the researcher is an individual in search of knowledge, knowledge is something that is gained and therefore knowledge may be owned by an individual. An indigenous paradigm comes from the fundamental belief that knowledge is relational. Knowledge is shared with all of creation. It is not just interpersonal relationships, or just with the research subjects I may be working with, but it is a relationship with all of creation. (Wilson, 2008, p. 56)

It is interesting to consider how this fits with the model of doctoral education and academic publication where the fundamental criterion is the original contribution to knowledge – a personal, individual contribution. Academia enforces even in its most unthinking ways some of the tenets of Western epistemologies over Indigenous ones, which is discussed further in a section below.

Moving on to the particular dimensions to which epistemological beliefs can attach, identified above as *certainty, simplicity, origins* and *justification*, *certainty of knowledge* refers to

> the extent to which knowledge is viewed as fixed or fluid. An individual may consider knowledge to be existing with certainty. In such cases, knowledge cannot be doubted, all experts would come up with the same answer to a question, and that answer would not change over time. At higher levels of development, individuals would be open to the idea that theories are modified over time as more information is gathered, and that knowledge is not certain or absolute. (Guilfoyle, McCormack and Erduran, 2020, p. 3)

Within this we can see the traces of different ontologies and epistemologies. Only if there is an objective reality could knowledge be viewed with absolute certainty and then only if we were absolutely confident in our ability to observe that reality. *Simplicity of knowledge* meanwhile refers to the belief about how simple or complex knowledge is. Is it simply an accumulation of facts, which are concrete, easily knowable and separate? Or is knowledge dependent on context, interrelational and complex? I suspect few people reading about epistemology could believe knowledge to be simple! The 'what works' drive within educational research, on the other hand, largely assumes knowledge to be both simple and certain: there is a 'right' way to do something, and if we know it, we can do it.

The *origins of knowledge* considers beliefs about the sources from which knowledge comes. An individual might hold an epistemological belief that knowledge is something outside the individual, which can be transmitted from expert to learner. The teacher is the authority on the knowledge and passes it onwards. A different epistemological belief places the construction of knowledge outside the individual, in the social interaction with others who might be more knowledgeable (see *Vygotsky* textbox) or might not.

Justification for knowing: 'This dimension is concerned with how individuals evaluate knowledge, how they use or evaluate evidence, authority, and expertise' (Guilfoyle, McCormack and Erduran, 2020, p. 3). This dimension is perhaps particularly relevant when we are thinking of epistemology in relation to research and research design. What will be the justification for the particular claim that is being made and at what point is it justifiable to make that claim to knowledge?

Peim (2018) highlights that in the social sciences we have a tendency to assume that empirical fieldwork – the generation of data – is key to research but challenges us to consider the need or otherwise for data as a fundamentally epistemological question. He points us to the general preference for the empirical over the theoretical (or 'speculative' thinking (2020, p. 37)), which can be seen even in the layout of this book, which turns to 'evidence' (or data) in Chapter 4 and leaves considering theory until Chapter 5 (into which no preference on my part should be read!). It is rare, for example, to find a doctoral thesis based entirely on theoretical work in education; the qualification is in some ways a licence for future empirical work. Yet it is worth considering Peim's point that this is an epistemological choice that has been made, rather than making it without consideration. As he points out,

> We don't set off on a quest for knowledge like intrepid and daring explorers approaching some strange terrain always for the first time. One of the problems for the researcher entering into the world of a given field of practice or into an already-established space of knowledge is that many have been there before. The field of knowledge is already peopled by established figures, concepts, data, interpretations, position, perspectives. Epistemology implies that the researcher must take this already-existing state of affairs into mind. … A critical epistemology will seek to call into question what is already fixed and determined. (Peim, 2020, p. 38)

Standpoint Epistemology

Standpoint epistemology theorizes the epistemological advantage that is gained by some groups by virtue of their position in society. Consider a group of young people, 50 per cent of whom went to boarding school, and 50 per cent of whom did not: the first group is easily and uncontroversially identifiable as more likely to know about boarding schools, (importantly for standpoint epistemology and research) to know of appropriate questions to ask about boarding schools in a research process and of appropriate sources to draw on. Standpoint epistemology therefore acknowledges the epistemic authority of experience. It works from the basic assumption that knowledge is socially situated, and that therefore marginalized people have some positional advantage in gaining some kinds of knowledge; and they are therefore more likely to be able to spot the relevant and important questions in research. Standpoint epistemology applies to class, gender, race and disability among other things. It ties into the historic political tradition of 'nothing about us, without us', which is a motto of the development of parliamentary democracy (as in Poland in 1505, or in America in the form of 'no taxation without representation') and has been adopted in disability rights movements and so on.

In standpoint epistemology no less than in the formal scientific method, however, absence of evidence is not evidence of absence. A fallacy has arisen from standpoint theory, which is essentially 'I am of x group; I have not had experience of prejudice, therefore prejudice against group x does not exist.' This is an oversimplification of an epistemology which seeks to consider lived experience as a valid source of knowledge and to use that to enable research to 'reverse the gaze' (Patel, 2016, p. 15, drawing on Du Bois (1898) (see *W. E. B. Du Bois* textbox)). Standpoint epistemology also does not obviate the need for research and analytical thought; it provides a theoretical justification and impetus to consult those who are most affected in any given situation.

2.1 W. E. B. Du Bois

W. E. B. Du Bois (1868–1963) was an American sociologist and highly influential turn-of-the-century writer on race, education and civil rights. He was the first African American to earn a doctorate from Harvard (in 1895). He ended up at Atlanta University, where he led a series of ground-breaking sociological studies of the lives of African Americans. He wrote widely and in 1903 his book *The Souls of Black Folk* collected together essays, memoir and fiction in what would become the classic study of race, culture and education in early-twentieth-century America. One of the arguments made in it is that African Americans should have wider access to higher education.

In the first paragraph of *The Souls of Black Folk* Du Bois voices the 'real question' asked of African Americans: 'How does it feel to be a problem?' ([1903] 2007, p. 7). This question is also challenged in his essay 'The Study of the Negro Problems' (1898); in both cases Du Bois's response is to ask us to 'reverse the gaze' (Patel, 2016, p. 15) and look not to Black people for the answer but to the societal structures that create the problems.

The first chapter of *The Souls of Black Folk* introduces the concept of 'double-consciousness', characterizing Black people as

> *a sort of seventh son, born with a veil and gifted with second-sight in this American world, – a world which yields him no true self-consciousness, but only lets him see himself through the revelation of the other world. It is a peculiar sensation, this double-consciousness, this sense of always looking at one's self through the eyes of others, of measuring one's soul by the tape of a world that looks on in amused contempt and pity. (Du Bois, [1903] 2007, p. 8)*

Double-consciousness continues to be an influential concept in race theory today. This book was only one of many; Du Bois was a prolific author. His writing shows his belief in the link between capitalism and racism and he became a prominent socialist as well as civil rights campaigner, eventually being targeted during the McCarthy period of American political history.

Epistemological Beliefs and Decentring the Global North

As noted above, both the doctoral process and the norms of academic publishing sustain a particular view of knowledge and research. Academia and universities institutionalize the production of knowledge in particular ways, and claim a monopoly on that production, something which has been described as 'a pillar of colonialism' (Batz, 2019, p. 103). Western academia 'was designed under an extractivist colonial logic that marginalizes, appropriates, destroys and attempts to delegitimize all other knowledge' (Batz, 2019, p. 105). Raewyn Connell describes in *Southern Theory* the ways in which the history of sociology (and the world) shaped the discipline to focus on theory which came out of the metropole, and excluded understandings from further afield, framing those of the Global South as subjects of research, not its proponents. She notes that this history means that sociological theory in general frames a universal which is based on only one-half of the world. As an example, she gives the concept of time in social theory: it offers 'the world-time of an intelligible historic succession (pre-modern to modern, pre-capitalist to capitalist, etc). This is time as experienced in the metropole. In colonised and settler societies, time involves fundamental discontinuity and unintelligible succession' (Connell, 2007, p. 45), because of the startling acts of violence and conquest which break off gradual evolutions of society and introduce massive dis-conjunctions. Yet the requirements of the academic world, as will be discussed in Chapter 9, are based around the understandings produced from the metropole, from the construction of social theory as it has been rationalized post hoc.

Descriptions of epistemic beliefs often distinguish between 'more sophisticated' or 'more naïve' beliefs (Guilfoyle, McCormack and Erduran, 2020, who also note that although these judgements are recognized not to be useful, researchers usually attempt to justify their use nonetheless). In using the language of value judgements, these descriptions encourage researchers to give more weight to Western epistemic beliefs, and to discount epistemic world views – and ways of creating and valuing knowledge – which come from Indigenous cultures. In doing so they further emphasize white Western research as the standard to which all should aspire, and prevent researchers from taking steps towards incorporating different traditions. For Indigenous researchers it can lead to the desire or need to assimilate and abandon traditional epistemic beliefs, or lead them to reject absolutely knowledge from a tradition which labels their own naïve. Wilson and Laing term the 'sustained effort to sever Indigenous peoples from traditional education and traditional knowledges' (via the promotion of Western-style educational norms) 'epistemicide' (2019, p. 133). These same issues can also lead to unethical and exploitative practices in the conduct of research, and to the dismissal of participant insight as being 'naïve' and therefore not worth incorporating – whether in the context of research among an Indigenous group to which the researcher does not belong, or in relation to a group considered less educated or less sophisticated for other reasons – children, for example.

It is important to note that the Indigenous, Aboriginal and Native epistemologies and ontologies *are* plural. There is no singular set of belief which is 'the Indigenous' viewpoint. As will continue to become clear, there are commonalities among Indigenous epistemologies, but they are not all identical. Similarly, although we talk of the theory of the Global South or *Southern Theory* as Connell (2007) has it, this is a shorthand for the many theories which emerge from the scholars of the Global South. In a related question of terminology, 'decolonisation' is an important theme in education worldwide. Tuck and Yang (2012) make an urgent case that 'Decolonisation is not a metaphor' (2012) – for many Indigenous and Native peoples their land is occupied by settler colonialism, has been for centuries and continues to be so (and in some cases such occupation is increasing via continuing extension of oil and gas networks). Decolonization in the academy and education tends to be about redressing historic imbalances in curriculum coverage, without considering the literal colonization that is, for example, the site of the school in New York – located on the traditional lands of the Algonquin people (Patel, 2016). (The fact that Great Britain is not a settler colony in some ways makes discussion of decolonization in education in Britain both more and less complex.) Part of the colonial project is the acquisition, categorization and sorting of material and intellectual goods, and research is by its nature complicit in that, in the ultimate expression of a Western epistemology which looks at the world as something to be pinned down, studied, analysed and sorted. The challenge for researchers who are anticolonial is to find ways to work around this tension.

Indigenous epistemologies tend to accept a broader range of sources of knowledge than those which are legitimized within Western epistemology. 'Dreams, visions, vision quests, and interactions with nature, along with insight and intuition are all salient to meaning and knowledge' (Welch, 2019, p. 63). McPherson and Rabb (2011) draw on an interview with a Blackfoot Métis man named Douglas Cardinal to demonstrate the parallels between the mystical experiences of the Native American which are frequently dismissed in a Western epistemology and other accepted embodied experiences which are accepted such as the near-death experience.

> In the case of the vision quest, phenomenological description allows us to discuss it without dismissing such experience as mere dream or hallucination,

> as many non-Natives might be tempted to do. At the same time, we are not required to admit that such experience is actually a glimpse into the spirit world, whatever that would mean. Note that many Native Americans believe that dreaming itself is a glimpse into the spirit world (60) … [And] to ask these kinds of questions [that interrogate the authenticity and reliability of Native embodied ways of knowing] is to miss the point. In one sense it really doesn't matter whether or not he was, in a technical sense, hallucinating. What is important is what you learn from such an experience, what you take away with you. (McPherson and Rabb, 2011, p. 62)

These epistemological concerns – how can we know what is to be known about the world – have implications for what is considered as and accepted as evidence or data, which we will discuss in Chapter 4.

As I have noted that Indigenous, Aboriginal and Native epistemologies are plural, so are Western epistemologies. There is sometimes a tendency to contrast Indigenous and Native epistemologies with the most positivist approaches in Western epistemology for effect, but there is much common ground to be found, although it is often framed in different ways. We might see particular coherence between interpretivist approaches and those of Native epistemologies. For example, Welch argues,

> Our individualized experiences of knowledge in and about the world, much of which evolved from the interplay between embodied tacit knowledge and intuition, is what constitutes both the phenomenological and the pluralist, polycentric components of Native ways of knowing. Universal, 'objective', knowledge as Western epistemology conceives it is not simply not possible, it's not even desired. The subjectivity of experiential knowledge that stems from our unique interactions is what gives us more authentic meanings of the world and more practical and shareable bits of knowledge that tie us together. (Welch, 2019, p. 64)

While the relational elements of this are not recognizable in most Western research, there is certainly an echo of the 'subjectivity of experiential knowledge' in some qualitative approaches in which the researcher is themselves the data collection tool (and indeed tool for the analysis of that data, as will be discussed in Chapter 7) and understanding of that subjectivity. The use of a particular version of social science to set the norms for all Western research (including in academic publishing) is problematic not only for some qualitative research, which is then held to norms which are inappropriate in terms of its ontological and epistemological basis, but also in terms of marginalizing and othering research coming out of Native, Indigenous or

Global Southern traditions as not meeting a supposedly objective standard. Hofer and Pintrich (1997) call for greater numbers of cross-cultural studies of epistemological theories both to understand where epistemological dimensions diverge and where there might be greater convergence. Such studies, it is to be hoped, could lead to greater acceptance of Indigenous research frameworks and concepts of knowledge. Kaomea (2001) discusses her own attempts to merge Indigenous and Western approaches as a Native Hawaiian researching within her own community, as a means to navigate some of the insider/outsider tensions she encounters. There are a number of voices now providing options and means for researchers from the Global North, from colonizer backgrounds, to engage with Indigenous and Native people on their own terms. Louis (2007) poses this as both an ethical and a practical requirement, as she argues that communities that have for a long time had research *done to* them are closing their doors to Western researchers who do not engage with Indigenous means of knowledge production and follow an acceptable set of values (as discussed further below).

Axiology

Axiology is only sometimes considered in educational research, but it is worth noting. Axiology is the study of values, and given the moral dimension to educational research identified by John Furlong (2013) and expanded on in Chapter 8 of this book, considering the axiological beliefs of the researcher is also relevant to our understandings of how we approach knowledge. While axiology looks at values as they apply to both ethics and aesthetics, only the first is relevant here. It should be noted that although I think it is a natural thing to consider one's values as a researcher, one of the reasons why axiology has not been routinely included in educational research textbooks is that in terms of a positivist epistemology knowledge is considered to be value-free and objective. As we explored in Chapter 1 there can be some anxiety about status in education as a discipline and this has sometimes meant some reluctance to give up the terms and concerns of the natural sciences with their status by association. Nevertheless, most researchers would admit that their choice of research questions and topics of investigation is at least partly value-led (Biddle and Schafft, 2015). Biddle and Schafft explore what a pragmatic axiology looks like, in relation to mixed-methods research which often operates on a base of pragmatism, and suggests it requires a recursive asking of 'what practical difference one action makes versus another' (2015, p. 327), in favour of a movement towards social good (which in itself is contested).

A particularly strong emphasis on axiology, even if not by name, tends to be a feature of research conducted with marginalized communities in particular. Louis (2007) identified four Rs of a relational axiology for researchers working with Indigenous communities – relational accountability, respectful (re)presentation, reciprocal appropriation, and rights and regulations. Relational accountability is the accountability to 'all our relations, be it air, water, rocks, trees, animals, insects, humans and so forth' (Steinhauer, 2002, p. 72). Respectful (re)presentation requires not only thinking carefully about the way you represent yourself and the people you are researching but also acting respectfully to your participants, and not insisting that your own ideas take precedence over them. 'It's about displaying characteristics of humility, generosity, and patience with the process and accepting decisions of Indigenous people in regard to the treatment of any knowledge shared. This is because not all knowledge shared is meant for a general audience' (Louis, 2007, p. 133). This concept is explored further in other contexts in Chapter 8. Reciprocal appropriation acknowledges that research is always appropriative, and pushes for benefits to accrue adequately to the Indigenous participants as well as the researcher. Finally, rights and regulations require research to recognize Indigenous people's 'intellectual property rights to "own" the knowledge they share with the researcher and to maintain control over all publication and reporting of that knowledge' (Louis, 2007, p. 133). This includes considering the kinds of language reporting is written in, and access to those reports for the Indigenous community (which is one of the ways that Kaomea (2001) found to navigate her position as Native Hawaiian academic working with her own community). These values are highly relatable in other areas of educational research (and others) as we consider who has access to the research which is done, incorporating not only academic publishing practices regarding journals but also academic writing conventions which may exclude those who could make the most use out of a piece of research.

Misaligning Ontology, Epistemology and Methodology

It should be clear by now that a researcher's ontology and epistemology/ies will have repercussions for the methodology/ies they adopt in conducting research. What you see as the ways in which we can have knowledge of reality will influence the kinds of data that you can collect and importantly the way that you approach that data with theory and analysis. Difficulties can arise, therefore, when ontology, epistemology, methodology and theory are not aligned in research. This can occur when a particular discipline is highly wedded to one set of beliefs but a particular project is utilizing an unusual methodology for that discipline, without sufficient awareness and groundwork. For example, psychology is strongly associated with the experiment, and most psychologists hold a more positivist epistemology, which can be problematic for those who wish to approach a psychological topic from a constructivist ontology but are influenced by the surrounding environment into taking a more positivist epistemological stance than is appropriate for such an ontology, despite following a qualitative methodology. This misalignment can cause difficulties for analysis of data as researchers become uncertain about how they can link up their data to their theoretical framework, or it can lead to published research where a reflexivity statement (see Chapter 6) espouses a constructivist approach but the entire attitude permeating the data belies that statement. Grix (2002) is very firm on the directionality of the relationship from ontology, onto epistemology, onto methodology, onto methods, to ensure alignment between them.

This directionality is disputed in relation to mixed-methods research, partly because the importance of justifying the possibility of combining methods was held to be more urgent than ontological considerations in the emergence of mixed methods (Biesta, 2010). Pragmatism – a 'what works' approach – is primarily the basis of mixed-methods research and implicitly reflects whatever ontology or epistemology is most relevant to the matter at hand. Giddings (2006) meanwhile critiques this version of mixed methods as 'positivism in drag' and particularly raises concerns over the quality and understanding of qualitative methods which are required by mixed methods. Mixed methods, usually considered to be a methodology despite the name, are dealt with at greater length in the next chapter.

One of the ways in which you can avoid such difficulties is to spend time reflecting on your understanding of reality and how it can be known early on. It is worth thinking, however, if struggling in the later stages of a project to make it all link up appropriately, if the problem is to do with a misalignment somewhere along the way between ontology, epistemology and methodology. It is also the reason why it is important to be honest with yourself about your beliefs in these matters. Your ontological and epistemological beliefs are a product of your entire experience and education to date and are deeply ingrained; changing them takes time, and simply picking a new one to follow is unlikely to be helpful. Working through what you *do* think about them will help you to understand your own work and that of others.

Conclusion

While the philosophical terminology of ontology, epistemology and axiology is often the most intimidating aspect of becoming an educational researcher, coming as it does as one of the first topics the researcher-in-training encounters, taking the time to reflect on the nature of reality and how we may know it is a worthwhile investment. Some doctoral theses contain lengthy meditations on the particular paradigms espoused by the author; few articles do much beyond a passing reference to a critical realist, a pragmatic or a constructivist approach. In a field as multidisciplinary as education, it is wise to be ready to judge research on its own terms, rather than holding it to account against standards that do not apply.

2.2 Antonio Gramsci

Antonio Gramsci (1891–1937) was an Italian communist leader and social theorist. He spent the last ten years of his life imprisoned by the fascist regime in Italy (after a trial at which the prosecutor declared that they must 'prevent this brain from functioning for 20 years') (Jones, 2006, p. 24). While in prison he filled over three thousand pages with writing on political and social theory and his collected works are called *The Prison Diaries* for that reason (see Gramsci, 1971, for selected extracts). Within the diaries, he developed the term 'hegemony' from its original place in the writings of Russian Marxists into a fully fledged social theory.

Hegemony, or 'cultural hegemony', is the inculcation of the ruling class's norms and values (their 'culture') to such an extent into the lives and minds of those who are ruled that they come to be accepted as universal norms. Gramsci recognized that 'social power is not a simple matter of domination on the one hand and subordination or resistance on the other' (Jones, 2006, p. 3) – instead there is a degree of consent by the subordinate to their being ruled. In terms of education we can see schools and universities as sites where cultural norms of the ruling classes are preferred over those of other, less dominant groups. We might cite, for example, the emphasis on Standard English use in schools in England (Cunningham, 2020) or the stigma attached to African American Vernacular English in US schools (both of which result in greater policing of economically disadvantaged students and Black students). In both of these cases the dominant norms are reinforced by the 'cultural institutions' of the mainstream media and their frequent moral panics over the language of children (Cushing, 2020).

The concept of cultural hegemony provides a useful counterpoint for popular contemporary educational concepts such as cultural literacy (Hirsch, 1987) and powerful knowledge (Young, 2009), in that it theorizes how we come to accept the idea that the knowledge valued by the elite should be the yardstick by which our education is measured as successful or not.

3
Fundamental Concepts of Design

Peter Smagorinsky describes the methodology of a study as the 'conceptual epicenter' of research writing (2008). In the methodology – the description of the research design, from research questions to specific methods – we think through the most important details of research, on the basis of which we can or cannot make claims about the world. Research design is the fundamental underpinning of any project, even as it draws on all the concepts outlined in this book. As this is not a methodological textbook, this chapter will not go into specific instructions for conducting different designs. Instead it explores some of the core concepts that underlie different approaches. The quality of the research design and how that is put into operation is more important than whether it comes from quantitative or qualitative or mixed-methods traditions, or any particularly epistemological paradigm. One concept which has become almost axiomatic in social research is the phrase T. S. Eliot attributes to Coleridge on good poetry, 'making the familiar strange, and the strange familiar' (1921, p. 1). Research design is key in ensuring that we move beyond what we know into exploring what else is out there to know. How the individual researcher can affect the research process is explored in Chapter 6; here we consider the design and methods themselves.

Bukve divides the research design into two distinct parts: the first task is 'clarifying the purpose of our project'; the second is 'forming a strategy for data construction' combining 'the choice of a basic perspective on data production with a specification of what methods and techniques we want to use for selecting, collecting, and analysing such data that the project needs' (2019, p. 74). The first part involves the introductory work of examining the literature and focusing on the research topic, before composing and refining the research questions.

Research Questions and Their Role

Generating research questions is typically framed as the beginning of the research project, although it is an open secret that research questions continue to be honed throughout a project. Much of social science is curiosity driven, although in education research there is a case to be made for research studies which follow the most useful paths for practitioners, rather than purely following the researcher's own interests. There is a balance to be struck here, naturally (and for further discussion on instrumental and blue skies research, see Chapter 8). White critiqued the relative lack of attention paid to research questions in educational research, while making the following claims for their value:

> Research questions represent an attempt to 'tame' curiosity. Pursuing curiosity is most productive when questions are not simply asked in a 'haphazard fashion' (Lewins, 1992, 8) but, rather, are posed in relation to what is already known about the topic of interest. The process of formulating, developing and refining research questions allows researchers to make connections with existing theories and previous empirical findings and helps avoid unnecessary repetition of, or overlap with, previous work. This process also allows researchers to clarify their ideas, to reflect on the definition and operationalization of important concepts, and to make links between the questions they aim to address and the most appropriate research design. (White, 2013, pp. 213–14)

In this rendering, creating the research question is the point at which a researcher makes sure their research is interesting, original, and that they can satisfactorily explain it to themselves – a necessary step before explaining it to others. Robson, meanwhile, drawing on Punch (1998) suggests that research questions should be:

- *Clear* They are unambiguous and easily understood
- *Specific* They are sufficiently specific for it to be clear what constitutes an answer
- *Answerable* We can see what data are needed to answer them and how those data will be collected
- *Interconnected* The questions are related in some meaningful way, forming a coherent whole
- *Substantively relevant* They are worthwhile, non-trivial questions, worthy of the research effort to be expended. (Robson, 2002, p. 59)

These are excellent principles, although in my experience following them too literally will result in essay-length questions which seek to clamp down on every tiny potential ambiguity and delineate methods within the questions themselves. The methodology section, however, the 'conceptual epicenter', will leave the reader clear on all of these points and, perhaps more importantly, the researcher themselves. The final point in Robson's list is an interesting one, often referred to as the 'so what?' question. This is related to the concept of impact which is explored in Chapter 8, and we should note here that there are questions we can generate data to answer, but we should pause to consider whether that is pointful. The second and third points – *specific* and *answerable* – are perhaps particularly pertinent to the research design. It is often a useful exercise to map sources of data to be generated through the design against the research questions, both to indicate if the design can answer the question and also if the question is strongly enough correlated to the design. The two can then be adjusted in parallel to create the strongest possible match between design and questions. One important point, emphasized by de Souza, Neri and Costa (2016) among others, is that a research question should not be one to which you already know the answer, or framed in such a way as to be simply seeking confirmation for pre-existing interpretations. After all, if research 'does not hold out the possibility of causing one to revise one's views, it is hard to see why it should be done at all' (Medawar, 1979, p. 94).

Research projects typically involve more than one question, most likely arranged around one or two main or overarching questions, with a small group of sub-questions. It is wise to restrict oneself to a small number of questions. As Bukve puts it, 'a shopping list of pell-mell questions is no good strategy for the job ahead' (2019, p. 205). In some projects, usually quantitative, the 'questions' can instead be represented by a series of hypotheses, usually providing a set of potential answers to an overarching question.

It is worth considering which questions are ones which can be answered by research. 'Should' questions, for example, often associated with policy or decision-making of other kinds such as pedagogies to be adopted, are not, strictly speaking, the domain of educational research because their answers may encompass a moral or pragmatic element – 'should schools utilise x method of teaching reading?' is dependent not only on the answer to the better research question 'does x method of teaching reading work (more effectively than existing methods)?' but also on the answer to 'how much do the materials for x method of teaching reading cost?' and 'does x method of teaching reading work differently for different students?' as well as many others. In philosophical research, however, should questions might well be the right kind of questions to ask.

Janesik (1998) uses the term 'methodolatry' to describe the 'slavish devotion to method', which means researchers begin with the method rather than allowing the research question to guide them to the most appropriate research design, something which Grix (2002) also warns against. It is a reasonable challenge, and we will discuss the similar issues in terms of theory in Chapter 5. However, it is also fair to state that if a researcher is embedded in a particular set of methods, they will be more likely to be interested in the kinds of questions that those methods can answer, and will therefore formulate those kinds of questions.

There are also some methodologies in which research questions are not honed down to specifics at the beginning of the design process, particularly ethnomethodological approaches such as Conversation Analysis. In Conversation Analysis we would instead take a general question like 'what happens in classroom interactions in mathematics lessons?' and collect naturally occurring data. The specific questions would then arise from what is noticed and made relevant in the data, so 'how are pauses operating in this classroom?' (Ethnomethodology is a descriptive set of research approaches which study the methods by which social groups constitute and govern themselves via interaction (including via text).) Similarly in some ethnographic or Grounded Theory[1] approaches the research questions might be quite general but honed iteratively through the data collection process.

Having identified the questions then, we can move on to the rest of the research design: 'a strategic framework for action that serves as a bridge between research questions and the execution or implementation of the research' (Durrheim, 2006, p. 34).

Identifying the Essential Elements of a Research Design

Grix (2002) identifies a logical and directional relationship between the building blocks of research. He moves from Ontology ('What's out there

---

[1] A note on Grounded Theory: Grounded Theory is a methodology, despite its name. It seeks to generate theory from data, but it describes a cyclical process of data collection, coding, theoretical sampling to collect more data, iteratively until saturation is reached and a theory can be generated. The classic text is Glaser and Strauss (1967).

to know?') to Epistemology ('What and how can we know about it?') to Methodology ('How can we go about acquiring that knowledge?') to Methods ('Which precise procedures can we use to acquire it?') to Sources ('Which data can we collect?') (2002, p. 180). As previously mentioned, this is not a methodological textbook and will not exhaustively discuss different methodologies or precise methods. However, it is important to note the distinction between the two, which Grix captures neatly. Some examples of how this works in practice are given in Table 3.1.

In the past we might have started by rehearsing the 'paradigm wars' between quantitative and qualitative, but doing so is largely unfruitful. (However, Alise and Teddlie (2010) noted that 'pure' disciplines like psychology adhered much more to purely quantitative research than 'applied' disciplines like education, where 16 per cent of the research they sampled employed mixed methods.) There are fundamental concepts which underlie both qualitative and quantitative methods, albeit often applied in slightly

Table 3.1 Examples of Methodologies Mapping to Methods

Methodology	Potential methods (not exhaustive)
Ethnography	Participant observation Non-participant observation Interviews Photovoice Collection of diaries Fieldnote writing
Case Study	Interviews Surveys Shadowing Documentary analysis Spatial diagrams
Practitioner or Action Research	Observation Surveys Assessment data Focus groups Classroom interaction data Student work Reflective diary
Intervention Study	Validation of measures Pre- and post-test Use of control group or matched comparison group Observation Interviews

different ways. The advent of mixed methods has also much to teach us about thinking of research design in stages. One key concept is triangulation, the use of data from different sources and/or methods of collection to cross-check against each other. Morgan (2019) writing in the *Journal of Mixed Methods Research* has suggested we have developed beyond triangulation as a key virtue of mixed methods, but also that the outcomes of triangulation – namely that different elements of data can be convergent, complementary or divergent – are worth holding on to. In other words you may want different data sources to back each other up, or to provide different sorts of evidence that work well together but are not saying the same thing, or you may want to have data sources that will challenge each other in order to make sure the conclusions you draw are as strong as possible. The different data sources might mean using different methods to collect data on the same topic (e.g. observing a class and then using stimulated recall to interview the teacher about what you saw), or asking two different sets of people (both teachers and students, for example, in a study of the classroom), or by looking at two different sites (so asking teachers in more than one school or more than one subject). Thinking of data in this way highlights the comparative approach that is key to many kinds of research.

Mixed-methods research has formalized different patterns of research design that enable these types of multiple data collection. The notation system used (Morse, 2003) indicates whether a project is QUAL or QUAN oriented (with capitals used to indicate the dominant aspect of the design, and lowercase for the less dominant aspect, e.g. quan), and whether the different elements are conducted simultaneously/concurrently, which is designated by a plus (+) sign, or if they are conducted sequentially, in which case the sequence is denoted by an arrow symbol (→). So we might have QUAL + quan, a parallel design in which the qualitative aspect is dominant, or QUAN → qual, a sequential design in which the quantitative element is dominant and the lesser qualitative aspect happens after the quantitative stage. The logical extension of this shows you the different designs that are possible. In addition a mixed-methods research project might be a conversion design, in which a qualitative element is subsequently 'quantitized' or a quantitative element 'qualitized' (Teddlie and Tashakkori, 2009, p. 149). Quantitizing is more common, as it is relatively easy to conduct frequency counts on interview data, for example, and use that to report the data. Qualitizing is less common, although Teddlie and Tashakkori give examples of studies that utilize multiple quantitative demographic variables to create qualitative profiles of 'typical' participants, which they consider to be an eligible form of data transformation. There is some debate if one can refer to 'mixed methods' if the methods do not conform to one of these designs, or the mixture does not include both quantitative and qualitative research methods. It may be preferable therefore to refer to 'multiple methods' in order to avoid this controversy.

> 'Numbers and a story' succinctly illustrate the appeal of MMR [mixed methods research], because the combination of both general numeric findings and specific cases exemplifying those findings generate a synergy that neither can alone. It is the generation of new knowledge that goes beyond the sum of the QUAL and QUAN components that makes MMR so valuable in understanding social phenomena. (Teddlie and Sammons, 2010, p. 116)

Mixed-methods research does not go unchallenged as an approach, with some concern over the validity of mixing different methods on an ad hoc basis (Morse and Niehaus, 2009). (See Chapter 4 for a discussion of the concept of validity.) Denzin (2012) covers some of the historical debate over mixed methods and particularly challenges its adherents to adopt more of the critical approaches of the qualitative tradition.

There are a number of different specific research designs which are worth mentioning by name. In education the cohort study may be particularly applicable, in which a group of participants who have shared a life event, such as birth or graduation, grouped by date and location, are recruited and studied longitudinally. The Millennium Cohort Study, for example, is following the lives of nineteen thousand people born in the UK in 2000–2. Data are collected at regular intervals allowing tracing of the life course and large statistical analyses to be conducted. Longitudinal studies take repeated observations of the same group over a long time period, usually of a minimum of a year. The Effective Provision of Pre-school Education (EPPE) project, for example, recruited a cohort of three thousand children who were then followed between ages three and seven, gathering data on outcomes, backgrounds, settings and many more variables (Sylva, Melhuish, Sammons, Blatchford-Siraj and Taggart, 2004). Longitudinal studies have a particular value in educational research where the impacts of interventions may not be seen for a long time, or may be intended to have an impact a long time into the future. Longitudinal research, for example, enables researchers to test if there is an advantage to starting foreign language learning early (Jaekel, Schurig, Florian and Ritter, 2017) (not according to their data), or the long-term effect of mentorship on encouraging under-represented minorities into STEM careers (Estrada, Hernandez and Schultz, 2018) (positive, according to their data).

Cross-sectional designs take a different approach to looking at difference over time by recruiting participants at different phases but studying them at the same time point. So, for example, Woodcock and Reupert (2012) studied the behaviour management strategies of trainee primary teachers in the first, second, third and fourth years of training on a single course (in the Australian model), finding the greatest difference between the first and second years in corrective strategies, and between the third and fourth in terms of their preventative strategies. The advantage of a cross-sectional design is that it enables researchers to study a breadth of participants in a short time frame, as opposed to a longitudinal one which can take years.

Experimental and quasi-experimental designs test the power of interventions with pre- and post-test measures, typically seeking to establish change over the period of the intervention. Experimental implies random assignment of participants to treatment or non-treatment groups, whereas quasi-experiments will often use pre-existing groups. While experimental design is easy to establish in a laboratory it is not always so simple in the real world of education, particularly if the intervention is not at the level of the individual child. Quasi-experiments are also sometimes called 'natural experiments' where one group has been exposed to a particular measure when another has not. Klapp (2015), for example, analysed data from Sweden from 8,558 students born in 1967; depending on the municipality in which they lived these students either did or did not receive a grade at the end of Year 6. Klapp found that boys and lower attaining pupils who received grades at the end of Year 6 made less progress than similar pupils who did not (including potentially dropping out); for girls receiving a grade had a positive long-term effect. No definitive explanation of this effect is known, but the study hypothesized that boys and low-attaining pupils were more likely to overestimate their level of performance, and hence be demotivated by the grade, while for girls the reverse was often true.

Some methodologies imply particular forms of research design, including Action Research which requires repeated cycles of action, evaluation and adjustment, or Grounded Theory which requires iterative data generation phases with interspersed analysis and refinement of methods and instruments until saturation is reached. Participatory Action Research's design feature is a focus on co-creation of research with the participants. Case Study Design is considered in the section 'What Is a Case?' While specific research designs follow a set of conventions, the concepts and questions underlying those conventions remain the same across designs.

3.1 Jean Piaget

Jean Piaget (1896–1980) was a Swiss psychologist who worked in the field of child development. He conceptualized children as problem solvers who perform experiments, make observations about the world and rearranged their knowledge accordingly. Development is the product of the combination of biological maturation and experiential learning of the world. His developmental stage theory sees development as a series of set stages which occur at roughly the same chronological intervals for the majority of children: the sensorimotor stage (birth to two); the preoperational stage (two to seven); the concrete operational stage (seven to eleven); and the formal operational stage (eleven and up). The preoperational stage is subdivided into the symbolic function substage when children are able to think in images and symbols (which you can recognize as imaginary play) and the intuitive thought substage, in which children begin to use early reasoning, which leads to curiosity. This is recognizable in the repeated 'why' questions of children of around age four. Piaget argued that these stages represented a qualitative shift in the way children thought.

The consequence of Piaget's observation of children and theorization of how they learn is an emphasis on child-centred learning in the early years. He himself recognized the tension between how he conceptualized children's learning, which would suggest a smooth trajectory, and the developmental stage theory which he remains famous for. He has also been critiqued for undervaluing the role of the environment around the child. Nevertheless he remains influential in the field of early childhood, although his ideas are often combined with those of Dewey and Vygotsky (see textboxes) when applied in practice. Another idea of Piaget's which is significant for applied linguistics is that language has to follow cognitive development. That is to say, you cannot use colour words before you have developed the concept of colour. Before you can say something is 'bigger' you need to have developed a concept of both size and relativity in objects.

Creative and Arts-Based Research Approaches

As discussed in Chapters 1 and 2, there is some anxiety about status on the part of the field of education in general in relation to its older siblings in the social sciences. This, in turn, leads to perhaps greater anxiety about creative and arts-based research methods in educational research than in other fields of research. However, creative approaches and arts-based methods have a long history in education itself. In both beginning anthropology classes and beginning creative writing workshops, it is not uncommon for students to find themselves instructed to go out into some public place – often a coffee shop – and simply observe, taking notes. The aim for both is to 'cultivate an attitude of curiosity' (Anderson, 2006, p. 21). Greenwood (2012) draws on three different arts-based approaches to educational research to explore the potential of the paradigm for researchers; she sees rigour in the ways in which arts-based research refines and fine-tunes enquiry with participants iteratively. The first of three cases she uses (Te Aika and Greenwood, 2009) was a two-day applied theatre workshop to explore Maori issues with a group on a year-long course in Maori language, focused on Maori education, combining Western approaches with traditional Indigenous performance techniques. Her participants found the dramatic format directing their thoughts in new direction, particularly introducing complexity into previously apparently simple issues. Both Greenwood and her participants found considerable parallels between the arts-based approach and Participatory Action Research, in terms of co-creation, a learning intention and the fusion of research and consequent action (Greenwood, 2012).

Arts-based enquiry is perhaps of particular use as a means of community inclusion in research, and as a tool for political activism (Finley, 2005), but it also enables the researcher to draw on embodied modes of knowledge, and to generate new and different ways of knowing the world. For Greenwood,

> it seems evident that working in the aesthetic can be a very effective way of anchoring knowledge, particularly if it involves bodily participation and choice. Knowledge held in this way is arguably more ready to be called into action than if it is purely verbally cognitive. But do we also know something more? With others who educate through the arts, I would argue that there is more, and that the more is significant, but that we cannot always explain what the more is. It is the more that we sometimes call magic. (Greenwood, 2012, p. 18)

Arts-based research designs are often intrinsically bound up in pedagogy or development of the participants in one way or another. They draw on existing modes of arts development in drama, photography, creative writing or visual arts, and utilize both process and product as data and outcome.

Narrative research sits somewhat on the cusp of arts-based approaches, as it asks for participants' narratives in order to address a research question. Worth (2019), for example, draws on extensive oral histories of British women's lives during the mid-twentieth century to consider their use of post-secondary education after a period of employment to achieve social mobility. Oral history has certain parallels with Conversation Analysis as the data come first, rather than the specific research question, and the researcher seeks to discover what lies within it. Jerome Bruner's classic piece 'Life as Narrative' explores the idea that at any point we talk about our lives we are constructing a narrative (1987), which means we may be influenced by rules of narrative convention and shape our stories accordingly. This means that narratives in research have to be understood as constructed, something which is discussed further in Chapter 4, and which will affect how they are analysed. Harper defines creative writing as something that '*brings into being*' (2019, p. 12, emphasis in the original), a definition which is useful for thinking about any participant-generated data, whether spoken or written, which produces that sense of life and vibrancy.

Selection of Data Sources (Sampling?)

A sample is a sub-set of a population and the term comes from quantitative research. If your population is, for example, high school maths teachers in Alabama, then your sample might be 10 per cent of those teachers. *Sampling*, on the other hand, is the strategy which you use to identify that group. In quantitative research it implies random sampling or probability sampling to produce a sample that is representative of the population as a whole, which is what enables you to generalize from the results of a small sample to the whole population. These terms are used in slightly different ways depending on the study methodology and research questions, but they are widespread throughout educational research. Yin (2014) argues that the use of the term *sampling* implies the statistical properties of a probability sample and the ability to generalize and that we should therefore use the term *selection* where that is more appropriate. Some qualitative researchers choose to simply talk of 'participants' and 'recruitment' rather than use the terminology at all, which seems to me to be more honest. As Yin points out, it is similarly important to be careful about implying knowledge of an overall population when talking about the findings from a group of participants – common words such as 'unique' and 'typical' need to be carefully handled (2014, p. xxiv).

Probability sampling, or random sampling, describes a strategy whereby every member in a population has an equal chance of being selected for the study and the selection is done at random. Statistically we can then infer characteristics from the sample to the population. Random sampling can be simple, in which the sample is usually selected by random number generation – or picked out of a hat. Alternatively the sample can be generated using a systematic method, that is, picking every *n*th member from a list. Stratified sampling, however, divides the population into mutually exclusive groups and then generates a random sample or a systematic sample from each group in order to form the whole sample, ensuring adequate representation from each group. It might also be used to boost the overall number taken from a subgroup for sufficient statistical power.

Theoretical and purposive sampling are terms for choosing participants using a set of criteria, drawn from theory or from the literature, in order to maximize the relevance of the sample to the phenomenon being studied. It is these kinds of sampling which cause Yin to suggest we should use the term 'selection', because they do not enable a probability sample which can be generalized to the population. To give an example, Torres (2014) identified a purposive sample of twenty teachers who had recently left teaching positions in New York charter schools. He recruited via networks – a newsletter that went to Teach for America alumni and also via personal connections – and sought a sample which had 'variation in terms of age (between 24–35 years), years of teaching experience, subject and grade taught, and age of the charter school' (Torres, 2014, p. 7). He also sought some variation in perceived teaching effectiveness, as shown by whether teachers were asked to leave or offered an incentive to stay, and a split in the sample between charter schools in management organizations and standalone schools (his topic was teacher autonomy, and he suggested that this characteristic of schools was likely to have an impact on teacher experiences). Could Torres have generated a random sample? In order to do so he would have needed to have a list of all teachers leaving New York charter schools in the year of his study, and then invited only those picked through random sampling (and almost certainly then worked his way through at least one replacement sample in order to recruit enough participants). Practically, in terms of access to the population, it would have been very difficult, and in terms of recruitment it would have been similarly difficult to persuade his randomly generated sample of people to take part. Rather than statistical representativeness, purposive sampling might aim for theoretical representativeness.

The practical difficulties of random sampling in many qualitative studies have to be weighed against the possibility of systematic bias introduced by participants being largely made up of volunteers. (A voluntary sample is made up of everyone who responds to an invitation to take part – the difference in a purposive sample is selecting for certain characteristics, or a spread of characteristics within that sample.) It is always possible that respondents to a study invitation will have a particular interest in the phenomenon, or have a particular angle they wish to push. Torres's participants might have responded because they wanted to criticize charter schools; it is perhaps slightly less likely that they responded because they were particularly in favour, but in many studies it is the extremes of opinion that encourage people to respond. Other systematic biases might be introduced through the modes of recruitment – Torres reports that twelve of his twenty participants were white female Teach for America alumni. Had he not utilized other networks than the alumni newsletter, that would indeed have introduced a systematic bias. As it is, the representation in the sample is not inconsistent with recruitment patterns in New York charter schools. For a further discussion of the concept of 'bias' and whether it's one that should even be applied to qualitative research, see section 'Bias' below.

Theoretical sampling is a term mostly found in the Grounded Theory literature, where the selection is made on the basis of theoretical hypothecation. Further sampling is done on the basis of seeking 'saturation', so sampling becomes an iterative process in which new participants, sites or informants are recruited because of what has been discovered already in the research, until each new case is adding near to zero new information. For example, it might become clear in a study of teachers' use of feedback in schools that teachers in practical subjects such as art, music or technology had different views to those in core academic subjects, and that more interviews in those subjects were needed to ensure a complete understanding, but further interviews simply confirm what has already been found. Theoretical sampling is also the closest to what is done in case study research when it is based around a unique case – so, for example, when a researcher goes to study the first of a new type of school.

Convenience sampling is realistically the most used sampling technique in educational research, because it dominates research done by teacher-researchers (explored further in Chapter 6), where teachers conduct practitioner research in their own contexts. Convenience sampling might less euphemistically be termed 'I got access where I could'. It might reflect geographical convenience (schools which are close to the researcher) or the networks of the researcher in terms of which organizations they could gain access to, or which gatekeepers they already know. Convenience sampling has the most problems in terms of the possibility of bias, whether systematic or not, but without it much research would never be done at all. Snowball sampling is similar, in that it 'snowballs' from one participant to another, recruiting those who are known to the original participants. Snowballing is sometimes necessary for recruitment among particular hard-to-reach groups, such as adoptive families (Ruggiero and Johnson, 2009), or is utilized for social network analysis, as in von der Fehr, Sølberg and Bruun's (2018) study of science education actors (i.e. not just teachers) in Danish municipalities.

It is important to note that in many forms of research bias in participant selection is simply not relevant, such as when the participants predate the design, for example, when a study is of a particular group, location or activity; or when the population is small and constitutes the set of participants; or when a study is pursuing particular methods with no intent to generalize to a wider population, perhaps with emancipatory purposes in mind. However, in any study the most important question is what data do I need and what sources will I get it from? The research design will use a recruitment strategy to generate those sources and select within them for the best quality data available to the researcher.

3.2 Lev Vygotsky

Lev Vygotsky (1896–1934) was a Russian psychologist, working in the field of child development, who argued that the individual develops through a two-way relationship between the individual and the society around them. His work forms the basis for socio-cultural activity theory and has a core of adherents in educational research around the world. His reputation has grown steadily posthumously after his death at only thirty-seven, of the tuberculosis which plagued him throughout his life.

> The key concept from his work for educationalists more generally is the Zone of Proximal Development (ZPD). The ZPD represents the ideal target area for learning – outside what the child knows already, but not so far outside it that the target is unattainable. Vygotsky defines it as the 'distance between the actual developmental level as determined by independent problem solving and the level of potential development as determined through problem-solving under adult guidance or in collaboration with more capable peers' (1978, p. 86). In learning the child makes use of the 'More Knowledgeable Other' (MKO), which might be a peer or a teacher. Vygotsky's ideas in this space put him in conflict with Piaget (see textbox) and his ideas of stage-based development.
>
> Less well known but also very useful for educational research is Vygotsky's concept of dual affect (1976): the experience of being both yourself and another at the same time. The example which Vygotsky gives is of a child playing doctors: 'a child can be both themselves and a patient, both themselves and a doctor. This "double subjectivity" allows the children the safe space to experiment emotionally: through the development of empathy they can experience fear (e.g. of an injection) but can withdraw from that fear at any time' (Elliott and Dingwall, 2017, p. 70). Dual affect has a number of applications, such as in informal education interventions with young people who have been excluded from formal education.

What Is a Case?

Case study research is a specific methodology which centres around one or more 'cases'. The identification of a case, however, is not exclusive to case study, nor does having identified a case or cases in your research mean that you are doing case study. Ethnographies, for example, frequently focus on a particular case that could also be studied via the case study. Platt (1992) suggests that the case study emerges as a method in sociology (and therefore later in other social sciences) as an inheritance from social workers' case histories which became the data for early sociologists. Charles Cooley, one of the founding fathers of American sociology, said the following of case studies:

> We aim to see human life as an actual dramatic activity, and to participate also in those mental processes which are a part of human function and are

accessible to sympathetic observation by the aid of gesture and language. ... This is what I understand by case study: a direct and all-around study of life-histories, as distinguished from the indirect, partial and somewhat abstract information bearing upon such histories with which we often have to be content. (Cooley, 1930, pp. 316–17)

It is worth discussing what makes a case at this point as it can be a fraught issue in both reading and conducting research. Yin, whose books on case study research are compulsory reading if you intend to work with this methodology, notes that there are at least two different parts to be considered: 'defining the case and bounding the case' (2018, p. 28). While in the early days the case was a person, modern case studies can be of organizations, schools, communities, education programmes, social movements and so on. The case is not the phenomenon under consideration, but a site for studying that phenomenon – a difference which can be subtle or can be important. So the phenomenon of privatization of education worldwide might involve the case of private online tutoring companies in China; the phenomenon of transgender students' experiences of transitioning as teenagers might involve several cases of individual students.

Defining the case includes considering the geographical and chronological location of a case; bounding the case then involves making sure it is clear who is included and who is not. Bounding is intended to 'determine the scope of your data collection and, in particular, how you will distinguish data about the subject of your case study (the "phenomenon") from data external to the case (the "context")' (Yin, 2018, p. 31). This is a useful idea to take into any research design: What exactly is the phenomenon you are investigating? What data sources are relevant to that phenomenon? What is of use? What is merely context?

In some examples, the uniqueness of the case is what makes it an intriguing site for research. Green (2009), for example, conducted ethnographic research in a particular Christian City Technology College in England because it was an early example of a school with an explicit Bible-based ethos in the UK, and therefore had intrinsic interest attached to it.

Some studies utilize multiple cases. It is useful to think back to Cooley's views of the strength of the case study to realize that there must be a fairly low number of case studies beyond which the data are not rich enough to call it a case study, at which point we might start to think not of the 'case' but of the 'unit of analysis' (discussed in Chapter 7). Some case studies are comparative, with the cases being similar (e.g. two schools) but with enough difference to be interesting in terms of data generation. Other case study designs involve the 'nested case study' so that the cases are not at the same taxonomic level; for example, we might have a case of a teacher, inside a case of subject department, inside the case of a school. Chong and Graham (2013) refer to this as the 'Russian Doll' approach, which captures nicely the variety of levels that might be needed. It is also reminiscent of Bronfenbrenner's ecological systems theory (see *Urie Bronfenbrenner* textbox).

Bias

Sackett (1979) defined bias as 'any process at any stage of inference which tends to produce results or conclusions that differ systematically from the truth' (p. 60). Bias as a concept comes from a more positivist epistemological position: that there is a single truth to discover. For many qualitative researchers it is not a concept which they recognize; trustworthiness and rigour are more important concepts which raise some of the same areas of interest. Galdas suggests that allegations of 'bias' in qualitative research particularly reflect a concern with the extent to which a researcher's own concerns and opinions are reflected in the research but that this is fallacious: 'those carrying out qualitative research are an integral part of the process and final product, and separation from this is neither possible nor desirable' (2017, p. 2). The concern must be with whether the researcher has been appropriately 'transparent and reflexive' (Galdas, 2017, p. 2). Bias is one of the topics that causes friction between practitioners of qualitative and quantitative methods, and particularly in relation to the review of research for publication. In this section I have continued to use the word 'bias' to describe types of systematic influence on research data which might cause the results to skew one way, but it is not a universally accepted term.

Selection bias is bias introduced during the selection of participants. It is not necessarily introduced through deliberate selection criteria. Shadish, Clark and Steiner (2008) conducted a randomized trial to look at the effect of randomized versus non-randomized allocation of participants in an experimental study, giving maths and vocabulary training to university students. There was a far larger difference between groups in the non-randomized experiment than in the randomized, suggesting selection bias did have an effect, although the researchers also demonstrated that they were able to counter the effects of most of the bias via statistical post hoc adjustments. One reason for the development of methods to impute missing data rather than simply excluding all cases with missing data was to avoid the systematic bias that was therefore being introduced. Even in randomized controlled trials there may be selection bias if the entire sample is predisposed to benefit, particularly if the control group does not receive treatment at all. For example,

> The ubiquitous and ethical practice of securing parental consent for study participation may introduce bias, because youth for whom parents provide active consent are more likely to have higher grades and test scores and are less likely to have frequent absences, receive free or reduced lunch, or engage in high-risk health behaviors compared with those for whom merely passive consent is provided (i.e., do not opt out of a study). (Cook, 2014, p. 235)

Selection bias can also be introduced via the means of recruitment to the study, sometimes known as self-selection bias. Calls for respondents to an online survey are likely to result in people who are interested in the topic, which may be innocent, or they may have a particular view one way or another which they wish to make the case for, as discussed above. In either case they are not the 'average' person. Cohort studies, which study a large group of participants, born on the same day or over the same small period of time, longitudinally across years, are particularly vulnerable to participants self-selecting out (Biele et al., 2019). Self-selection bias can also be a problem for interventions based around extracurricular activities, dependent on the way recruitment is conducted (e.g. Vallett, Lamb and Annetta, 2018). Quantitative researchers are constantly developing statistical methods to compensate for systematic bias introduced by selection or self-selection bias.

One form of bias (or challenge to rigour) which is more common in qualitative research is social acceptability bias, when individuals edit their responses based on what is perceived to be acceptable to the interviewer or to society more generally. This touches on issues that will be discussed further in Chapter 6, relating to how the researcher responds to the participant. Social acceptability bias may have a smaller effect on internet-based research, where there is no direct contact, and data are anonymous at the point of collection. It can be more of a problem in practitioner research or other contexts where the researcher is well known to participants, particularly if they are in a position of some power and their views are known. This calls into question the validity of the data. Cook suggests a similar problem arises if interventions are not double blinded as effects can be introduced 'such as participants and interventionists in the treatment group trying harder (i.e., performance bias) and observers/assessors evaluating outcomes differentially as a function of group identity (i.e., reporting or observer bias)' (Cook, 2014, p. 235).

Other forms of bias can be introduced at the post-study stage. 'Cherry-picking' (Wagenmakers, Wetzels, Borsboom, van der Maas and Kievit, 2012) is a form of reporting bias where researchers only report the results of analyses that support their hypotheses and omit the rest. One proposal to prevent this has been the introduction of registered reports – where researchers provide plans of proposed research and analyses for review before conducting the research, perhaps most notably in psychology. However, even this is no guarantee: Dwan et al. (2008) reviewed studies that compared published research with the pre-registered reports, which showed between 13 per cent and 31 per cent of primary outcomes named in the registered reports were omitted from the publication of those studies. Publication bias presents a further problem as novelty and statistical significance are more likely to result in publication in journals than negative results, non-significant results or replication studies (see discussion in Chapter 4).

Generalizability and Transferability

As discussed above, the sampling choices of any design are fundamental in being able to claim generalizability from that project to a wider population. Generalizability is generally sought after from quantitative studies, but may be pursued through qualitative methods as well if careful sampling procedures are undertaken to select participants. Hedges (2013) argues that even large experiments, however, can rarely support generalizations to populations that are sufficient for the researchers to make recommendations for practice or policy. This moves us into the field of evidence-based practice (or policy) which is discussed in the next chapter.

In terms of design and the aims for a research study, qualitative research or research that does not follow a random or representative sampling strategy might instead look for transferability to another context. Transferability must be argued for on a theoretical or methodological basis on the individual level and context is extremely important in enabling or preventing transferability. One good example of problems of transferability is educational policy borrowing; Harris and Jones (2018) use an example of school leadership and policy borrowing in seven educational systems to demonstrate that borrowing policy from other countries without sufficient consideration of the context may bring unintended and unfortunate consequences.

The goal of research is not always to generalize or transfer the findings, however. Unique cases, for example, may be of interest in and of themselves as discussed above, or in Participatory Action Research a key aim may be the transformative potential of involvement in the research project itself. A key question is what kind of claims are being made from the data that have been generated, and that generalizability is not being claimed where it is not warranted. Where non-representative samples have been generated claims can only be made about the sample, not the population: not '10% of teachers say' but '10% of respondents say'.

Conclusion

Research design takes the research from research question, set in the context of the existing knowledge on a topic, through the choice of methodology to specific methods. It requires thinking about how data will be generated and how that data map onto the research questions. Whatever research design is followed, there are underlying issues as to how the research identifies the participants, what the phenomenon is that they are investigating and how it is defined, and how combinations of methods will be organized. The next step is to think about how evidence answers those questions, to which we turn in Chapter 4.

3.3 B. F. Skinner

B. F. Skinner (1904–1990) was an American psychologist who largely established the theory of behaviourism. Behaviourism depends on conditioning, where behaviours are reinforced through positive or negative stimuli in order to elicit the desired outcomes. Behaviours may be respondent, that is, elicited by a stimulus, and then strengthened through conditioning. Pavlov's dogs are the classic example: they drool because they are presented with food, and at the same time a bell is rung. After enough time they will drool in response to the bell ringing because of the association. Operant behaviours, on the other hand, arise naturally and are then reinforced by conditioning to promote or deter them. The majority of Skinner's research took place with rats, although it has been utilized widely in the field of human behaviour.

Behaviourism is one of the main drivers of discipline methods in schools today around the world where behaviours are either reinforced positively with praise or negatively with punishment. Not for nothing is discipline in schools more frequently referred to as 'behaviour management'. Skinner is not frequently referenced in educational research now, but the underlying principles of behaviourism are extensively referred to, if not by name. His work is particularly relevant to early childhood development where learning is often generated via repeated reinforcement – parents repeating sounds which appear to be words back to a child who is yet to talk, for example, on the principle that this will encourage the child to make those word-sounds more.

4

What Counts as Evidence?

Epistemic authority is the principle of who has the right and ability to validate knowledge. Someone – or something – which is presumed to have epistemic authority is considered trustworthy, someone whose claims you can accept without validating them yourself. A key question for research is how it gains that epistemic authority – what counts as evidence? This chapter considers some key concepts – rigour, validity, reliability, significance – for educational research and epistemic authority. It goes on to think about the constructed nature of data and how that affects the way we think about data and make claims. In turn this leads us to consider the role of 'evidence-based practice' in education and the so-called 'gold standard' of research evidence, the randomized controlled trial (RCT).

Whetung and Wakefield (2019), in discussing Whetung's experiences as an Indigenous scholar researching her own community, highlight the discomfort created by her progress through the institutional ethics process which did not acknowledge that there might be Indigenous researchers of their own societies and areas. Whetung relates the tension of feeling that she must either be colonizing researcher *or* an Indigenous community member, because there was no acknowledgement that anyone could be both. She goes on to write, 'more than this, the university operates from a knowledge-supremacy position where it dis-embeds knowledge that is rooted outside of the academy to bring it into the academy by validating some aspects of it as "research"' (Whetung and Wakefield, 2019, p. 148). This raises some difficulties for the producer and consumer of research – what counts as evidence?

As a researcher who began as a classroom teacher I might relate something which I know to be true through my own experience, but that has to be in an appropriate context, or it can be dismissed by a reviewer as being assertion, without evidence. I might say something is true, but a research claim would need someone other than the researcher to have said it and for it then to be reported as the belief of a research participant. Embedded knowledge from researcher backgrounds can only be evidence in certain contexts. This is in some ways a fundamental principle of research: it does not simply consist of opinion pieces based on 'what I think': it must draw on external evidence, whether that is data or logical argument (in the case of theory). Different research traditions consider different sources for authority, whether that is the authority of the researcher, the writing or delegated from the participants. For example,

> Within cultural anthropology our case for ethnographic authority and knowledge involves showing the immediacy of '"being there": showing that you the researcher, the author, were in the field long enough to produce professional research. Good research might not always lead to good writing, but it is surely a precondition.' (McGranahan, 2020, p. 2)

For others, epistemic authority stems directly from the research design and methodology. Rigour refers to any set of criteria for trustworthiness in research, which differ according to the tradition that research draws on. Rigour requires clarity, transparency, honesty, acting according to stated methodology and analysis, and reporting appropriately. Two key issues, with which we begin, are validity and reliability.

Validity and Reliability

Validity, roughly speaking, is the extent to which what you are measuring or can measure is what you say you are measuring. For example, in England children at the end of Year 1 of school have to take a Phonics Test, in which they 'read' a series of pseudo words, that is, words which are not in English but are made up of plausible phonemes. This is not a valid test of reading (because children who can read fluently can fail the test), but of whether children can use the systematic synthetic phonics approach to decode words; it is a measure which is testing whether schools are using the mandated approach to reading instruction (Carter, 2020). In research we speak of 'validating' measures and scales used to assess everything from motivation, to empathy, to vocabulary and many more. This means checking that what the scale is purporting to assess is what it is actually assessing. Validity is an important technical term in assessment (see Newton and Shaw's (2014) extensive exploration) and those technical aspects transfer across to measures in educational assessment that can be defined as assessment. Validity in research more generally is framed in a number of other ways.

Campbell (1957) distinguished between internal and external validity: internal validity was the extent to which there was confidence that the findings were true for the group in the research; external validity was the degree to which the results could generalize to the population from which the sample was taken. The former can be increased by introducing features to the design which eliminate alternative explanations for the finding (so, e.g. controlling for specific characteristics) and the latter by following particular procedures in selecting the participants for a study. External validity can be divided into population validity (as described) or ecological validity – the extent to which findings would be valid across other conditions, such as settings (Bracht and Glass, 1968).

Although validity begins in the quantitative realm it applies equally to the qualitative. Richards warns qualitative researchers against 'throwing out the idea of validity with the rather murky and now decidedly tepid bathwater of the debate with quantitative research!' (2015, p. 214). In relation to non-quantitative research, Johnson (1997) suggests three types of validity: descriptive validity, that is, the factual accuracy; interpretative validity, that is, the extent to which the interpretations reflect the thoughts, experiences and views of the participants; and theoretical validity, that is, the fit between theory and data. Lather (1986) had three different types, explicitly addressing research with an ideological purpose (or 'political' as it is framed in Chapter 9): face validity, construct validity and catalytic validity. Face validity is the extent to which the results are recognizable to readers with experience of the research context; it might require member checking of data with the study participants (see Chapter 7) or consulting with a small group who share key characteristics with the participants. Lather defines construct validity as 'a systematized reflexivity, which gives some indication of how a priori theory has been changed by the logic of the data' (1986, p. 67). (Construct validity has a different meaning in assessment theory.) Her 'catalytic validity' is the extent to which the research facilitated transformation from the participants, a concern which is unlikely to trouble those not undertaking explicitly political research.

Reliability, on the other hand, is the extent to which results are consistent, either over time or between different researchers. Between researchers we might be looking at administration of a validated measure – do different researchers administer that measure in the same way as each other? (In educational research this might be a test administered in person, or an observation schedule for recording classroom behaviour, or the application of a coding frame to a set of data, to give three examples.) Over time we ask those same questions of the same researcher – if you do any given research activity on day 1, do you do it in the same way on day 30? If we ask the same question, do we get the same answer? Reliability is a feature not only of a researcher but of a research instrument: if we give the same test to someone thirty days apart, do they get the same result (all other confounding variables aside)?

One way to test the validity and reliability of the findings of a previous study is to replicate it. If you can reproduce a finding with a different sample, then it increases the confidence in its accuracy. Replications are an important part of research in all fields, but they tend to be less popular than looking at new studies for a number of reasons, including the fundability of the projects, the personal status the researcher stands to gain and the criterion of novelty for journal acceptance (Sterling, Rosenbaum and Weinkam, 1995). Makel and Plucker (2014) analysed the complete publication history of hundred educational research journals to examine replication rates; out of 164,589 articles examined they found 0.13 per cent were replications and forty-three journals contained no replications whatsoever. The majority of the replications were successful, but nearly half were carried out by the same team who made the original finding; replications were significantly more likely to be successful ($p < 0.001$) if one or more of the original authors was also an author on the replication.

This low level of replication is significant because of what has been called the replication crisis, or the reproducibility crisis, in psychology, in which a number of high-profile, highly cited experiments failed to replicate satisfactorily (with one study suggesting only a third of psychological replications were successful (Open Science Collaboration, 2015)). One example which is pertinent to education is the delightfully named 'Marshmallow Test', based on a number of experiments on self-control in children in the 1960s. Shoda, Mischel and Peake (1990) conducted a follow-up study in which pre-school children's ability to delay gratification, in the form of resisting eating a marshmallow, with the promise of a further marshmallow if they could wait until the researcher returned, was compared with their teen academic achievement and socio-emotional behaviours and a strong bivariate correlation was found. A replication by Watts, Duncan and Quan (2018) of that experiment was successful *but* showed that controlling for family background, home environment and early cognitive ability, two-thirds of the effect disappeared. In other words, your likelihood of being able to delay marshmallow gratification at age four was partially dependent on your normal access to sweets (a validity problem). The effect of the original study had been confounded by links between socio-economic status and academic attainment.

The replicability crisis may have other causes than poor science. Silberzahn et al. (2018) and Botvinik-Nezer et al. (2020) both gave multiple research teams (twenty-nine and seventy, respectively) the same data set and research questions/hypotheses and in both experiments the results obtained by differing teams were highly varied because of the wide array of analytical techniques they used. Hoffman et al. (2021) argue that because there are usually a 'large variety of possible analysis strategies acceptable according to the scientific standards of the field' (p. 1), part of the replication crisis is caused by these hugely varying approaches. They provide a set of guidelines for quantitative researchers to potentially increase replicability based on the findings.

Replicability is a term which largely applies to experimental studies where the measures are quantitative, where there is a clear procedure which can be repeated in an exact repeat of the original. There is also conceptual replication, where a different project is designed to test the same hypothesis. In qualitative work we might talk instead of retroductability (Wodak, 2014). She introduces the term 'retroductable' as a translation of the German word *nachwollziehbar* and defines it as meaning that 'analyses must be transparent, selections and interpretations justified, and value positions made explicit' (Wodak, 2014, p. 312). In other words, in research where the researcher themselves functions as a tool of analysis and interpretation, and indeed of data generation, the conditions required for replicability are not possible. Instead, we look for enough information to trace back through the research the decisions and analyses that were made so that we can see that they were appropriate. In doing so we judge research according to its own paradigm and principles: quantitative research intends to be as 'objective' as possible; qualitative research looks to the construction of the world by individuals and acknowledges the researcher as part of that process. Retroductability summarizes the ways in which others have suggested qualitative research may gain trustworthiness and credibility. How

> do you decide if the [anthropological] research is valid? Ethnographic research cannot be replicated in a laboratory sense. Instead, we have different markers of credibility such as correspondence with related scholarship. Other classic markers of validity are thick ethnography, rigorous theory and excellent writing. All of these can be persuasive. (McGranahan, 2020, pp. 6–7)

The word 'persuasive' here needs unpacking: it may seem somewhat unscientific, but to an extent it is what all research publications seek to achieve. We are persuaded that the researchers have acted appropriately, with intellectual rigour and with honesty, and that what they have found is significant in some way. In other cases, such as research whose outcome is a creative product of some kind, the value is not defined in terms of validity and reliability: again we look to judge research by its own paradigm. Interestingly, McGranahan also suggests the acknowledgements of an ethnography are an overlooked but key site for validity judgements, as authors reveal the extent of their 'being there' (2020, p. 7).

> ## 4.1 Abraham Maslow
>
> Abraham Maslow (1908–1970) was an American psychologist whose theory of motivation, known as Maslow's hierarchy of needs (1943), remains widely referred even today. Maslow argued that humans have to fulfil basic needs before they can address more complex needs. He ranked the hierarchy as moving from 'physiological', 'safety', 'belonging and love', 'social needs' or 'esteem', to 'self-actualization'. Although Maslow originally framed these as requiring the lower level to be completely satisfied before someone could move on to a higher level, later revisions suggest rather that the levels overlap, but also that the lower levels can take precedence at any time. In other words, if you lose the roof over your head ('safety') then that becomes an urgent motivation for you.
>
> There is little to no empirical evidence for these needs as specific psychological constructs, or the existence of a hierarchy in the way that humans respond to them for motivation (Wahba and Bridwell, 1976). Some research continues to use Maslow's categorization as a taxonomy, as an analytical lens (e.g. Abbas, 2020; or Crandall et al., 2020, which found that belonging and love in the form of parent–child connectedness was more important for understanding adolescent depression than more 'basic' needs in Maslow's understanding).
>
> In 1938 Maslow spent six weeks living with the Blackfeet Nation near Alberta in Canada. His hierarchy of needs draws strongly on Siksika (Blackfeet Nation) teachings, but he did not acknowledge this in his writing. In Siksika teaching, the aim is for not self-actualization but community-actualization, and then for cultural perpetuity. It is possible that one of the reasons Maslow omitted these needs was

because of his understanding of European-American society as being more highly oriented towards the individual; it is notable, however, that he did credit a number of other (white) psychologists whose work he built on while not mentioning the Blackfoot teachers he had spent time with.

Significance

A further term which needs defining in research terms is significance. While the lay meaning of something being 'significant' is that it is important, in research terms the word almost always refers to statistical significance. The statistical significance of a result is the likelihood that the result from the data was obtained due to the cause identified rather than by chance. The higher the statistical significance, the smaller the possibility that the result was obtained by chance. The most common measure of this is 'p' (the probability that the null hypothesis is true); a p value of less than 0.05 (i.e. less than 5 per cent) is generally held to be statistically significant. The use of this word as an extremely frequent technical term means that it is best to avoid it outside the context of statistics; a claim that something is 'significant' is likely to be read as meaning statistically significant even if the meaning intended is 'important'.

Understanding Data as Constructed

Although we commonly refer to 'data collection' in research, data 'generation' is a more accurate account of what we do. This, like many other terms, is a legacy of the positivist versus constructivist argument.

> The term *generation* is intended to encapsulate the variety of ways in which the researcher, social world, and data interact in qualitative inquiry. Data are not considered to be 'out there' just waiting to be collected; rather, data are produced from their sources using qualitative research methods. (Given, 2008, p. 192)

Perhaps it is a mark of my own particular epistemological leanings that I would suggest most quantitative data are also generated not collected. Take, for example, Pittas and Nunes (2017) who look at whether children's dialect awareness is a long-term predictor for spelling and reading. The children were assessed with '(three dialect awareness measures) and five control measures (the similarities sub-test from the WISC-III, as an estimate of verbal IQ, one measure of phonological awareness and three measures morphological awareness)' (Pittas and Nunes, 2017, p. 3). Those data did not exist before the researchers administered the tests, and would not have existed if they had not. Secondary data analysis might be an exception, in that the data have already been generated, but they may still have to be collated, combined, cleaned and so on.

There might also be an argument for the exception of what is called 'naturally occurring data' which includes recordings of normal classroom speech for Conversation Analysis, or discourse analysis carried out on documents: that is, data that would come into existence whether or not the researcher was there to see it. (Although decisions about the delimitation of those data sets contribute to a sense of generation, not of collection, there is also a question of whether the knowledge of being recorded changes what people say.)

This idea of generation rather than collection has implications for how we understand data. They are constructed in particular circumstances which affect what they say. Chapter 6 considers some of these issues in relation to the particular researcher, and the relationship between researcher and researched, but it is also true of documents which do not have the same interaction with the researcher. 'Documents are not neutral, transparent reflections of organizational or occupational life' (Atkinson and Coffey, 2010, p. 77). Rather, they are constructed to achieve particular aims, for particular audiences, even if that audience is only the author: 'A diary is a form of identity practice and self-production. ... The life led and the life recorded are not the same thing' (Bayley, 2016, p. x).

Visual data similarly are not a simplistic record of time or place. Koh (2016) examines advertising for tutorial schools in Hong Kong. These 'naturally occurring' data are gathered, yet are evidently constructed for a particular persuasive purpose, with the relation of words and text providing rich material for Koh's media analysis.

> Like other modes of representation – textual, oral, visual – photographs are not innocent, tell-all records that offer an unmediated view of the past. ... which cannot be understood as 'all-seeing' pictures of an event or classroom, or as simply capturing things as they really were in a naturalistic record. Rather, photographs can be staged and stylised, some elements foregrounded

or backgrounded in the composition, and even with supposedly candid and random photographs, some things are excluded from view. And, of course, the same image evokes different emotional and analytical responses from viewers and takes on new significance with every re-reading. (McLeod, Goad, Willis and Darian-Smith, 2016, p. 19)

McLeod, Goad, Willis and Darian-Smith (2016) capture the idea, more common in arts-related research, that meaning even of objects is co-created at the level of the observer and the object, so that data are constructed at two levels, at the level of generation and at the level of encounter with them for the purpose of analysis. Blum-Ross discusses utilizing participatory filmmaking with young people as part of her ethnographic methods set, and emphasizes that everyone needs to understand the representational nature of such data, rather than accepting them as 'unproblematically "real"' (2013, p. 5). Think about utilizing student note-taking as evidence for what happened during a lesson or lecture. For one thing each student's notes will be an incomplete account, only showing what they did not already know, or what they found interesting, or what they had time to write down, or what they heard. Alternatively, if you interview policy makers about their part in the creation of a particular education policy, they will have other interests in terms of consolidating their legacies. Natow (2020) suggests that triangulation from other data sources is essential in elite interviews in order to identify biases and inaccuracies in what they have said. However, this assumes that the purpose of the research is a descriptive 'what happened': some research is more interested in the construction of narratives by participants. McIntyre and Hobson (2016) looked at the ways in which student teachers talked about their experiences with mentors from outside their own school environment, as opposed to inside the school environment and showed that they could be more honest about their problems, as opposed to constructing an identity of competence for someone who was both mentor and influential professional superior. Understanding the constructed nature of their data enabled them to make a recommendation for support for beginning teachers outside of the school hierarchy in which they are embedded.

Jerome Bruner (see textbox) theorized the idea of life as narrative (1987). An easy way to conceptualize this is to think of the job application letter and curriculum vitae. When you write an application for a job, you tailor your account of your life teleologically – that is, as if it had all been leading up to this point. Even if you have only just decided you want to do whatever the job is, you recount your life experiences as preparation for that role. We narrate our lives constantly in big and small ways. Bruner's idea stems from the idea that as humans we have no other way to relate lived experience than as narrative. In addition,

> Narrative imitates life, life imitates narrative. 'Life' in this sense is the same kind of construction of the human imagination as 'a narrative' is. It is constructed by human beings through active ratiocination, by the same kind of ratiocination through which we construct narratives. (Bruner, 1987, p. 692)

So the kinds of narratives – the kinds of stories – we tell about our own lives also help us to understand them and alter how we act. In research we frequently ask people to relate their experience to create data, whether in small ways or in big ways like oral histories. In either case their responses are shaped by all sorts of factors including our understandings of what a story looks like. This is a warning, not of bias but of the factors that go into our construction of any kind of communication, and which must be understood as part of the data we generate. 'Stories economically communicate experience, ideas and emotions and help make sense of potentially perplexing situations' (Gabriel and Connoll, 2010, p. 507).

Evidence-Informed/Evidence-Based Practice

Evidence-based practice in education follows the model of evidence-based practice in medicine and has been a trend in education since the end of the twentieth century. Davies (1999) establishes two levels of evidence-based practice – the first is the availability of evidence in a systematic way to educational professionals who can evaluate that evidence and judge its relevance to their own environment and needs. The final point is interesting in the context of the term 'evidence-based practice' having come to mean a 'what works' approach where there is assumed to be a universal answer and in a societal context where social media, particularly 'EduTwitter', has entrenched divisions between different approaches espoused by different groups. The need for appropriate contextual relevance is one of Biesta's (2020) challenges to the 'what works' narrative of educational research. He also argues that it is a problematic model given the nature of teaching as an endeavour:

> The model of professional action implied in evidence-based practice – that is, the idea of education as a treatment or intervention that is a causal means to bring about particular, preestablished ends – is not appropriate for the field of education. What is needed for education is a model of professional action that acknowledges the noncausal nature of educational interaction and the fact that the means and ends of education are internally rather than externally related. What is needed, in other words, is an acknowledgment of the fact that education is a moral practice, rather than a technical or technological one. (Biesta, 2007, p. 10)

Such a view of education means that teachers must be the ultimate arbiters of what is appropriate in their classrooms. This is largely in line with Donald McIntyre's concept of practical theorizing (1993) which sees a reciprocal relationship between theory (including research evidence) and practice. He talks of this in relation to teacher education in a way that reflects Biesta's conceptions of teaching and offers a model for the embedding of research into teaching in a non-forced way, accepting the variations between classes, teachers and contexts:

> The theoretical knowledge which we offer student teachers should be treated by them as tentative, inadequate and constantly to be questioned and, where appropriate, falsified; but it should also be knowledge which we offer them because we believe it to be of practical value to them as teachers. Our commitment to the process of experimentation and falsification should be equalled by our commitment to making available to our students theoretical knowledge which they will mostly, with refinement, be able usefully to assimilate to their professional thinking. (McIntyre, 1993, p. 41)

This also avoids another potential pitfall of the evidence-based practice approach which is that in siting the agency and expertise with the teacher, there is less chance of resistance based on differing personal experience from what the evidence base says. There is no need to say 'that cannot be true because it is not true in my classroom' if you are able to say 'to work in my classroom, these adjustments need to be made' and make them.

Davies's second level of evidence-based practice is the consequent need to establish a sound basis of research evidence where existing evidence is weak. One of the trends in educational research over the last twenty years has been the increase in carrying out systematic reviews and meta-analyses (again following the example of medicine), which seek to gather together the best available evidence to draw conclusions on the basis of a much larger data set than any one study could provide. At the time of writing the

International Database of Education Systematic Reviews is in the first phase of its operation, working to catalogue systematic reviews in the sub-field of language education (idesr.org), with the aim of enabling educationalists the world over to identify existing systematic reviews and their evidence base rapidly. Systematic reviews follow strict exclusion and inclusion criteria on the basis of focus of study, the nature of the sample and other quality criteria. Meta-analyses can then be conducted using the outcomes of these studies and creating an overall measure of, for example, the effectiveness of a particular intervention. The nature of the methodology tends to advantage quantitative over qualitative evidence.

Davies's first level of evidence-based practice in education also required teachers to be research-literate and able to evaluate research for themselves. Two major barriers arise to this requirement: first is the fact that much research is not available to people outside academia, which means that the teachers cannot evaluate it at all, and the second is the increasing pressures on teachers the world over to increase attainment, counter social problems, deal with mental health epidemics among young people and other priorities which take their time and prevent most from having the time to look for and evaluate research which is rarely written in a way to make it comprehensible to the non-academic. There is a more positive side: there are subject associations in many countries which do make research available to their members; there are a great number of practitioners involved in research in their own classrooms; open access is becoming more incentivized; and more researchers are working towards producing versions of their research which can be used by practitioners. However, time pressures do create particular issues relating to the oversimplification of and consequent implementation of research in ways which do not realize its original potential.

One extremely popular piece of research in schools is Carol Dweck's work on mindset (2006). Briefly, her research shows that 'Individuals who believe their talents can be developed (through hard work, good strategies, and input from others) have a growth mindset. They tend to achieve more than those with a more fixed mindset (those who believe their talents are innate gifts)' (Dweck, 2016). However, she has noted that in becoming popular the original idea has become distorted (2016); knowing that a growth mindset promotes greater learning gains does not necessarily translate well into being able to develop growth mindsets, and given that mindsets are deeply held, it is perfectly possible for students and teachers to espouse out loud a growth mindset as mandated by their school, but less easy to tweak behaviour and attitudes to cohere with that espousal. Similarly, the version of Bourdieu's cultural capital (1977) (see *Pierre Bourdieu* textbox) that was institutionalized into the English education system by the schools' inspectorate Ofsted (2019) and consequently circulated among teachers bears far more relation to E. D. Hirsch's Cultural Literacy (1987) than to Bourdieu. Cultural capital is certainly not, in its original incarnation, viable as an intervention to decrease attainment gaps between students from different social backgrounds, as it has become viewed in English schools. The difficulty comes when very popular research is oversimplified beyond the point of usefulness, and the effect is no longer felt, so effort is being expended to no end. In addition, as Hedges (2013) notes, implementation research shows that even interventions which work well in a laboratory or small-scale setting do not always translate well to a large-scale implementation, and indeed may not be feasible as a result. This leads to disappointment and can lead to a rejection of research evidence in general.

The 'Gold Standard'

For many the 'gold standard' of research remains that which comes out of a positivist, cause-and-effect paradigm, that is, large-scale quantitative research. This is seen as the highest standard of evidence that can be attained, modelled after the experimental hard sciences. In both the United States and the UK, in recent years there has been an emphasis on RCT as a methodology, promoted by analogy with medical research and promoted by government sources, such as the report *Building Evidence into Education* (Goldacre, 2013), commissioned from a medical doctor. As a result, a large part of funding for educational research available from the UK government was diverted via the Education Endowment Fund into RCT-based research and meta-analyses which drew almost exclusively on existing RCT evidence. RCT *is* a key method for the evaluation of interventions but that does not mean it is or should be the exclusive research method in educational research. Concerns that similar moves in the United States on the part of the National Research Council might restrict what could be considered 'scientific' were raised by Erickson and Gutierrez (2002).

However, in terms of 'what counts as evidence?' this emphasis relates to one key way in which evidence is judged – its ability to enact change, particularly in educational policy. Large-scale quantitative evidence is seen as powerful and convincing. Numbers are convincing for rhetorical reasons, to quote a 'pessimistic' view (McConway, 2016, p. 49) of the role they play in media coverage of research and in policy making. 'Numbers are not construed in the same way as other, equally factual and trustworthy, information' (McConway, 2016, p. 52); instead, they carry greater psychological weight. Statistical data on populations are also important in ensuring the visibility of particular groups. Walter and Andersen discuss the 'Canadian census's inability to enumerate Aboriginal sociality' (2016, p. 111) which renders some First Nations problems invisible to policy makers, for example. There is also a role for the specific, qualitative research in policy making, and making the case for policy change, however. Qualitative research enables the detailed story to be told, and as explored above, humans have a natural affinity to narrative.

The 'gold standard' will be addressed further in Chapter 9.

Conclusion

Many different types of data find their way into educational research but it is not what data they are that matters but how they are handled. To become evidence they depend on the framing given by the researcher, in that the framing shows their source, their validity (in a broad sense of the word) and why the consumer of research should rely on them.

4.2 Jerome Bruner

Jerome Bruner (1915–2016) was an American psychologist who specialized in cognitive and educational psychology. He was born blind due to cataracts but had restorative surgery as a young child. His theory of learning is a constructivist one, and influenced by Lev Vygotsky (see textbox). One of his principal concepts was the idea of scaffolding which has become firmly embedded in modern educational practices. Based on his observation of language acquisition, Bruner made a distinction between interactional environments where support for the learner facilitates learning, like joint picture book reading or parent–child 'caretaker' speech, and environments where support is not given, like the reading of a bedtime story.

The level of support needed can be increased or reduced depending on the needs of the child in the particular learning experience. Effectively scaffolding provides the difference between the inner and outer boundaries of the Zone of Proximal Development proposed by Vygotsky. The key to successful learning is the removing of scaffolding when it is no longer needed, so that the student is able to achieve the same outcome alone.

Bruner also proposed the spiral curriculum, in which the same concepts, skills or topics are revisited periodically, with increased difficulty or sophistication each time. This is the basis where each science is taught in each year, in progressive levels of difficulty, as in the UK, as opposed to splitting them and teaching each science in one grade, as in the United States. The principles of the spiral curriculum suggest that it is possible to teach even quite sophisticated material with the right structuring and instruction to even quite young children. The combined effect of Bruner's thinking is in contrast to the idea of developmental stages; for him development is not qualitatively different, it is just that the child requires different levels of support at different ages.

Bruner was a prolific author and educator; there are many contexts in which you may find his work cited in education. His essay 'Life as Narrative' (1987), and the subsequent developments of it, for example, are widely used in thinking about narrative data in qualitative research.

5
Theory as the Beginning and End of Research

This chapter considers the three major ways in which theory interacts with empirical research: as the source for design; as an analytical tool; and as an end product, when research leads to the creation of a theory. It will consider the different 'levels' of theory, at the micro- (concept), meso- (middle range theory) and macro- (Grand Theory) levels. We will consider the role a theoretical framework plays, and what use it is. We will also consider how the overlapping of different disciplines, in education in particular, means that there may be several different theoretical concepts which are effectively describing the same thing from different approaches. Theory and data exist in an ongoing symbiotic relationship in research:

> Theory is supposed to 'fit' data – either by design, where a lack of fit should lead to rejections or revisions of a theory, or by default, where theory is understood as emerging from the data. Theory and data are thus seen as 'external', two different entities that can and should be related while still being recognized as separate. (Alvesson and Kärreman, 2011, p. 3)

Throughout this book textboxes have been used to showcase particular theorists. These theorists are those who are of particular relevance in education and whose work is frequently referred to by researchers. They provide a brief introduction to a 'who's who?' of theorists in educational research to support recognition when they are mentioned in passing in this book and elsewhere. It is not a comprehensive list and they may reveal some of my own biases in who I think needs to be known. Certainly at one point or another in my early career I have come up against most of their names in a context where I was clearly expected to know who they were. Others I have selected because they are increasingly important in educational research as it is now, or with reference to an understanding of the construction of a theoretical canon which does not always recognize those with marginalized identities even if they came up with an idea first. The ordering in the book is chronological by date of birth.

What Is Theory?

> Like so many words that are bandied about, the word theory threatens to become meaningless. Because its referents are so diverse – including everything from minor working hypotheses, through comprehensive but vague and unordered speculations, to axiomatic systems of thought – use of the word often obscures rather than creates understanding. (Merton, 1967, p. 39)

Theory is a level of abstraction which gives us a lens to look at the specific data we have to understand them better, which enables us to say things not just about the specific situation we are in and which offers some level of explanation. As Durkheim said, over a century ago, 'the words of everyday language, like the concepts they express, are always susceptible of more than one meaning, and the scholar employing them in their accepted use without further definition would risk serious misunderstanding' (1897, p. 41). It is somewhat challenging that 'theory' is one of the words that is bandied about and used to mean many different things – or rather, to mean several different orders of magnitude of the same things. In this section we will discuss how theory as a whole is defined, but to avoid Durkheim's trap I will say now that I have chosen to distinguish between levels of theory at the Grand Theory scale (e.g. Marxism), which is the macro level; middle range theory which works at the level of the individual phenomenon; and theory on the micro level where I think the term 'concept' or 'lens' is a better fit than 'theory', where we use it to interrogate data in close encounters.

Theory can sometimes be intimidating because of the terminology employed both in writing it and writing about it. Take Kerlinger's definition:

> A set of interrelated constructs, definitions, and propositions that presents a systematic view of phenomena by specifying relations among variables, with the purpose of explaining and predicting phenomenon. (Kerlinger, 1986, p. 9)

Here, we get a sense that theory is relational: it looks between variables (or people). It is not just about the moment in hand but has a wider relevance. I prefer Tuhiwai Smith's definition which is longer but clearer:

> At the very least [theory] helps make sense of reality. It enables us to make assumptions and predictions about the world in which we live. It contains within it a method or methods for selecting and arranging, for prioritising and legitimating what we see and do. Theory enables us to deal with contradictions and uncertainties ... It also helps us to interpret what is being told to us, and to predict the consequences of what is promised ... If it is a good theory, it also allows for new ideas and ways of looking at things to be incorporated constantly without the need to seek constantly for new theories. (Tuhiwai Smith, 1999, p. 38)

This final point she makes is a useful one – theory must withstand the addition of new data, new relationships, which can be incorporated, rather than entirely shifting the terrain. (Such huge shifts do occur, as set out in Thomas Kuhn's *The Structure of Scientific Revolutions* (1962), but they are the exception rather than the rule.[1]) Kettley similarly argues that new material must be explicable in the context of the theory, rather than requiring it to be extended:

> First, the purpose of a total theory is the compact arrangement of concepts used in description, analysis and explanation allowing the simultaneous inspection of interpretations. Secondly, the production of a total theory must avoid the ad hoc integration of new concepts into the explanation, since concepts must be logically derived one from another. Thirdly, a total theory is an accumulation of interpretations, which allows new stories to be built on its foundations. If extensions of the theory are required, necessitating new foundations, it is suspect in terms of its explanatory utility. Fourthly, empirical investigation and the analysis of data are promoted by sound total theories, because they suggest the arrangement or cross-tabulation of concepts in an attempt to explain. Finally, the procedure involved in the construction of a total theory must be explicit, approximating the rigour of statistics, enabling the critical inspection of abstractions. (Kettley, 2010, p. 23, after Merton, 1968)

Kettley also has high standards for the construction of theory, requiring its logical steps to be clearly visible and set out for inspection, so that false

---

[1] Kuhn's work is the origin of the idea of 'paradigm shift' and although his book is on the philosophy of science, it is frequently referenced in social sciences and is therefore worth knowing about. It argues for periods of gradual cumulative progress, or stable science, which are interrupted by discoveries of such magnitude that there is a 'paradigm shift' which changes the rules of the game. Einstein's General Theory of Relativity would be one such paradigm shift.

equivalences and logical fallacies may be identified and rejected, and the theory strengthened or disbanded as a result.

At this stage it is worthwhile addressing the difference between a taxonomy and a theory, and specifically Bloom's taxonomy (Bloom, Engelhart, Furst, Hill and Krathwohl, 1956) which holds such a steadfast place in educational practice. The taxonomy classifies intended learning outcomes and was originally developed at the behest of Benjamin Bloom as a useful tool to aid in writing examination items that each tested the same objective in order to facilitate a bank of such items that could be drawn on by different universities (Krathwohl, 2002). The original six categories were: Knowledge, Comprehension, Application, Analysis, Synthesis and Evaluation, although each was also divided into a number of subcategories which are completely omitted in the taxonomy's use in school classrooms today. Knowledge, for example, contains three sub-divisions, each with a number of categories beneath them. Comprehension, often considered a relatively simple category, contains: 2.1 Translation, 2.2 Interpretation, and 2.3 Extrapolation (Krathwohl, 2002, p. 213). Taxonomies are hierarchical systems for the classification of things based on observable characteristics. The difference from theory is that this does not provide us with further insight into the categories once they have been sorted. A theory as analytical lens provides us a further lever to understand a mechanism or a relation: a taxonomy *is* a mechanism. It is for this reason that Bloom's taxonomy is not an educational theory, nor was it ever intended to be. Theory to me is a tool – a tool for looking at the world, or at a phenomenon as a whole, or at specific data.

When Does Theory Happen?

> For a scientist [a point of view on what to observe] is provided by his theoretical interests, the special problem under investigation, his conjectures and anticipations, and the theories which he accepts as a kind of background: his frame of reference, his 'horizon of expectation'. (Popper, [1963] 2002, p. 62)

Theory plays an essential role in all research. It can stimulate the origins of a project; provide a helping hand in the design, execution or analysis phases; and can be the outcome of educational research. Theory acts as a framework to a research study (a background understanding of the research field, topic and data); as a tool for analysis – either on a large or a small scale; and as the outcome of data analysis – generating explanations for relationships between data and concepts. Most published articles make some sort of 'theoretical contribution': an abstraction that goes beyond just the data they have produced; in quantitative research that might be a generalization to the population, or a causal explanation. Below there are examples of research where theory generates research questions (e.g. Roussel, Joulia, Tricot and Sweller, 2017), or where it is used as an analytic device to understand data (e.g. Rose and McKinley, 2018).

Biesta advocates a pragmatic approach to theory (not in terms of pragmatism as a theory), which he contrasts to a 'confessional' approach (p. 8) in which one begins from the theory, taking a position via the form of a confession ('I am a post structuralist'):

> While it is true that one can never start from nowhere and that in this regard there may be sense in laying one's cards on the table, this shouldn't mean that one should do this in a confessional way, that is, as a matter of literally *taking* the position ... To compare it with carpentry, while a hammer can be a very appropriate tool for some tasks, it is entirely useless for other tasks, which shows that confessing oneself as being a *hammering* carpenter would seriously limit one's ability at being a *good* carpenter. (2020, p. 9)

I must disagree to some extent, in that there are certainly researchers who operate purely from one theoretical standpoint, one Grand Theory, and that it is essential that they should confess this openly. In their cases (take, e.g. socio-cultural activity theory), the theory comes first and all questions are viewed through this light. Other researchers could and do see the same problem through different lenses. While to a large extent I also advocate for a pragmatic approach to theory (and method) in education, it is important to acknowledge that some people work within the same grand theoretical framework (or apparently atheoretical framework) for their entire careers which does not necessarily make them less good carpenters, but merely more specialized ones. And if they are specialized in this way, then it is essential that I know that when looking at their work, and that they know it, when writing about their research and conclusions.

Perhaps a more common encounter with theory, particularly theory-as-concept as discussed below, is to discover a need for it during or towards the end of the analytical process. Discovering an unexpected phenomenon leads to the need to seek for potential explanatory theory. In published research the conventions of the genre mean that the chronology of such actions (analysis, then theory) is misrepresented (as theory (then methods) then analysis) which can be deceptive for the beginning researcher. In my first published article I reported a phenomenon where examiners, marking scripts, would talk aloud to an imagined version of the candidate, usually commiserating about how they were going to have to give them a low mark, but reassuring the imaginary student that they (the marker) were a kind and just person (Elliott, 2013). In seeking an explanation for this I found Festinger's cognitive dissonance theory (1957), which suggests that when we hold two contrasting beliefs it causes dissonance, and we seek to resolve it by somehow reconciling the beliefs. In this case the examiners were seeking to reassert their identities as teachers, allied with students, empathetic to the consequences of the poor marks they were giving for those students, by framing the necessity of maintaining the accuracy of the marking process as part of an identity that looked for justice and fair assessment for all students. As a naïve beginner in the world of academic publishing, I did not bring in Festinger until the discussion section of my paper, reflecting the process I had been through: the reviewers firmly told me to fully explore the literature and theory on which I was drawing in the appropriate section of the article, namely the literature review. These conventions camouflage the way the research process works (not only in terms of when you address theory and literature but also in terms of the iterative process that analysis often is, and the ways research questions are revised). To return to Biesta's point above, and to reiterate it in this context also, it is important with theory as with interpretations of data to test their appropriateness to destruction: the analysis process should look to disrupt the explanation (or theory) that comes first to mind, in order to ensure that there is not a better explanation (or theory) that can be found. As Kettley argues, 'theory per se never constitutes a barrier to research and social explanation; rather the incorrect application of existing theory results in weak research' (2010, p. 5).

Despite the potential fetishization of empirical work in educational research (Peim, 2018), there are also those who argue the other direction (naturally!) but at the same time underline the fact that we are always engaged in theory:

> There is far too much mystique about theory. For reasons that are not fully apparent to me, social science and, in particular, sociology, valorizes its theoreticians far more greatly than those who engage in the whole process of generating data and sorting out what it might mean. Yet while theorists are parasitic upon empirical researchers, those engaged in empirical research are actually forced to be theorists as well. For whether it is recognized or not,

generating new data is always a theoretically driven activity, it is just that in some cases the theory remains unexamined when it should be subjected to scrutiny. (Walford, 2001, p. 147)

As with many of the aspects of educational research, Walford reminds us that it is important to be reflexive and aware of what it is we are doing in relation to theory and theorizing. With reference to the final sentence of this question, it is interesting to ask whether there is such a thing as non-theoretical research. Many researchers argue that theory is always present, whether it is implicit or explicit (Merriam, 2001; Rocco and Plakhotnik, 2009; Peim, 2019), and I tend to agree. Large-scale quantitative research has theory implicit in the variables which are measured and put into relation and in the ways that measures are created and validated. Qualitative research must at least draw on theoretical concepts in the analysis of data and the development of arguments.

5.1 Urie Bronfenbrenner

Urie Bronfenbrenner (1917–2005) is the originator of ecological systems theory. He was born in Russia but his family emigrated to the United States when he was six, where he received all of his education. He was a developmental psychologist who revolutionized the field by raising the significance of ecological and societal factors in child development. To be simplistic, a child living in a rural community will have different developmental influences than one growing up in an inner-city tower-block; different networks of peer relationships will provide different input.

The key concept of ecological systems theory which continues to be extremely influential in educational research is generally shown in a diagram of concentric circles, working outwards from the individual to the microsystem, the mesosystem, the exosystem and the macrosystem (Bronfenbrenner, 1977). (These labels are often replaced by the specific items which are being considered in each layer.) The microsystem consists of their immediate environment, such as their family, their peers, their schools. The mesosystem is a series of connections between these – so, for example, when parents and teachers communicate, representing how individual influences are connected in various ways. The mesosystem also connects the microsystem to the exosystem, which is the indirect environment – such as the extended family, the neighbourhood, the parents' workplaces or the school's context such as being in a chain of schools, or the regulations governing its conduct. The macrosystem is the wider societal context of cultures and values, that is, the national societal context (or international) and the socio-economic context. Outside all of these circles comes the chronosystem – that is, the change over time in the environments affecting the child.

Different researchers will put different contexts in each layer of the model, enabling them to focus on their specific levels of interest. The strength of the model is its ability to show the ways in which interactions between different contexts affect the individual at the centre, and also the macro context of societal discourse. Bronfenbrenner and Ceci (1994) renamed the model the Bioecological model, taking into account biological and biopsychological effects. Most researchers not working directly in child development use the earlier model – and have expanded it beyond its original applications. Paat (2013) applies ecological systems theory to working with immigrant children and their families in the United States, looking, for example, at the different implications of living in ethnically similar or ethnically diverse neighbourhoods. Ecological systems theory is widespread when researchers want to consider nested contexts for their research questions.

Grand Theory

Grand Theory is the level at which the layperson thinks of theory: Marxism, Feminism, Critical Race Theory, Critical Pedagogy, Neoliberalism and so on. Grand Theory crosses disciplines and fields, working across social science and humanities. The term starts out as a pejorative term coined by C. Wright Mills in *The Sociological Imagination* (1959) for theory which is too abstract, too far removed from the realities of life. Although I have used the term here to distinguish between different levels, this is also just called 'theory'; the point is that it is working at systemic levels.

As an example, take Intersectionality, a term coined by Kimberlé Williams Crenshaw in her Black Feminist analysis of the interactions of race and gender in antidiscrimination law (1989) (see textbox). In coining the term she crystallized a number of thoughts and practices that had been in place among Black Feminist writers for a long time. Intersectionality works as a theory of analysis: it allows consideration of multiple causes of oppression at once, rather than holding them separately. It theorizes that, for example, being Black and female will mean that you have different experiences than just being Black, or just being female, but also works for sexuality, disability, class and a number of other intersections. Intersectionality is a natural fit for quantitative research which thinks about educational attainment differences between groups; it does not mean, however, that we should only consider discrimination in relation to highly specific groups. Intersectionality works at the Grand Theory level, looking at how societal relations work on a large scale, although it can also be used as a middle range analytical tool, but it does not work at the level of the individual: 'I'm intersectional' does not make sense.

Grand Theory can be used as a framework for many kinds of research. Bagley and Castro-Salazar (2012) used Critical Race Theory fused with life history and performance as data and methods, to generate an arts-based performance text called Undocumented Historias with undocumented American students of Mexican origin. They argue that the combination provides a powerful framework to work with educationally and socially marginalized groups, and follow Denzin who claims that 'performance text is the single most powerful way for ethnography to recover yet interrogate the meaning of lived experience' (1999, p. 94). The role of the theory here is to provide a focus for the performance text, honing it with reference to that 'critical' aspect which challenges power relations, in this case in relation to race. In contrast Huber and Cueva (2012) who also use Critical Race Theory, as well as Chicana feminist theory, utilize these as analytical frameworks which generate concepts such as *conocimiento* (critical awakenings) (Anzaldúa, 2002) which form tools to analyse and unlock their data.

Kettley (2010) specifically warns against the 'deification' (p. 33) of Grand Theory in education research, where it may interfere with the very purpose of the research – the generation of sound explanations. He has high expectations of theory as providing 'powerful explanations' – 'the work of the educational researcher is, after all, to pursue social explanations, effective understandings of collective cognition and behaviour, unlimited by societal locations' (Kettley, 2010, p. 43). He acknowledges that therefore 'individual accounts of experience' (2010, p. 43) will not always align with the overall social explanation, because individuals are limited in time and space. My feeling is that Kettley is too hard on educationalists, and fails to recognize the constraints in which they operate: he wants education research to be able to fulfil the ambitions that consecutive governments in many countries across the world have had for the education system, namely to fix the societal ills and problems of structural inequality.

Middle Range Theory

Middle range theory 'seeks to explain a limited instance of a given form of social behaviour' (Kettley, 2010, p. 17). The term was developed by sociologist Robert K. Merton (1968). Some middle range theory is explicitly linked to a specific discipline, so there are educational theories and theorists. Figured Worlds (Holland, Lachicotte, Skinner and Cain, 1998) and the specifically educational Communities of Practice (Lave and Wenger, 1991, see textbox *Jean Lave and Etienne Wenger*) come under this heading. Middle range theory links empirical phenomena with some level of abstraction, seeking to consolidate phenomena and their explanations into a coherent overarching explanation. Most research studies will require some middle range theory as well as or instead of using a Grand Theory.

One increasingly popular middle range theory in educational practice is cognitive load theory. Cognitive load theory applies knowledge of working memory limits to the learning process, given that material must first pass through working memory before being committed to long-term memory. Sweller (1988) argued that cognitive load could be reduced using instructional design. Roussel, Joulia, Tricot and Sweller (2017) applied cognitive load theory to design three experiments on the efficacy of Content and Language Integrated Learning (CLIL – where subject content is taught in a target foreign language). Cognitive load theory led them to hypothesize that without direct foreign language instructional support, the delivery of new content in the foreign language could interfere with rather than support learning. They conducted experiments with higher education students in varied conditions, varied languages and varied subjects to test this hypothesis. The results supported their hypothesis, with consequent recommendations for teachers of CLIL. Here the middle range theory generated the research question, but middle range theory is just as likely to support data analysis. Fish and Syed (2018) demonstrate another approach to middle range theory, when they apply Bronfenbrenner's ecological systems theory (see *Urie Bronfenbrenner* textbox) to the experiences of Native Americans at higher education institutions, using the theory to recast the situation from a different perspective, thus generating new insights.

Concepts

Concepts are the lowest level of theory, working at the level of tools (the metaphor of 'tools' is itself a concept taken from Vygotsky (see textbox)), with which you can prise open data. You might also hear the word 'lens' in relation to this, although lenses can also be on the level of Grand Theory, implying a coloration to everything you are seeing. These concepts are often everyday words which need defining according to literature, but they are sometimes not; for example, 'masks', 'push-pull model', 'deficit model' and so on.

Rose and McKinley (2018), for example, analyse a particular initiative to internationalize Japanese higher education. They draw on the (theoretical) concepts of internationalization, globalization and Englishization; the research is not informed by Grand Theory but by specific useful 'tools' from the literature, which enable them to analyse and conceptualize the moves within the initiative. Sundaram and Sauntson used the concept of silence as a tool to unpick the ways in which government documents and young women themselves talk about sex and relationships education and specifically pleasure: 'Absences in texts are potentially as significant and meaningful as what is present' (2016, p. 242). Theory-as-concept often arises out of the data themselves, as inductive analysis demonstrates what is important within the data, and the use of a particular word or metaphor will suggest particular concepts from the literature. In Elliott and Dingwall (2017) we considered how drama interventions allowed students at risk of disengagement to practise being 'other', as participants described in various ways the idea of a mask which could be put on and taken off. The mask itself was a useful theoretical concept with which we could then explore the data, but it also led us to the Vygotskyan concept of *perezhivanie*, which Peter Smagorinsky (2011) translates as 'emotional experience'. The metaphorical mask the students put on enabled them to gain the emotional experience of being someone other than their contested and constrained selves. At a middle range theory level we then looked at Gee's identity theory and discourse identity (2001), which is the identity an individual is placed into by the discourses around them.

These examples amply demonstrate that theory-as-concept is fundamental to the function of educational research, as it forms the basis of the toolkit with which we analyse data and group them in order to form new relationships and generate new understandings of phenomena. Theory-as-concept is not exclusive of middle range theory or Grand Theory, and indeed it is possible for all three to co-exist in one research project. As with ontology and epistemology, the need is for them to act together coherently. Theory-as-concept is closest to the concrete experience, and as we move up to middle range and Grand Theory we move increasingly towards the abstract (Anfara and Mertz, 2006).

5.2 Paulo Freire

Paulo Freire (1921–1977) was a Brazilian educator whose work *Pedagogy of the Oppressed* is one of the most influential works on education ever written. It promotes a critical pedagogy opposed to what Freire called the 'banking model' of education, in which teachers fill up empty vessels (children) with facts. Critical pedagogy critiques the view of the teacher as the sole holder of knowledge, and therefore power, instead proposing a model in which teachers and pupils learn from each other and discover a spirit of inquiry.

For Freire the purpose of life – and therefore education – is for individuals to become 'more human'. They can become dehumanized by oppression, injustice and exploitation, and *Pedagogy of the Oppressed* expresses a means by which the oppressed can be helped to fight back against their oppression and achieve their humanization. The form this took in practice in his life was organizing the education of the vast number of illiterate workers and peasants in north-eastern Brazil, through what he called 'cultural circles'. Literacy was one of the fundamental requirements for being able to vote in Brazilian presidential elections of the time, so through literacy a large class of previously disenfranchised rural workers would gain a political input. The focus on humanization, equality and enfranchisement was carried through in the terminology used: not students but 'participants', not teachers but 'co-ordinators'. Education was for the purpose of liberation.

Freire had embarked on training coordinators through a university and expanding his programme to target millions of poor Brazilians when the government of Brazil was overthrown by a military coup sponsored by the CIA in 1964, because of fears of communism. Freire himself was accused of being a communist, was fired from his job and had all his teaching materials confiscated as well as spending seventy-five days in prison. The new government considered his literacy project to be subversive and it was brought to a halt. Exiled from Brazil in 1964, Freire eventually restarted his literacy work in Chile.

Freire identifies the tools of the oppressors as being conquest, manipulation, divide and rule and cultural invasion; in contrast the tools that can be used to fight oppression are unity, compassion, organization and cultural synthesis. It is not hard to see how these tools apply to many educational debates today. Augusto Boal was highly influenced by Freire's ideas and developed them into the *Theatre of the Oppressed*, which emphasizes dialogue between audience and performer and remains influential in drama education today.

Theoretical Frameworks

The theoretical (or conceptual) framework of a research project is equivalent to a map generated from pre-existing theories and concepts, to enable you to travel across the terrain of your data generation and analysis. It can be drawn from one single theory or it can be constructed from concepts taken from a number of different theoretical areas. In creating a theoretical framework the researcher seeks to streamline and tame the theory on which they are drawing, and to provide an outline of only those pieces which are relevant to their projects. When it is a framework drawn mainly from the micro-end of the scale of theory, it makes sense to consider it a conceptual rather than a theoretical framework. It does the same job of getting the concepts aligned and ready for use.

The multiple disciplines which make up education all have their own theoretical traditions. As a result when undertaking educational research you can find that there are a number of different theories or concepts on which you could draw which are doing very similar or the same things, which have originated in different fields. When constructing my own doctoral research my primary theoretical framework was that of Tversky and Kahneman's cognitive heuristics (1974), drawn from psychology. The theory of cognitive heuristics provides an explanation of the ability of the human to make intuitive judgements when the cognitive load is beyond their rational capability, using three heuristics which involve assessing a decision against the information that they can bring to mind (*availability*), judging its *representativeness* against samples from their prior experience and then adjusting to fit the scenario currently in question (*anchoring and adjustment*) (Tversky and Kahneman, 1974). My study was of the ways that examiners made decisions when marking scripts from eighteen-year-olds in History and English. In assessment meanwhile, there is a theory called construct-referenced assessment (Wiliam, 1998), intended to be in contrast to criteria-referenced, that is, assessment against rubrics. Construct-referenced assessment theorizes a mental framework of internalized tacit standards, against which new examples are compared and slotted in at the appropriate point. It is possible to see how this is a specialized theory that works on similar principles – comparison against previous experience, which depends on the availability of previous examples, judging the representativeness of a script against constructs of grades, and adjusting appropriately. I utilized both theories in forming the theoretical framework for the research, as well as drawing on a very similar theory from the arts, that of connoisseurship, in which the second and third criteria for a connoisseur – 'the exercise of critical faculties is based on knowledge and experience' and 'there is an ability to make comparisons in relation to perceived qualities' (Robbins, 2008, p. 5) – are also clearly parallel to heuristics and construct-referencing.

One route when confronted with multiple theories is to do what I did and combine them into one theoretical framework. This could be a theoretical contribution on its own, particularly in a field like education where many researchers reach outside for theory. Alternatively, one theory is sufficient, so choose the one which has the most utility for your particular study, in enabling you to understand and explain your data. Or, if there is no difference in utility, other factors may come into play, such as matching the theory to those most commonly used in research around your topic. Biesta warns about the borrowing of theory in much the same way as educationalists warn against policy borrowing:

> If we disconnect a particular theory or philosophy from its context of origin, we end up giving it a status it never sought to have. Doing so runs the risk of putting us in a position in which we use *theory-as-truth* rather than *as-a-specific-answer-to-a-specific-question,* which, by the way, is a more precise and more specific approach than the idea of theory as a 'lens' or 'perspective'. (Biesta, 2020, p. 11)

I find this an interesting argument. The question that arises is, What is the 'context of origin'? Much theory in the psychology of learning, for example, is developed in laboratory experiments, and requires testing in the field before it can (or perhaps should) be applied in schools. We have already considered the idea that theory should be able to absorb new data and withstand it without falling apart or requiring the development of new theory. We might argue that learning is learning anywhere, and a theory of learning should therefore be transferable in context. However, theories of learning in the Global North do not take into account the role that land plays in Indigenous cultures (Connell, 2007), *including* its role in learning and education. It is possible to incorporate the land into some theories, such as Bronfenbrenner's ecological systems theory, and less easy in others, such as cognitive theories which would claim its irrelevance, and would therefore be inappropriate for that context. Not only because of the overriding of Indigenous cultures of Biesta's *theory-as-truth* in those instances but also for the less moral and more pragmatic reason that it conceals and represses the story that emerges from the data, rather than revealing and unfolding.

I adhere to Anfara and Metz's claim: 'A useful theory is one that tells an enlightening story about some phenomenon. It is a story that gives you new insights and broadens your understanding of the phenomenon' (Anfara and Mertz, 2006, p. xvii).

Building Theory

Having discussed the ways in which it is possible to borrow and transfer theory in order to enable you to use it to investigate your data, we turn to the production of new theory, the focus of Kettley's (2010) book *Building Theory in Educational Research*, in which he argues that there is a 'crisis' of theory building which 'arises from the failure to encourage original interpretation of data among new researchers. Cleaving to existing concepts and isolated paradigms is not imaginative thinking' (Kettley, 2010, p. 9). The production of new theory is the natural outcome of creating a level of abstraction from the concrete data without using existing theory at the middle range or above, and sometimes even so. Some research, such as that conducted using the methodology of Grounded Theory, is intended to create theory. Theory creation can also be the summation of a programme of research. But it can also be the result of any research study, on the micro level, as researchers seek to explain their data. It is the natural next step.

> Collecting and coding data does not, in and of itself, create awareness of social phenomena, because the data do not speak for themselves. Theory is

> not discovered in an external reality. Rather it is made up, invented or built through creative imagination and personal cognitive ability, which allows the researcher to explore the logical relationships and the causal connections between conceptual abstractions. Theory is always an artifice or contrivance. (Kettley, 2010, p. 9)

This to me speaks further of the demystification of theory: it is simply what we are doing when we think sufficiently deeply about our data.

Kettley also argues that most middle range theory development is insufficiently evidenced in the writing that proposes it: theory is asserted and demonstrated but the arrival at the original assertion is not documented. There is, he argues, 'a tendency to generate sound hypotheses, usually related to statistical generalities, which are not then comprehensively tested against robust primary data. There is also a failure to explain the interpretative processes used to derive concepts to build explanations' (Kettley, 2010, p. 21). In building theory, then, we need to adhere to the same standards as for explaining, justifying and testing analytical decisions about data.

Eisenhardt (1989) argues that the messy data generated by case study are ideal for promoting the creative work of theory building, because it throws up contradictions:

> That is, attempts to reconcile evidence across cases, types of data, and different investigators, and between cases and literature increase the likelihood of creative reframing into a new theoretical vision. Although a myth surrounding theory building from case studies is that the process is limited by investigators' preconceptions, in fact, just the opposite is true. This constant juxtaposition of conflicting realities tends to 'unfreeze' thinking, and so the process has the potential to generate theory with less researcher bias than theory built from incremental studies or arm-chair, axiomatic deduction. (Eisenhardt, 1989, p. 546)

This idea of messy data being helpful may seem counter-intuitive as it seems ideal to have neatly fitting data which slot perfectly into the pre-existing framework which we have created for it. Yet if it does, was there a point to doing the research? Many of the quotations throughout this chapter have referenced the creative possibilities inherent in theory, theory building and research in general. Retaining the possibilities both of messiness and creativity in the face of the tidying and streamlining of the narrative required by publication is part of the joy of research and theory.

Conclusion

Theory is sometimes a pejorative term in Education Research when speaking to practitioners or policy makers who want practical answers – solutions to problems in classrooms, instantly. But theory can provide practical answers, generating potential interventions and thoughtful explanations.

> Theory is a vehicle for 'thinking otherwise'; it is a platform for 'outrageous hypotheses' and for 'unleashing criticism'. Theory is destructive, disruptive and violent. It offers a language for challenge, and modes of thought, other than those articulated for us by dominant others. It provides a language of rigour and irony rather than contingency. The purpose of such theory is to de-familiarise present practices and categories, to make them seem less self-evident and necessary, and to open up spaces for the invention of new forms of experience. (Ball, 1995, p. 266)

Theory is not something to be afraid of, nor is it in opposition to the practice of research and of education; it is how we think about the concrete on the level of the abstract and how we understand the world relationally.

5.3 Frantz Fanon

Frantz Fanon (1925–1961) was a French West Indian psychiatrist and theorist from Martinique. He was an important theorist in relation to decolonization, and was a major influence on the Black Power movement in the United States. His major works are the books *Black Skin, White Masks* (1952), *A Dying Colonialism* (1959) and *The Wretched of the Earth* (1961). He took a psychoanalytic approach and considered colonial influence as it has been internalized as well as its external violence. Hence in *Black Skin, White Masks* he argues that Black people are never simply Black, they are always Black in opposition to whiteness, that is, that race is a social construct. He conceptualizes racial trauma and analyses the performance of 'white-ness' which Black people have to undertake to move through the world. Fanon also speaks in *Black Skin, White Masks* of the importance of language in attaining acceptance in the performance of whiteness.

> *To speak means to be in a position to use a certain syntax, to grasp the morphology of this or that language, but it means above all to*

> *assume a culture, to support the weight of a civilization. (Fanon, 1967, pp. 17–18)*
>
> In *The Wretched of the Earth* Fanon argued that violent resistance to colonization in order to achieve independence is justified. Colonization is achieved by military strength and therefore violent resistance is imposed by the colonizer on the colonized.
>
> Education is central to Fanon's analysis in that it is through education that the colonizers instigated the norms and hierarchies which caused the traumatic internalization of whiteness (and hence the repression of their Black selves). De-colonizers see the importance of reversing this hierarchy. Erica Burman has developed the application of Fanon's work for education in what she calls 'child as method' (2018), arguing that his work enables to understand many of the most pressing issues of education today, and forms a framework for anti-racist education and parenting.

6

The Body of the Researcher

Except for educational researchers who work only with secondary data sets, data generation is always embodied in some way, even in online contexts. This chapter considers the role of the individual researcher within research, in terms of both physical and conceptual presence. It introduces positionality and reflexivity and explores the impact that the researcher has on the design, data collection and data analysis processes, whether or not they acknowledge it. It will consider the relationship between researcher and participant and how different demographic characteristics can lead to increased effectiveness (or the opposite) in data collection. It will also consider the practitioner-researcher, which is an important case in the field of education.

Embodiment

> I like university professors, but you know … They're disembodied, you know, in a kind of literal way. They look upon their body as a form of transport for their heads. Don't they? It's a way of getting their head to meetings. (Robinson, 2006)

The distinction between mind and body has a long history, as far back as Aristotle and Plato, but it is most associated with René Descartes, the seventeenth-century European philosopher who gave his name to Cartesian Dualism, the concept that mind and body, while closely linked, are essentially separate. More recently, the concept of embodied cognition has come to the fore: the idea that cognition is a situated activity, one that takes place within a body, and to which the body contributes as well as the mind. To give an example: Ehrlich, Levine and Goldin-Meadow (2006) studied spatial problem solving in children aged five. What they found was that the more the children gestured about moving pieces while explaining how they solved the task, the better they performed on the test; gesture was helping with cognition. Similar effects have been found in adults (e.g. Chu and Kita, 2011). Southern theory and Indigenous epistemologies have long centred the embodied nature of knowing. Welch (2019) in bringing together the concepts of embodied cognition and Native American ways of knowing points out that 'emotion, like perception, manifests in the body at the deepest level; it is experienced not only consciously in the manner in which we most commonly recognize it, but also non-consciously' (pp. 59–60). She later gives the example of being exhausted by sheltering from a storm, merely experiencing it and the stimulation it provides to the emotions and the mind, to demonstrate the physicality of embodied cognition.

Arguments are still taking place with philosophers, psychologists and neuroscientists about the ins and outs of embodied cognition, but in the meantime it is useful to explore the idea of embodiment as it relates to research and data generation. We do not go into research sites as a disembodied mind, as described by Ken Robinson above, but as individuals whose characteristics, appearance and behaviour can all impact on the data generated. There is a well-known phenomenon where female instructors systematically receive lower student evaluation scores than male instructors (e.g. Mengel, Sauermann and Zölitz, 2019) and some research has shown an effect of perceived ethnicity as well (Chávez and Mitchell, 2020). The same kinds of unconscious judgements apply to relationships between researchers and participants, in both directions, and consequently affect both the data that are generated and the interpretations placed on that data.

> The recognition that one is an embodied being includes the acknowledgement that even in a situation of being an observer one is an involved observer – someone who is affected by and is affecting what is taking place. Being a researcher … requires that one becomes fully and thoughtfully involved. It is as if one is engaged in a dance of moving forward and moving back: one steps closer and steps away, has an effect and is affected, all as an embodied being. (Halling and Goldfarb, 1991, p. 328)

A few years ago I took part in a research study in which I was a participant observer in a drama intervention with eleven-year-olds. I spent an hour every week for six months doing a variety of activities, the most memorable of which was probably creating an ice-cream sundae machine with our bodies, although a regular warm-up game where one participant lay on the floor and others threw beanbags across a circle directly above their face was also a favourite. Taking part, among other things, created a rapport with the young participants, which improved the quality of the data generated by interviews at the end of the intervention; it made me understand much better the effects of the intervention on them, and the emotions that they were experiencing; and it embedded me in the group and reduced the observer effect.

Even in hard science the observer effect is acknowledged, and the act of observing changes that which is observed. Teachers in their early careers are frequently observed teaching by tutors from university, or more senior staff members acting as mentors or assessors. It is commonplace for the teacher being observed to note that their class behaved differently with a second (or third, etc.) adult in the room. Even the presence of a video camera or audio recorder can change the behaviour which is being recorded (leaving us to ask if any data which are collected non-covertly are really 'naturally occurring') (Ingram and Elliott, 2019). A video camera, however, does not have the same embodied nature as a person, and may be more easily ignored after a time.

There is an idea in educational research that if you want good data from children, you are better off utilizing women and preferably young ones to generate the data because they are more familiar figures, forming the majority of the teaching workforce and caregivers in nurseries and after-school settings. This is rather undermining if you are not a young female and hope to generate data with these sorts of participants! It is not necessarily true, however, and generating a rapport with participants is more important. In some cases, however, the characteristics of the researcher can make a difference, and needs to be considered ethically as well as for the effect on the data. In observing activities or interviewing in spaces which are regarded as 'safe spaces' by the participants, for example, the characteristics of the researcher matter. It might be inappropriate and counter-productive for a male researcher to go to a shelter for women escaping from domestic violence, for example.

In other instances it might not be as inappropriate but might have an effect on the data: imagine two researchers, one Black and one white, collecting data for the same research project on Black students' experiences of racial diversity in curriculum in schools. Requiring Black students to talk to a white researcher may create more of a burden on the participant, when talking about a racism-related topic because of the need to negotiate around (potential) white fragility, or because of the students' own previous experience of racism. That negotiation – that fear – also has the potential to reduce the richness of the data, another application of the 'social acceptability bias' as the participant edits themselves. Educational environments and their approved expressions of emotion put the onus on Black students to avoid triggering shame or denial on the part of white teachers and classmates (Thein, 2018); these are habits which are not necessarily or easily put aside when one leaves that classroom.

Race, gender, dis/ability and age are perhaps the most obvious characteristics that may impact on the researcher/researched relationship, but there are others. Clothing choice is another factor that impacts on the instant judgements that humans make of one another. If you are conducting fieldwork in an unfamiliar country then it is wise to educate yourself about the cultural norms of clothing, appearance and behaviour, for reasons both of safety and of good data generation.

Place and Space: The Situated Body

In Indigenous epistemologies the land is an important site of knowledge, and learning can be tied to the land in a reciprocal relationship that recognizes Indigenous peoples and their knowledge *as part of* the land (Simpson, 2004). The close tie between people and land, and knowing, is one of the reasons for the statement that 'decolonisation is not a metaphor' (Tuck and Yang, 2012).

> Spiritual places are destroyed and with them opportunities to maintain alliances with the essential forces of nature, the very alliances that are responsible for the transmission of Indigenous Knowledge. Opportunities for knowledge holders to pass their knowledge down to younger generations become fewer. As people have fewer reasons to go out on the land, there are fewer occasions for children to observe, experience, and learn from the natural world. (Simpson, 2004, p. 379)

Knowledge as situated and place as participant in knowledge generation and understanding is an important concept to consider.

Dingwall (2020) reports on an intervention with young people at risk of becoming disengaged using drama methods in a school. The space made available to the school was a normal classroom, but each week the group leaders and the students began the session by reconfiguring the room, pushing the tables back to the edges, stacking the chairs and clearing a space for a 'studio' in the middle of the room. The reconfigured space, for both students and staff, created a kind of levelling of status away from the normal spacing of desks and chairs, and produced a figurative and literal 'safe space' for the students to engage in the drama-based activities. In discussions of classroom practices there are fierce debates between rows of tables and chairs, groups of tables or u-shapes, and whether the teacher stands or sits, has a desk at the front or side, or where they move during teaching. Space and place matter enormously in education, whether for real or symbolic reasons, and the same is no less true of research and data generation.

Some data can only be generated in situ, in the classroom, on the playing field, in the playground, in the home. Others, notably interview data, can be generated in a variety of spaces, and the difference in those spaces makes a difference, practically and psychologically. Interviewing a teacher in their classroom, for example, might give access to examples of wall displays, or enable them to picture teaching more easily, or allow them to demonstrate particular movements. However, during the school day the classroom is prone to interruption, or the teacher might feel constrained about what they could say because of the presence of children, or because they did not feel comfortable critiquing the school management when there was a remote chance of being overheard. There are practical considerations too: sounds such as bells ringing or footsteps in the corridor can be separated out from a person speaking by the human ear, but an audio recording will make that impossible, so that the speech will no longer be audible over the contextual noise. Or, there will be interruptions: I have done at least two interviews with assistant principals where they have had responsibility for, and been interrupted by, children on internal exclusions carrying out work while we were talking. How might that change the data?

Equally, there are power dynamics to the places in which research data are generated. Interviewing an elite participant in their office – including a head teacher – can put the researcher in the position of supplicant. This may have a positive effect: the elite participant may be beneficent, bestowing information liberally. Or it may cause the opposite: the reminder of their status may prevent them answering questions. In either case they may be distracted or interrupted by the context of their normal working life. Interviewing children can be similarly affected by context, particularly if interviews are taking place in school; consider the difference that may be created by being in a large empty classroom, a small room usually used for intervention, the school library or the dining room. Interview data in particular are co-constructed in the dialogue between the interviewer and the interviewee(s) and place has an impact on who and how we are in any given moment. One method which has begun to take advantage of this is the 'walking interview' (see Jones, Bunce, Evans, Gibbs and Hein, 2008), utilized by Lynch and Mannion (2016) to investigate a type of education where place is integral – outdoor learning. Tusting, McCulloch, Bhatt, Hamilton and Barton (2019) utilized the walking interview as one of their methods in studying the writing practices of academics, asking for guided tours of workplaces which illuminated 'the influences of the material space, institutional resources, and working environment' (p. 19) on the writing practices of their participants. Space matters: we are not disembodied minds working in the cloud.

The impact that place has on the individual has become a focus of research itself, particularly through the use of photovoice and photo-elicitation research with young people, who are asked to take photographs of their environment as they go about their daily lives, or to take photographs of places that are important to them. Uses of such visual methods 'can generate, or perhaps more precisely have the potential to generate, new insights as they act as a "can opener" and tap into or bring to the fore memories, ideas or social worlds that may easily be missed, misinterpreted or seen as unimportant' (Leonard and McKnight, 2015, p. 630). Considering the locations, the situatedness of the research participants, by this account, becomes a tool to leverage an increased quality of data and an increased understanding of the participants. Leonard and McKnight also warn, however, that 'participants, intentionally or unintentionally, may produce images which show them and their surroundings in a positive light' (2015, p. 632). No data are purely a reflection of reality: it is a re-presentation of reality. Rasmussen (2004) utilizes photographs taken by Danish children to introduce the idea of 'children's places' as opposed to 'places for children' which are provided by and largely controlled by adults. The use of photographs taken by children to explore the spaces and places which they inhabit provides an insight into life as a child which would be difficult to gain via observation as an adult. In addition, the use of photovoice provides a means by which the young participants are able to author their own lives and data, and demonstrate their own understandings rather than being subject to the imposed interpretations of the adult researchers. Interestingly White (2020) in her ethnography of young Black people in Newham East London emphasizes the 'sonic landscapes' (p. 114) of place as important in generating understandings. She writes of the displacement of grime and rap from particular spaces as a way in which marginalization and segregation are operationalized, as these music genres 'support the production of local identities, but also connect to a global audience' (White, 2020, p. 54). She also introduces a 'hyper-local' framework, bringing the consideration of young lives down to a very small, specific neighbourhood and using that as a way to understand how those lives are constrained, contained and regulated in a way as to further marginalize them and reduce their future participation in economy and society.

One 'place' which is becoming increasingly common as a data generation site is the internet. Conducting interviews over videoconferencing became common during the pandemic, and raised a whole new set of practical and ethical considerations. When interviewing minors, for example, should their camera remain switched off? Should yours? Video calls take us into the private spaces of recipients' lives which they may not be happy to share, and while some people have become adept at using software settings to show artificial backdrops, many others have not. Richards, Clark and Boggis (2015) note the complexities of interviewing children in their homes (discussed in Chapter 8): in video interviews there may be no way around some of those complexities.

Other internet-based research involves the gathering of data in chat rooms or forums, a set of research sites which has generated a very large field of literature on the ethics of such research over the past decade. Hudson and Bruckman (2004), for example, found that if they revealed they were studying a chat, in one of three different ways, they were often ejected from the chatroom, the participants effectively refusing their consent. They were far less likely to be ejected if they did not make those statements, but this raises other issues. Convery and Cox (2012) note that one of the complexities of the situation is the somewhat less than clear distinction between private spaces (where fully informed consent would be required) and public spaces (where it might not) in internet-based research. Hudson and Bruckman also argued that members of 'public online environments often act as if these environments were private' (2005, p. 298). This has consequences not only for the ethics of the research but also for understanding the data. Kelpi (2018) analysed youth narratives regarding internet anonymity and found that it increased interactional courage – which can have both positive effects, increasing relational intimacy, and negative effects, linked to harassment and bullying. From the point of view of data we must ask ourselves whether statements made under the aegis of anonymity are 'truer' because the speakers do not fear repercussion, or if they are less true because they do not represent what the speaker would say in person. In any case, statements made on the internet are constructed for a particular time and audience. However, they can remain accessible for years, which has other repercussions for consent (how can you contact long-defunct user accounts?). In theory the public accessibility of data makes it a public forum, but if you need a username and password to access it, is it still public?

Reflexivity and Positionality

Reflexivity and positionality are closely entwined, but they are different concepts, although either can be used as a title when researchers discuss both. This pair of related terms has risen to prominence in social sciences in recent years. As Mann says, 'in an era of increasingly multi-disciplinary, mixed-methods and multi-methods research, it is crucial to contemplate synergies, relations, and the points of congruence and dissonance' (2016, p. 11). How much truer is this in a field which is composed of overlapping disciplines, and in which colleagues may have many different starting points, or use the same terms to mean different things?

> In place of images of scientific work that suggest a unity of method and theoretical outlook among colleagues, we are increasingly confronted with the reality of difference among ourselves and the unavoidable necessity of dialogue across these lines of difference. (Drew, Raymond and Weinberg, 2006, p. 102)

Initially we will discuss and define these two concepts and their use before exploring some of the common issues which come up when people engage in reflexivity. Mann offers the following definition of reflexivity in research interviewing:

> Reflexivity is a conscious process of thought and articulation centred on the dynamics of subjectivities in relation to the interviewer, the interviewee(s), and the research focus and methodology. (2016, p. 15)

That it is conscious is important; it is an explicit and intentional act of thinking about the relations (the relative positions) between the researcher and the researched, and how that research happens. Edge (2011) highlights the bi-directionality between the researcher and the research, in that just as the researcher has an effect on the study, so the research has an effect on the person doing it.

Positionality is to some extent one of the subjects about which the researcher is reflexive: it is the idea that who we are in the world, our views and beliefs (including but not limited to our ontology and epistemology), shape how we understand that world. It is effectively a shorthand for many of the issues discussed in this chapter. In understanding our own position, we are able to be thoughtfully reflexive about how that position affects our research. Much of the extant literature on positionality and reflexivity is in the area of qualitative research, but it is important to note that the same concepts apply in quantitative research, even in secondary data analysis. Your position influences what relationships between variables you might think to look for, how you write about the analyses that you have done, what questions and hypotheses you pose in the first place. It is also worthwhile engaging in reflexivity while *consuming* research as well as producing it, recognizing how and why you are reacting to and evaluating what is said by others.

Mann (2016, p. 17) identified the following dimensions of reflexivity in the research literature with a reflexive focus: it is an essential element of research (Flood, 1995); it takes stock of the interviewer's actions and role (Temple and Edwards, 2002); it means standing outside the research process (O'Leary, 2004); it is ongoing and evolving (Clark and Dervin, 2014); it deals with the impact of identities and relationships (Temple and Edwards, 2002); it is about understanding the self in relation to knowledge (Berger, 2015); it is about interrogating representation (Woolgar, 1988); it is a source of data (Takeda, 2013); and it requires the researcher to question their interpretations and how they came about (Hertz, 1997). Together these dimensions reflect the scale and breadth of the process of reflexivity, although others have warned researchers should avoid overindulging in this thinking at the expense of engaging in 'navel-gazing' (Sparkes, 2000, p. 21; Finlay, 2002, p. 215).

To 'stand outside' (O'Leary, 2004, p. 11) the research you are conducting is not necessarily an easy feat. Etherington offers four questions to assist the researcher in their hunt for reflexivity:

1. How has my personal history led me to my interest in this topic?
2. What are my presuppositions about knowledge in this field?
3. How am I positioned in relation to this knowledge?
4. How does my gender/social class/ethnicity/culture influence my positioning in relation to this topic/my informants? (2004, p. 11)

These questions help take us beyond the simple and easy analysis of position which considers the 'insider' position of researching within your own context. Many educational researchers begin by conducting research projects where they have some elements of the insider position: English as a foreign language teachers researching applied linguistics; school teachers researching teaching; nursery workers researching child development. Reflexivity asks us to remember this, but it also challenges us not to be too carried away with the idea. Linda Tuhiwai Smith makes the excellent point:

> Really, in practice, there is no inside. Even if you are a researcher in your own community, by being a researcher, you're positioned in relation to the community in a complicated way. You might know the community. You might have the language of the community. You might have relationships in the community. But the role of research always positions you in a somewhat different space with different responsibilities, including ethical responsibilities and intellectual responsibilities. (Tuhiwai Smith, 2019, p. 12)

She goes on to say that beyond insider/outsider concepts we need to think about 'boundaries, borders, liminality and intersectionality' (2019, p. 13). She is speaking in relation to Indigenous researchers but I would argue these are concepts everyone should be thinking about. Though these thoughts might be isolating, they are not necessarily bad for research, in that they help return us to that state of making the familiar strange. Reflexivity is asking us to make sure that we are not making assumptions in our research decisions and analysis, based on our beliefs about our understanding of data from our personal histories. For example, if you are an ex-teacher, you may have more sympathy for the accounts of teachers than of other participants; reflexivity asks us to notice this and account for it.

Personal histories are instrumental in the development of our minds. bell hooks writes of

> marginality as much more than a site of deprivation ... it is also the site of radical possibility, a space of resistance. It was this marginality that I was naming as a central location for the production of a counter hegemonic discourse that is not just found in words but in habits of being and the way one lives. As such, I was not speaking of a marginality one wishes to lose, to give up, or surrender as part of moving into the center, but rather as a site one stays in, clings to even, because it nourishes one's capacity to resist. It offers the possibility of radical perspectives from which to see and create, to imagine alternatives, new worlds. (hooks, 1990, p. 341)

Marginalization creates a sort of permanent liminality, in this account, which creates a productive tension in the ways in which the world is viewed. hooks emphasizes the possibility of radicality, but we might just as well consider the potential for new insights, and the strengths of a diverse research community that can draw on all these insights. It is this capacity which forms the basis of Participatory Action Research (PAR), discussed below.

Questions which are important for reflexivity are covered throughout the book. We might consider here, for example, questions of language and translation (see Chapter 7); questions of the ethics of encouraging an interviewee to believe you agree with them (see Chapter 8); or how we align our ontology, epistemology and methodologies (Chapters 2 and 3). Xerri (2018) relates his experiences of reflexivity while working as a teacher-researcher, utilizing a series of reflexive practices in order to defend the trustworthiness of his research given that he was researching within his own context (see below for further discussion of the practitioner-researcher). He utilized reflexive diaries, discussions with a mentor and member checking with an explicit eye to his dual role throughout.

How, then, do we ensure reflexivity? The existence of a small paragraph with that heading located in the methodology does not guarantee anything more than a post hoc reflection on a few token issues. Mann suggests research diaries as a way to keep track, and reflexivity is certainly a key component of ethnographic field notes. Emerson, Fretz and Shaw note also that field notes themselves must be the subject of analyses of reflexivity, but emphasize that good ethnographic field notes 'reflect understandings gained through subjecting oneself to the logic of others' social worlds, a logic that comes to partially constitute the lens through which the ethnographer views and understands these worlds' (2011, p. 247), returning us to the concept of the bi-directional effect highlighted by Edge (2011). Emerson, Fretz and Shaw describe the normal behaviour of the ethnographer to explain how this partial constitution occurs: 'the more the ethnographer involves himself in others' social worlds, the more he subjects his own presuppositions, his own ways of doing and giving meaning to events and behavior, to the challenges of members' everyday lives' (2011, p. 247). This also partially describes how reflexivity might act during data analysis in any research, demonstrating the 'challenge' that we must make to our interpretations based on our understandings of our own world views, and those of others. Though some seek to dismiss reflexivity as navel-gazing, it is a way to strengthen research and its conclusions, and particularly to challenge false assertions of objectivity. For more discussion on this, see Chapter 7.

> ### 6.1 Michel Foucault
>
> Michel Foucault (1926–1984) was a French philosopher who wrote a range of works which deal with the relationship between knowledge and power. One of his key ideas was that power is constituted through discourse and that is implicated in what is constructed as knowledge (Foucault, 1990), which has been extremely influential in the development of (Foucauldian) Critical Discourse Analysis (FCDA). This is a productive methodology for the analysis of education policy, and the construction of particular societal tropes by media or politicians. A discourse is a 'system of statements which cohere around common meanings and values' (Hollway, 1983, p. 131). One discourse in education is that of meritocracy – the idea that talent is rewarded (critiqued in Sandel, 2020). FCDA enables researchers to explore power dynamics in texts we might more normally think of as being neutral – such as Bazzul's (2014) analysis of biology textbooks and their construction of neoliberalist subjects. FCDA is also adaptive: Galuvao (2018) describes using a Foucauldian toolbox to create a version of CDA for the Samoan context (Tofā'a'anolasi) which he used to uncover previously unacknowledged issues in reading assessments in New Zealand primary schools for Samoan students.
>
> One key work for educationalists is Foucault's *Discipline and Punish* (1977) which begins with an analysis of the history of prisons before expanding that to consider how the role of discipline in society is used to create docile bodies via its institutions – not only prisons but also in the army, factories and schools. He draws on the idea of panopticon originated by Jeremy Bentham – the idea of constant surveillance from all directions. *Discipline and Punish* functions better as a theoretical analysis of political and social power than as a literal history of prisons. Foucault campaigned for penal reform, and criticized human rights abuses and racism.

The Practitioner-Researcher

The practitioner-researcher is a specific case of how the embodiment of the researcher matters in education. Practitioner research is carried out when educators of various kinds research their own practice, some of whom follow the specific design approach of action research with its cycles of action, evaluation and refinement. The strength of practitioner research is that it is designed for a particular context, working with a group of students of whom the researcher has close knowledge; interventions are delivered by someone who is invested in their design and effectiveness, and will put energy into ensuring their successful delivery, and with whom the students are familiar and have an existing relationship. These strengths are also their weakness, in that interventions designed in this way may not transfer across contexts well, as the body of the practitioner is tied up in their operation and their success (or otherwise).

> The producer of the material is not seen as separate from the material but part of it – because they are part of what they are researching. They will not attempt to finalise an interpretation or produce conclusive findings. There may not be an expectation of analysing material so much as speaking from within complex, shifting practice in a deeply reflective and subjective manner. (Simon, 2018, p. 42)

Practitioner research rarely reaches the research literature, for a variety of reasons, including but not limited to its small scale and its specific situatedness, both within a school, class or university, within a community of students and teacher, in a particular geographical and socio-economic context. This provides challenges for the question of generalizability – or in this case transferability – to another context. The outcome may not be as important as the process of conducting the research, however, requiring as it does a level of reflection and analysis of practice from the researcher which can have an impact on the quality of teaching beyond the outcome of the specific intervention or equivalent. Simon's idea of 'speaking from within complex, shifting practice' may in fact be of more interest to other practitioners than the more normative educational research; practitioner-researchers focus on topics of particular interest to them in their roles as educators, which is another factor increasing their interest to fellow teachers and lecturers. Some further discussion of practitioner research, focused on ethics, can be found in Chapter 8.

Participatory Action Research

> PAR is an empirical methodological approach in which people directly affected by a problem under investigation engage as co-researchers in the research process, which includes action, or intervention, into the problem.

> While PAR shares similar approaches with student voice research, it embodies particular empirical assumptions and methodological strategies that differ from other approaches to social science research. PAR researchers believe that local co-researchers possess expert knowledge derived from their everyday participation in the contexts under investigation and their direct engagement with the issues under study. Local actors, they believe, can provide unique insight into the issues and how they should be investigated. (Rodriguez and Brown, 2009, p. 23)

Because PAR centres the co-researchers (participants) it is a uniquely situated and embodied form of research, which draws on that embodiment and situatedness as a form of expertise in the problem under consideration. It partakes in 'pedagogical and methodological processes that not only gather and present the viewpoints of marginalized youth but further their understandings of how they can make their voices matter – that is, a shift from simply having a voice to being actual agents of change' (Rodriguez and Brown, 2009, p. 22).

As a result of its historical focus on marginalized youth, usually through race, poverty, gender or a mixture, PAR is an explicitly political form of research of the sort discussed in Chapter 9. It has outcomes other than the research itself: in order to utilize co-creators of research, PAR projects provide training in research skills to the participants. These may not only be of use economically but also 'personally transformative' as the participants gain the ability to 'critically interrogate their everyday life and collectively reflect upon personal experiences' (Cahill, 2007, p. 328). Stovall and Delgado (2009) give an account of actually using PAR as a method of delivering a high school law class in Chicago, which additionally allowed pedagogical content to focus upon the legal issues that were most likely to face their students.

The focus of PAR on the marginalized means that the co-researchers are often those with politicized bodies, by which I mean bodies which communicate identities outside the hegemony, and bodies which are more policed by society than others. Examples include women who wear the hijab, Black boys, users of mobility aids (particularly part-time users of wheelchairs or sticks) and gender non-conforming people of all kinds. It is this marginalization, as bell hooks identified, that gives particular insight and drives some of the most powerful PAR, speaking directly to the ways in which the co-creators inhabit politicized bodies in everyday life.

Conclusion

This chapter has sought to explore the effect of the researcher on research, and of the research on the researcher. It has emphasized the physical presence of researchers and participants and spaces in which research takes place, which are sometimes ignored in favour of more abstract considerations. We have explored the concepts of reflexivity and positionality and noted the importance of keeping them in mind throughout research as a means of strengthening it. We have also noted that although this is a focus mainly in the literature on qualitative research it also applies to quantitative research, even in secondary data analysis. Further discussion of some of the aspects raised in this chapter can be seen in Chapters 8 and 9, particularly the practitioner-researcher and PAR.

6.2 Pierre Bourdieu

Pierre Bourdieu was a French sociologist (1930–2002) two of whose theories are commonly adopted by educationalists: the concepts of *field* and *habitus*; and his theory of capital and class distinction (with various forms of capital adopted by analogy with financial capital). Deployed to Algeria on military service, he remained there as a lecturer following his year's service and undertook anthropological fieldwork. The resulting *Sociology of Algeria* made his reputation in France.

Habitus is a complex, multilayered concept in Bourdieu's writings (Reay, 2004). An individual's habitus comprises their personal history, but also the history of the community and class of which they are a part; it is embodied in the way they physically exist in the world; it includes possibilities for action, but also excludes particular possibilities on the basis of histories. Habitus is 'a mixture of the embodied, the instinctual and the unthought, [as well as] the "life of the mind", the reflective as well as the pre-reflective' (Reay, 2004, p. 441). Correspondingly a field is the system of social positions into which an individual can be inserted:

> social reality exists, so to speak, twice, in things and in minds, in fields and in habitus, outside and inside social agents. And when habitus encounters a social world of which it is the product, it is like a 'fish in water': it does not feel the weight of the water and it

> takes the world about itself for granted. (Bourdieu and Wacquant, 1992, p. 127)

Capital, meanwhile, is the sum of assets in different forms that individuals accrue, and which form a key part of class distinction. Economic capital – money – leads by analogy to social capital (e.g. networks, college legacies, etc.), cultural capital (such as qualifications, success in particular educational subjects) and symbolic capital (such as prestige). Class distinctions predict these forms of capital, provide them and then are reproduced by them. Being able to translate economic capital into attending a good university and gaining a degree (cultural capital) disguises to some extent the level of class reproduction. Cultural capital has become embedded in the popular educational consciousness as the forms of cultural participation – going to the theatre, attending museums, listening to classical music – associated with higher socio-economic status. In Bourdieuan terms, however, cultural capital is not associated exclusively with high-brow culture; different class distinctions and societal groups carry their own forms of cultural capital.

7
Data Analysis

Analysing data involves making a series of decisions (Elliott, 2018); those decisions may be unconscious and instinctive, but they are decisions nonetheless and it is essential that the reflexive researcher identifies those decision-making points, both in order to maximize the quality of their research and also to prevent unintended bias creeping into their work. When reading research it is often possible to see those decisions to which thought has been given, and those to which it has not.

Analysis, broadly speaking, is getting to know your data, and reducing a large data set, whether quantitative or qualitative, to a form in which they can be understood and reported economically. 'Text data are dense data, and it takes a long time to go through them and make sense of them' (Creswell, 2015, p. 152), but the same is no less true of quantitative data. We analyse and present data in ways that enable others to see the story that we have seen in those data; analysis is finding the woods in the trees. Goodwin (1994) describes this as the development of a 'professional vision' directed towards your data.

This 'professional vision' is developed in the context of a number of issues that we have already mentioned and others that will be explored in the final two chapters. Choices about data analysis should be consistent with the epistemological positioning of the research, as should the way it is written up. The positionality of the researcher is just as cogent to consider during the analysis phase as the data generation stage. This chapter considers some of the key concepts and debates in analysis of data, including the unit of analysis, the decision to pursue a priori or emergent analysis, member checking, establishing the reliability of the analysis, issues of language and translation, and writing about analysis. Finally we consider some non-standard ways to present data that reflect some of the creative approaches possible in educational research today.

The Unit of Analysis

The unit of analysis in a study governs what the analysis is *about*; it is not necessarily the same as the unit of observation. It is easiest to explain this by exemplification: you can collect data on student scores, which is done on the individual level, making the student the unit of observation. However, if you then aggregate those scores to consider them on the class level then the class becomes the unit of analysis. Alternatively, you might interview multiple teachers in clusters from different schools: the teacher is the unit of observation, but there is a choice as to whether to make the teacher or the school the unit of analysis. The unit of analysis reflects the research questions posed by a study and the level of claims that are made. If we are asking about school ethos, perhaps the unit of analysis is the school; if we are asking about how individuals adopt to the school ethos, then the unit of analysis is the teacher. They might be nested within schools, so we would be interested to know that all the teachers in school A feel the same, but that that is different to the teachers in schools B, C and so on, but we are still analysing the data at the level of the teacher. In contrast the unit of observation is largely decided by the methods which are used to generate the data.

Units of analysis can be people, groups, documents, artefacts or interactions. While units of observation can be on a sub-level from the units of analysis, the opposite is not true. So while you can collect student data to aggregate into class level data for analysis, you cannot take the class level observation and use it as the basis of research where the student is the unit of analysis.

A priori versus Emergent Analysis

Analysis in both quantitative and qualitative data can be a priori – based on pre-existing plans, frameworks and decisions – or emergent – based on what emerges from the data. In quantitative research emergent analysis can be somewhat problematic.

So-called 'p hacking' is a form of data analysis which involves running vast number of analyses of quantitative data in order to find results that can be presented as statistically significant. Doing so hugely increases the chance of false positives. If we remember that a 'p' value is the probability that a result has arisen by chance, and a 'statistically significant' result is one of

0.05 or smaller, that is to say only 5 per cent of the samples would have that result by chance, then the greater the number of analyses run, the greater the probability that eventually these results will appear by chance, as opposed to being because of an underlying relationship. Running a large number of analyses but only reporting the statistically significant ones disguises this. 'P hacking' is also called 'significance chasing'.

For this reason it is important for quantitative analyses to be run on theoretically driven (hypothesis-driven) lines, so that a statistically significant result is less likely to appear by chance. It also means that if we do find a relationship in quantitative data we can theorize a reason for the relationship. Replicating significant results in other data sets also confirms the likelihood of a real relationship existing. It is useful, therefore, to read quantitative research with an eye to how many analyses were run on the data, and how the researchers write about it. Most writing up of research leaves something out, but careful reading should provide clues as to the ways in which results were obtained. Strong hypothecation based on the literature or theory is also a mark that p hacking has not been involved.

In qualitative research, both emergent (also known as inductive) and a priori (also known as deductive) analyses are entirely normal, and indeed it is not unusual to find both within the same project. The decision of which to follow can be directed by the research question or the epistemological framework.

> At one end of the continuum we can have prespecified codes or more general coding frameworks. At the other end, we can start coding with no prespecified codes, and let the data suggest initial codes. *This decision is not independent of other such decisions concerning research questions, conceptual framework and the structuring of data generally.* (Punch, 2014, p. 174, my emphasis)

A large project with multiple coders is likely to use an a priori framework with a pre-designed coding book because it provides a direct path to reliability (see below); that is not to say that such projects do not use emergent codes for analysis, although those that do are likely to codify them quickly into a coding framework. If a research design is testing a theory against empirical data, it will need preset codes derived from that theory, although some methodologists recommend allowing for opening up to additional emergent codes even in the context of a priori coding schemes (e.g. Cresswell, 2013). In contrast researchers with a deeply held commitment to an interpretivist epistemology, and from particular traditions like grounded theory, are likely to prefer emergent codes. Emergent or inductive analysis is based on categories and codes which emerge from the data: individual words from participants' voices; patterns in the data; or even concepts which you have been sensitized to during the process of reading the literature for research. Emergent analysis still requires formal codification at some stage during the analysis, in order to ensure that all data have been considered in the light of all potential analytical categories.

In either case, a priori or emergent analysis, whether working in broad brush themes or specific, specialized codes, naming is a key activity which affects how the researcher and the reader think of them.

> A code in qualitative inquiry is most often a word or short phrase that symbolically assigns a summative, salient, essence-capturing and/or evocative attribute for a portion of language-based or visual data. (Saldaña, 2016, p. 4)

'Summative, salient, essence-capturing and/or evocative' is a high bar but it is important to remember that it is these labels which capture the reduction of data and will ultimately be used to structure reporting of data. Choices of code and theme names are closely related to research questions and to the precise procedures of data analysis. A priori codes set beforehand can be categorized and made consistent within categories, so that they follow the same naming protocols. Emergent codes, on the other hand, may require post hoc adjustment to make them consistent (such as being all processes, or all nouns); such adjustment needs not to make them no longer applicable to the data they describe. Miles, Huberman and Saldaña argue that making sure codes are part of a coherent whole is important: they should 'have some conceptual and structural unity. Codes should relate to one another in coherent, study-important ways; they should be part of a unified structure' (2014, p. 82).

One main debate which is referenced elsewhere in the book is the question of whether or not to use in vivo codes, that is, code labels lifted from the exact words of participants. Creswell calls these the 'best' code labels because 'you start to build codes and later themes that resonate with your participants' (2015, p. 160). He notes,

> Other types of code labels would be a term you make up on the basis of your personal experiences (e.g., stressed out) or a good social science or health science label based on theory (e.g., efficacy). Still, 'in vivo codes' are best because they move you towards the voices of participants, which you want to reflect in your realistic final report. (Creswell, 2015, p. 160)

A counterpoint is provided by Rapley who suggests that utilizing in vivo codes 'confuses the analytic phase with the phase of presentation of your argument to others. In notes to yourself and in publications, you will probably end up using verbatim quotes, and so give others access to these "voices"' (2011, p. 282). Miles, Huberman and Saldaña, on the other hand, argue that 'phrases that are used repeatedly by participants are good leads; they often point to regularities or patterns in the setting' (2014, p. 74). Particular epistemological or political commitment on the part of the researcher may be part of the decision, so that, for example, some researchers working from emancipatory paradigms would prefer in vivo codes as closer representations of the communities whom they seek to represent and work with. Using words from the participants can also keep interpretation closer to the data and give it greater face validity, which brings us to the next concept: member checking.

Member Checking

Member checking is a procedure known by various different names: participant checking, participant validation, respondent validation. The effect is to return the transcripts, interpretations or analyses to participants for them to 'check' them, whether for accuracy, resonance or agreement. This can be a rewarding or a distressing process for the participant (Birt, Scott, Cavers, Campbell and Walter, 2016), as they revisit data which were traumatic, or are embarrassed at verbatim renderings of their speech, or find comfort in finding their experiences reflected in those of others in the study. Candela (2019) considers this in the context of her study of mathematics teachers; on being shown the analysis two of her three participants found the portraits of themselves in her analysis and in their own words to be disturbing, even if not inaccurate. One resolved to re-read the transcription regularly to remind himself not to lower cognitive challenge inappropriately.

Some researchers see member checking as an important ethical step (and see Chapter 8 for its relevance in terms of research with Indigenous communities) while others (including Birt et al., 2016) argue that the process of interpretation which is an essential part of the analytical process in qualitative research means that member checking is inappropriate, in that the researcher can gain insight into what has been said, from their understanding of theory, literature and the rest of the data, and by virtue of simply not being the participant, to which the participant themselves does not have access. By providing a form of 'face validity' member checking may serve to obscure more surprising results. Alternatively, some elite participants may not agree to be part of research without the right to veto their own material. Member checking may or may not imply that right, or that a researcher will change their interpretation upon a participant's challenge.

Reilly (2013) reports asking participants to create 'found poems' from their transcripts that reflected their thoughts and feelings about using poetry as a personal and organizational learning tool (i.e. answered the same research question as the original study). With one research assistant she undertook a traditional coding analytic process, and with another a thematic analysis of the found poems; they found similar representations in each analytical set. However, 'the found poems are a richer and more potent evocation of the themes than the dry and desiccated traditional categories of open coding' (Reilly, 2013, p. 12), which Reilly reports as intensifying her personal difficulties over how data should be represented. She also notes,

> Found poems may provide an avenue for participants who diverge from the representations of the researcher to express more explicitly what they think and feel. Providing an alternate view of their reality, participants' dissident voices could stand along side those who are in agreement, creating a sense of multivocality and multisubjectivity. (Reilly, 2013, p. 14)

This is an interesting point: while analysis usually seeks to tell the overarching story a 'minority report', as it were, can be an important counter-balance to the dominant story, and prevent over-reliance on one interpretation.

7.1 Jean Lave and Etienne Wenger

Jean Lave is an American social anthropologist (1939–), whose most famous work was completed with her former student Etienne Wenger (1952–), on the topics of situated learning and communities of practice (CoP). Situated learning considers learning in the social situation in which it occurs. Lave showed that shoppers in California who could do the mathematics needed to compare prices in situ were less able to do the same mathematics in the form of a test (Lave, 1988). This developed into the theory of situated learning: individuals take part in legitimate peripheral practice on the edge of CoP and are gradually apprenticed into the knowledge of that community of practice (Lave and Wenger, 1991). Their original work was a study of the learning of apprentices in traditional tailoring in Africa. Legitimate peripheral practice means newcomers undertaking low-risk tasks in the interests of the community, through which they gain familiarity with the practices, vocabulary and knowledge of the community.

CoP was then further developed by Wenger in his book *Communities of Practice* (1998). A CoP is a group of people who engage in the practice of something together and learn together. CoP has become a hugely popular educational theory used to consider the transition of adult students into higher education (O'Donnell and Tobbell, 2007); the reproduction of early childhood education norms (Fleer, 2003); medical education (Cruess, Cruess and Steinert, 2018); and online and blended learning (Smith, Hayes and Shea, 2017), to name but a few. CoP incorporates both formal and informal learning environments. The key criterion is a group of practitioners, united by interest in the practice, who maintain a community over time, in which individuals can participate with gradually increasing mastery.

Reliability in Analysis

Reliability has already been discussed in Chapter 4, but in this section I will focus on reliability in the context of analysis. As previously explored, conceptions of reliability are largely taken from quantitative research:

> Reliability is generally defined as the consistency of a measure, or the degree to which scores approximate each other across multiple assessments of an instrument or multiple ratings of the same event. (Syed and Nelson, 2015)

When we turn to analysis, the question of reliability applies in two ways: consistency between researchers (or inter-rater reliability), and consistency over time with the same researcher. It is possible to calculate statistical levels of agreement between two raters or coders, and in quantitative research it would be normal for this to be reported. Where an individual researcher is conducting a study it would still be common for a proportion of the coding to be checked by another person (supervisor, colleague, research assistant), as a measure of validity as opposed to reliability. Richards (2015) argues that qualitative researchers base their claims for credibility on very different grounds and with different standards than those of quantitative research, and therefore reporting of statistical levels of agreement would not be appropriate.

If, however, it is appropriate or necessary to calculate levels of coder agreement, then certain questions need to be answered in order to make it feasible, and these are questions which it might be desirable to answer anyway. Should every word in a data set be coded? What size is a 'chunk' of data which can be coded? Can a segment of data be coded more than once, that is labelled with more than one code? In a large project with a large number of coders, just as it is more essential to have a precise coding manual agreed on, it may also be more desirable to check inter-rater reliability whether that be by statistical means or not. It might be more useful to conduct a qualitative analysis and consider which codes are least agreed on by coders. Is there an obvious reason, such as an unclear definition, or an overlap with another code? Are all coders understanding the constructs in the same way? Are they all coding the same density of codes?

However, as Richards says,

> being reliable (to use the adjective) beats being unreliable. If a category is used in different ways, you will be unable to *rely* on it to bring you all the relevant data. Hence, you may wish to ensure that you yourself are reliably interpreting a code the same way across time, or that you can *rely* on your colleagues to use it the same way. (2015, p. 117, emphasis in the original)

She also, however, sounds a note of caution with the use of inter-coder reliability or consistency tests. Over time, researchers develop their understanding of the data, so consistency over time might be unlikely, or counter-intuitively, a bad thing. Consistency between two coders, meanwhile, is not necessarily desirable as in some qualitative research you might deliberately aim to have researchers with different perspectives on the data, or from different disciplines.

A priori or emergent codes should be defined in a framework or codebook as 'clear operational definitions are indispensable' (Miles, Huberman and Saldaña, 2014, p. 84), whether or not those definitions will be used to test reliability. Refining and outlining these definitions might be another way to either increase reliability or to improve the validity and credibility of the research as a whole:

> Definitions become sharper when two researchers code the same data set and discuss their initial difficulties. A disagreement shows that a definition has to be expanded or otherwise amended. Time spent on this task is not hair-splitting but reaps real rewards by bringing you to an equivocal, common vision of what the codes mean and which blocks of data best fit which code. (Miles, Huberman and Saldaña, 2014, p. 84)

It is surprisingly rare to find coding decisions explicated clearly in qualitative research, despite their key role in establishing trustworthiness.

Language and Translation

A choice made at the design stage is what language to work with participants in, if the researcher has competence to interview in the participants' mother tongue, or if participants speak a lingua franca (usually English), or if an interpreter is required. Bilingual researchers may also generate data in both languages, sometimes within the same interview, which adds another level of complexity to the decisions about translation discussed below. If an interpreter is required the data have been through a further level of mediation and must be considered as such. In educational research one likely example is a student who is fluent in English having to translate for their parents who are not; it is easy to see how such a situation might lead to a student mediating the translation through filters of social acceptability, or editing because of a fear of consequences. Goitom raises a further, ethical, issue in relation to languages spoken by small numbers of people in a country where the majority language is something else. In relation to Amharic, the language spoken by the Ethiopian community in Canada of which she is a part, and in which she researches, she says,

> In the Canadian context, working with translators who are from the same community as the participants poses significant ethical challenges. When one participates in the research activity, it is done with the assurance that their identity is protected. To hire translators from the participants' community to transcribe the data would risk exposing their identities. Even with the signing of confidentiality agreements, participants and potential translators remain members of the same community, thus risking exposure. (Goitom, 2020, p. 552)

Cormier (2018) figures the researcher as linguistic insider/outsider, explicitly considering her positionality as a French-minority speaker in Canada, who also speaks the language of the majority, and researches second language education. Even as linguistic insider the relationship between researcher and participants may be affected: Hallion Bres (2006) relates that as a Francophone speaker from France she perceived her Francophone Canadian speakers as speaking more formally with her, which affected her data given that her research was on the morphosyntactic features of the dialect.

One question for the researcher working with participants in another language (or languages) than the one they are writing in is at what point do you translate the data? There are three main options:

1. translate data at the point of transcription
2. translate data after transcription (or for documents after collection) but before analysis
3. analyse in original language but translate for presentation in the research write-up

Each of these has its advantages and disadvantages, and the first two options only apply if you have decided to transcribe your entire data set. A final question is if all words can be translated, or if some should be left untranslated but explained, if there is not an equivalent in the target language, or if the original word carries connotations that the translated word does not offer, and that will materially change the reader's understanding of what has been said. Halai (2007, p. 344) describes the texts she produced from her bilingual Urdu and English data as 'transmuted' to capture the sense that they were both reflections of the original and recreations in some way. She describes translation as 'a boundary crossing between two cultures' (2007, p. 345), which incorporates the idea that translation is not just about linguistic equivalence but about ideas and cultural knowledge as well. Goitom describes the 'words and phrases that derive from particular poetic and traditional ecclesiastical idioms' (2020, p. 553) which are used by her interviewees, which must of necessity be translated into English, yet have no equivalences that can convey the same web of meanings. Her solution requires an additional layer of work to be done in the moment of data generation:

> I often write down Amharic words used by participants and their corresponding meaning as I understand them. I then ask for clarification in that moment by engaging in a discussion with the participant on how we are both relating to that word/phrase/metaphor in the context of the discussion in order to arrive at some level of clarity around what this means to them in light of what is being narrated. (Goitom, 2020, p. 553)

In doing this, Goitom is maintaining fidelity to her participants and maximizing the rigour of her (translated) data.

One standard for translation in research is that of forward–backward translation, in which a text is first translated into one language, and then translated independently back into the original language. This is the approach utilized as the first step in the preparation of the OECD PISA items (demonstrating that interviews and other qualitative research methods are not the only contexts in which translation and language matter). International large-scale assessments like the OECD PISA programme aim to compare educational attainment in different countries, and require lengthy translation processes. Two source texts, one each in French and English, are prepared, via a process of forward–backward translation and reconciliation, then the recommended approach is to translate those two texts independently into the target language, and then reconcile a final version from the two translations (OECD, 2009). El Masri, Baird and Graesser (2016) nevertheless argue that language difficulty effects can be introduced, taking as their example the PISA science items from 2006, and comparing the difficulty of reading the text in each language. Translation is not, as this example shows, a simple technical question. In English we have the word 'dog' and the word 'canine' as near synonyms but at vastly different levels of reading and comprehension difficulty. Another language may only have one of those options: to translate 'dog' as the equivalent of 'canine' is to imply a potentially greater level of sophistication, to introduce a level of difficulty which was not in the original, and possibly to change the connotations of what has been said.

If analysing data which remain in the original language, questions then arise over the coding that should be used. There are not only issues of appropriateness of using English coding labels on data in another language but also the extra level of cognitive difficulty introduced into the task for the researcher who has to work simultaneously in both languages. If a researcher is working with 'in vivo' codes, then they will naturally arise in the original language. Decisions around these issues will also affect the level of checking that can be done with other researchers to improve the rigour of analysis.

7.2 Gayatri Chakravorty Spivak

Gayatri Chakravorty Spivak (1942–) is a literary scholar and feminist critic. She was born and raised in Calcutta, India, before moving to the United States to undertake graduate study. She is the author of the classic essay of postcolonial theory 'Can the Subaltern Speak?' This draws on the work of Antonio Gramsci (see textbox) and his coining of the term 'subaltern', but the popularization of the term stems from Spivak's work. Subaltern designates the native populations of countries under colonial rule, who are excluded from power and over whom the hegemony exercise power. Spivak cautions against reading this as a synonym for 'oppressed'; it is specifically those dispossessed by colonial rule.

'Can the Subaltern Speak?' addresses the ways in which the intellectual domination of the West displaces ways of knowing which are held by other cultures; in order to participate in the dominant intellectual culture the subaltern must adopt the formulations and approaches of that culture, and are thus never able to express their own ways of knowing. Spivak also brings attention to the ongoing economic inequality between the historical colonizer and the historical colonized, in terms of the ways that international extractive capitalism work.

Spivak uses the example of *sati*, the historical Hindu practice of widows committing suicide by self-immolation on their husband's pyre, to demonstrate how colonizers' rendering of their actions cuts off historical continuity and reshapes what we might call 'general' knowledge according to those dominant colonizers' viewpoints. The British presented the banning of *sati* as essentially a rescuing of women, protection provided by the paternal colonizing power. Spivak's analysis of Hindu law and linguistics of the terms demonstrates the much deeper and richer history of the practice, linked to the ability to escape reincarnation as female. The significance of her work is in asking us to consider how research creates its object as 'Other' and disavows the potential for the subaltern to speak.

Writing about Data Analysis

Key to reproducibility, retroductability and general trust in the findings of a research study is the way in which researchers write about their methodology, and their data analysis process. Much published research skims over the data analysis with quick references, for example, to 'discourse analysis' or 'thematic analysis' despite the fact that each of these comprises a vast range of analytic methods and decisions.

> The objective is to produce a meaningful account of the phenomenon that addresses key aspects of the research question, and to produce this account in a systematic and transparent way so that the reader can see how concepts, themes or categories were developed. Other researchers might well have

devised alternative themes or developed different categories, but they should be able to see how the researcher(s) 'got there' and be able to assess the value of the analysis. (Spencer, Ritchie, Ormston, O'Connor and Barnard, 2014, p. 278)

In preparation for writing about data analysis, it is invaluable to keep clear records of decisions made at every stage, including the emergence of codes, changes in code books and iterations of coding 'as part of your continuing report on the story of your project' (Richards, 2015, p. 121). (This principle also extends to every stage of the research journey.) Coding frameworks and definitions are rarely articulated in the writing up of research in the form of journal articles, but it is indispensable to do so in dissertations and theses. It is not unknown to write to researchers who have used a particular measure or coding framework and ask if it is possible to use it, with due citation; sharing of these items enables reproducibility and the accumulation of greater evidence bases over time than is possible with a single study.

Quantitative research follows fairly similar conventions for the reporting of data analysis, which are governed by norms of journal submission guidelines and by the procedures of different quantitative methods, although we have already noted the potential problems of 'cherry-picking' in Chapter 3 (Wagenmakers, Wetzels, Borsboom, van der Maas and Kievit, 2012). Above all, quantitative research features numbers; the question for qualitative research is to count or not to count? This question usually emerges when reporting data and particularly in relation to publishing qualitative research in journals which are more accustomed to quantitative methods. If a researcher decides not to count it is almost inevitable that a reviewer will insist on having absolute numbers in the journal article before they will consent to its being publishable. I will not enter into the arguments about the standards to which qualitative research is held by largely quantitative journals, but it is worth mentioning that qualitative researchers often have to choose between being pragmatic (in the lay sense of the word) and be published in the journal they want, or to hold to higher principles about their beliefs about what qualitative research should or should not do.

That is to say, providing numbers to indicate the frequency or magnitude of a code or pattern is against the principle of some qualitative researchers (Creswell, 2013), particularly those who are at the very interpretivist end of epistemology; for others a more pragmatic approach is that counting enables a systematic approach to reporting data. Counting might also provide an indicator if a particular code should appear in the write-up of a study: Harding (2013) suggests that if a quarter of participants in a study share a code then it is worth consideration in the final analysis, as a rule of thumb.

Yet, depending on the research questions and methodology, a sense of how widespread a phenomenon is might be more significant than simple numbers. In a study of exam reform we interviewed three teachers within a school, with a sample of fifteen or so schools (Ingram, Elliott, Morin, Randhawa and Brown, 2018). It was important to the study to know across how many teachers and across how many schools certain responses came up – a code applied to six teachers in two schools was likely to be less worthy of detailed consideration than one applied to six teachers in six schools.

When writing about analysis, the introduction of counts may also induce the researcher and the reader to overlook the significance (not statistical!) of an idea that appears only once in a data set. Saldaña warns that the 'unique' code or one that appears just two or three times in a data set may be the key to unlocking the analysis, but he also warns,

> Unfortunately, that same number of just one, two, or three instances of a code may also suggest something unimportant, inconsequential, and unrelated to your research questions and purpose. The analyst must reconcile which one of these possibilities is at work. (Saldaña, 2016, p. 25)

There are no easy answers to be had in educational research decision-making.

Writing up research can be a site of particular anxiety for researchers. For every Geoffrey Walford with his 'compulsive writing' (2001, p. 165) there are a dozen other researchers worrying about writing. Howard S. Becker's *Writing for Social Scientists* (2007) is an excellent resource for those who do struggle. One of his themes is persona and authority, a key issue for writing research when how it is written is part of the justification for its trustworthiness.

> Living as an intellectual or academic makes people want to appear smart, in the sense of clever or intelligent, to themselves and others. But not only smart. They also want to appear knowledgeable or worldly or sophisticated or down-home or professional – all sorts of things, many of which they can hint at in the details of their writing. They hope that being taken for such a person will make what they say believable. (Becker, 2007, pp. 31–2)

Such ambitions, particularly the need to present a persona of authority and intelligence, can breed a particular type of writing that obscures rather than clarifies, that is more interested in impressing than it is in communicating. While a certain level of technicality is unavoidable, my feeling is that clear explanation and honesty is the best way to make research transparent, and also accessible to the greatest number of individuals. In educational research where the end-users of research may be practitioners rather than other researchers that is important for other reasons, but since writing about methodology and data analysis is a key component of trustworthiness, clarity and honesty are indispensable.

Creative Presentation of Data

We have already discussed the idea of making the familiar strange. One of the techniques which can be used to create a sense of distance or alienation from data and to enable readers to see it in a new light is the creation of found poems from data extracts. Found poetry is a technique whereby a writer makes a collage of phrases, words or sentences 'found' in another context, such as graffiti in public toilets. Within research it is a way of presenting data verbatim, but in such a way that the reader does not skim over a block quotation. Katherine Collins (2021, p. 134) created found poetry from interview transcripts with migrants about national identity:

Metanastis
all of these words: immigrant, migrant, ex-pat, refugee.
Anybody who goes from one country to another is metanastis.
It's neutral; it's just that's what you are, if you go
from one country to another; I can't see why
you'd differentiate. And I do see among British ex-pats,
as they like to call themselves. This word,
ex-pats. It affects the way people think.
It's not used for a Nigerian who comes to Britain.

The spacing and line breaks of poetry provide specific signals to the reader about the text they are engaging with, and give weight to the statements made in this way. It is perhaps particularly useful in terms of engaging the public with research, in a format which is familiar from school education. Another increasingly popular method of non-traditional dissemination of research to public rather than academic audiences is via the medium of stand-up comedy, exploiting the genre's history of social observation

(Fox, 2021). Similarly devising plays around research data is a long-standing way of engaging the public with social research (e.g. Rossiter et al., 2008).

Another non-standard way to present data and conclusions, perhaps less unconventionally, is through the dialogue format. Edmiston and Sobjack (2017), for example, present a case study of four eleven- and twelve-year-olds with emotional and behavioural difficulties participating in a dramatic enquiry project based on Homer. The dialogue is between Brian Edmiston (a professor of drama education) and Laura Sobjack (the class teacher of the children who collaborated with Edmiston for the drama project); in using the dialogic format the reader gains a sense of the exploratory nature of the study and the contributions which each of the two research partners made to the research in interpreting the data. In part the dialogue re-rehearses what has already happened, as the participants relate things they have talked over during the project.

Laura: I remember thinking, as James and Karl swung imaginary swords toward one another with great vigour, this is not going to end well! They had a long history of problems with each other during the time they had been together in the EBD unit having learned how to push each other's buttons. James was more of an overt bully, and Karl was sneakier, but they both had it in for each other.

Brian: They were approaching each other with teacher permission to pretend to maim but you were worried they might actually hurt each other. (Ediston and Sobjack, 2017, p. 55)

The dialogue gives a greater sense of the research 'in the moment' and is more lively than a traditional presentation of data analysis might be. In some ways this makes it more accessible and useful for practitioners than traditional research reporting. The comments of the class teacher (Laura) explain what the practices brought into the classroom were, and how that concerned her as a teacher, while Brian glosses that concern with a more traditional academic framing. Laura's commentary also helps to give the practical information which a teacher would need to replicate the practices of the drama-based enquiry being reported into their own classroom:

Laura: When we started to decode I also appreciated how you said anyone could say 'Stop' if they wanted to ask about the meaning of any word, that we'd figure out meaning together, and when you noted you hadn't known the names of the Trojan warriors. That put everyone on a more equal footing.

Brian: I always try to lower my status early on to signal that I want us to share power as much as possible. (Edmiston and Sobjack, 2017, p. 54)

This last sentence is then footnoted with reference to Dorothy Heathcote, the drama education practitioner and researcher, which situates the dialogue within the academic discourse. This structure is still relatively unusual to find within a journal article, however, although it is more accepted in book chapters (e.g. Whetung and Wakefield (2019) which is discussed in Chapter 8).

Conclusion

If the methodology is the 'conceptual epicentre' (Smagorinsky, 2008) of the research study, data analysis provides its practical heart, where the meat of the study emerges. Data analysis is always a process of making decisions, and in this chapter we have identified some of the aspects in which those decisions are particularly salient, whether you are planning your own research or looking to see how others have conducted theirs.

7.3 Howard Gardner

Howard Gardner (1943–) is an American developmental psychologist. His most influential work in education has been his theory of multiple intelligences. This proposes that intelligence is not a single general entity but one which consists of differing levels of ability in eight different domains: linguistic, logical-mathematical, musical, spatial, kinaesthetic, interpersonal, intrapersonal and naturalistic. The last of these was not included in his original book on the subject but has been added to encompass the intelligence of the naturalist – or the hunter-gatherer (1995).

It is readily recognizable that these categories have also had a great deal of influence on the non-educational world and general perceptions of intelligence. Gardner's theory of multiple intelligences has also been widely challenged on the basis of lack of experimental evidence; most of them have a strong correlation with g – general intelligence, with the exception of bodily-kinaesthetic. Multiple intelligence also has clear links to learning styles (visual, audio, kinaesthetic, etc.) which have been very influential in teaching but have also been comprehensively debunked (Sharp, Bowker and Byrne, 2008).

More recently Gardner has been senior director of Harvard's Project Zero, a large-scale project now over fifty years old with a focus on the arts and creativity in education and more broadly.

8

Research as an Ethical Practice

The ethical dimension of research is an important one, which has become institutionalized throughout the world as universities and funding bodies seek to quality assure research studies through ethical procedures. This chapter, however, is not about ethical procedures and processes but about ethical practice. As Furlong argues, there is 'a strong moral dimension to much of the research undertaken in education; the moral commitment to make a difference that is still a hugely important force in defining the field' (2013, p. 10). Concomitant to that comes a responsibility to think and act ethically, not merely outsourcing that to an ethics board; additionally 'ethical approval' is a step between research design and data collection, and does not offer the support needed to work through ethical dilemmas in the field. Whetung and Wakefield (2019) note the urge to 'codify' and 'write everything out' so that in fulfilling the procedures the researcher gains an insurance policy against being accused of unethical work. They also note that university ethics procedures are 'grounded in – and normaliz[e] – the university as the arbiter of what is ethical in creating knowledge' (Whetung and Wakefield, 2019, p. 150). Richards, Clark and Boggis (2015) consider university ethics frameworks with a Foucauldian eye (see *Michel Foucault* textbox), conceptualizing them as disciplinary strategies of control within academia.

This chapter, rather than engaging with university ethics procedures, explores some of the larger ethical issues in relation to research in education, problematizing some of the current practices. It considers purely instrumental research and the role of blue skies curiosity-driven research, asking what questions are worth asking, new questions of ethics prompted by the climate crisis and the responsibilities of researchers to the communities they study. We will explore hierarchical power relationships, and issues of anonymity, consent and rapport.

Impact – what Is the Point of Research?

Impact in research is defined by the UK research councils as 'the demonstrable contribution that excellent research makes to society and the economy'.[1] Impact is one of the dimensions on which research is assessed in the UK Research Excellence Framework (Watermeyer, 2016). In some respects it formalizes the demands made by the last of Robson's criteria for research questions – that they must be *substantively relevant* (2002, p. 59) – the 'so what' dimension of research design. In education we might site impact within the moral and ethical dimensions of research, in that researchers by and large are engaged with the potential of education for increasing social justice. In the United States, the 'No Child Left Behind' and in the UK the 'Closing the Gap' agendas explicitly laid the responsibility for a decrease in inequality on the shoulders of schools. The requirement for research to have 'impact' in education ties in with this responsibility, and the increasing expectations on teachers' shoulders to make up for structural inequalities between families of different races, different economic backgrounds and many others. We might argue that if a research project shows that teachers could make a major change to their students' outcomes (including but not limited to their attainment outcomes) by adding a particular practice, then we also need to think about what they should then omit to allow resources for that practice. Ethics is not only about the students' outcomes but also about the quality of life for teachers. In general, however, we could argue that the use of impact as a criterion for the excellence of research aligns with the motives behind educational research at large.

In contrast, Laing, Smith and Todd (2018) argue that the impact agenda, though framed as neutral, is in fact a neoliberal driver, favouring particular models of implementation and evaluation, in particular away from forms of research which depend on critical theory. The use of metrics as a means to monitor value for money in education (and many other areas of public life) is an almost inescapable neoliberal mechanism (Baird and Elliott, 2018),

---

[1] https://esrc.ukri.org/research/impact-toolkit/what-is-impact/. Accessed 10 January 2022.

although Khazragui and Hudson (2015) have argued that impact assessment itself is largely reliant on persuasive narrative accounts rather than reliable metrics. Large-scale research based on quantitative measures coheres with a model of metrics-driven quality assurance. Randomized controlled trials (RCTs) which measure the effectiveness of an intervention that could raise attainment, according to the metrics which govern the system, become hugely desirable as a result. Fancourt notes that UK government policy promoting RCTs in education 'aimed to enable schools to make research-informed decisions, so that time and money were not wasted on irrelevant or ineffective strategies – a "what works" rationale' (2017, p. 161).

The impact agenda, then, could be seen as working in tandem with more direct pressures in favour of 'gold standard' research such as the Random Controlled Trial (see also Chapters 4 and 9) to drive public funding towards research which delivers immediate and implementable solutions, and which is in 'the public interest'. This is problematic because it ignores the potential of 'blue skies research' to produce unexpected innovation, or impact which may not be seen for decades – such as Peter Higgs's theoretization of the Higgs Boson in 1964, whose existence was finally demonstrated in 2012 at CERN, after the physicist had retired, and caused him to be awarded the Nobel Prize in 2013. It may also, as has been argued by Kettley (2010), lead to research being funded which is less likely to have large ambitions of wholesale revolution in education, and more likely to merely provide incremental improvements within a system which does not and cannot deliver social justice. Following the path, suggested by some, of ensuring that educational research priorities are determined by what teachers want to know carries a similar potential risk. For example, it might tie research too closely to the existing system, and make it less likely to consider completely different approaches which might revolutionize the fairness of education.

Blue skies research is largely defined as research which does not have any immediate application, often theoretical.

> Blue-skies research has become synonymous with basic research, fundamental research or pure research, although the term pure leads us into all sorts of semantic trouble. What turns blue sky research from 'fanciful' to 'fanciable' are the semantic links that many establish between blue-sky research, 'curiosity' and 'serendipity', imagination, passion. But some may still see it as 'not practical or profitable'. (Nerlich, 2012, n.p.)

It is easy to see where this might lead us in the hard sciences – indeed the rapid development of Covid vaccines in late 2020 was due to blue skies research in mRNA vaccines that had already been done. In education we might look to some of the foundational work on classroom interaction done through Conversation Analysis. In the early 1970s Mary Budd Rowe recorded a number of science lessons in small groups and measured the length of 'wait time' before teachers spoke again after asking a question (Rowe, 1972, 1974). This research in itself was not instrumental or intended to have direct impact – Rowe was exploring classroom discussion and found that teachers typically wait less than a second before answering their own questions. Over ten years later she herself started to publish on ways that that discovery could be instrumentalized in instruction (Rowe, 1986), and manipulating 'wait time' has become an accepted technique in classroom teaching (Ingram and Elliott, 2016). We might also locate blue skies research in education within theoretical development unbounded by empirical application, whether or not that is then used in empirical work. A case in point would be Harry Daniels's work on the sociology of pedagogy (e.g. 2009) bringing together the work of Basil Bernstein and Lev Vygotsky. He uses Bernstein's analysis of classification and framing as ways to describe institutions to supplement Vygotskyan theory in order to 'take account of ways the practices of a community, such as a school and the family, are structured by their institutional context' (Daniels, 2009, p. 35).

The middle ground between extreme instrumental research which looks to create immediate impact, typically in the form of raising achievement scores and fully blue skies research, is the more exploratory research which seeks to understand and explain phenomena and which is the necessary prerequisite for the design of interventions to be evaluated through RCTs. The raising of attainment measured through standardized scores might seem to be the very height of ethical research: it has an immediate impact on individual lives and is improving the very foundation of education – learning itself. One might also argue that in doing so it simply reinforces the very unethical system which relies on standardized attainment scores which underpin a failing meritocratic system (Sandel, 2020) and reinforces social and educational disadvantage, ossifying it down the generations. Both positions have their merits (the irony of the word) and exemplify why arguments about ethical research are rarely black and white or easily resolved.

One important consideration is the ethical obligations to participants in research in terms of the use of their data. There is a strong ethical case to say that you should only collect data which you can and will use; is there an ethical case to suggest that blue skies research, with less likelihood of short-term real-world impact, does not accord with the principle of minimizing the burden to participants if the research is not going to have an impact? A similar dilemma emerges with RCTs: if an intervention can reasonably be expected to have a positive effect, then how do we justify not giving that intervention to the entire group that volunteered for the trial (see Morrison 2001; Hammersley 2008)? Various answers are posed for this: one is that we do not know until we have actually completed the trial that the intervention is indeed beneficial (Haynes, Service, Goldacre, and Torgerson, 2012). Another is that many studies provide an alternative treatment to ensure that benefits that are seen are not merely a 'halo effect' (Thorndike, 1920) where just being given a different treatment and being studied has an impact on the participants. This would be the equivalent of giving a control group a placebo in a medical trial, so, for example, an RCT evaluating a specific reading catch-up one-to-one intervention might give a control group an alternative where the students read one-to-one with an adult but did not follow the other pedagogies of the intervention. The alternative is still beneficial. A third alternative is that some studies propose giving the treatment to the control group after the first study has finished, so that in volunteering for a trial you will receive the intervention, but not necessarily in the first wave. If the intervention is shown not to be beneficial, then the second group could avoid it altogether. To return to the question of ethics and blue skies research, it is debatable whether the participant sees an immediate benefit to participation even for research that is intended to have a rapid impact: participants in research largely act from motives of interest (as in curiosity) and the potential for causing change (e.g. Clark, 2010).

Finally it is worth noting that although much educational research is framed via an ethic of social justice, the link to how that justice will be brought about is less clear.

> Left unarticulated, there often seems to be a tacit theory of change that through critique, through the articulation of wrong or malignancy in society, that transformation will occur. However, calling attention to something does not automatically mean its transformation. (Patel, 2016, pp. 1–2)

The philosophy of research puts the emphasis on knowledge before action; Patel simply raises the challenge to all of us as to what we do with that knowledge once we have gained it. An ethical practice of educational research might require action to follow the deliberate creation of impact for the societies and individuals whom we have researched.

Responsibilities in Researching with and in Indigenous and Vulnerable Communities

Vulnerable populations include: 'people who are incarcerated or formerly incarcerated, use illegal drugs, suffer from intergenerational poverty and structural inequality, have health issues or transmittable diseases, or engaged in activities that are unconventional in contemporary society' (Boeri and Shukla, 2019, p. 3). Indigenous communities are often affected by structural inequality and racism. In educational research vulnerable groups also include some (but not all) children, such as those who are looked after by the state, have special educational needs or disabilities, or are groomed by adults for sexual purposes or for drug distribution. Working with vulnerable populations carries with it an additional set of responsibilities.

Tuhiwai Smith writes of European PhD students approaching Indigenous communities in New Zealand informally, and how, by attending a community event and being invited into someone's home – building networks and access in what the Europeans would consider a normal way – the student then puts hosting responsibilities, including sponsoring of the researcher into the wider community, upon the person who unwittingly invited them into their home, through the types of guesting protocols of the Indigenous community, through what she calls the 'subterfuge of innocence' (Tuhiwai Smith, 2019, p. 12). This is of course deeply unethical, even if the PhD student does not know what they are doing. It is the responsibility of the researcher to do the reading before they go into the field so that they are not putting obligations upon people who have not had that choice. The researcher as guest is not confined to these kinds of contexts: many educational researchers might visit children in their homes to conduct research and again take on dual roles (Richards, Clark and Boggis, 2015). Whereas in the first example the obligations fall on the researched and are thus unethical, in the latter example the obligations fall more on the researcher to fulfil the role of guest if treated as such, sometimes at the expense of the quality of the data that are produced. Richards, Clark and Boggis also note that while researching children in their homes is largely figured in the literature as being more ethical as it is conducive to feelings of confidence and control in the children, this makes assumptions about the lives of those children and frames them as having specific kinds of home lives – which may alter the data that are generated.

Pacheco-Vega and Parizeau (2018) consider, among other ethical challenges and opportunities associated with researching in vulnerable communities, the question of incentivization, and what can be offered without being coercive or extractive. Educational research rarely uses incentives to encourage participation, partly because of the nature of working with children, but when working with disadvantaged communities there is a strong argument to be made for recompensing them for their effort in participation. Pacheco-Vega and Parizeau draw on the idea of 'doubly engaged' (Skocpol, 2003) research which

> requires researchers to be self-reflective, autocritical, and engaged with the needs of those communities that they are studying. Investigating the challenges facing vulnerable communities also demands the deployment of specific research methods that not only engage the scholar but also ensure that target populations are protected, both in their well-being and in their livelihood. (2018, p. 2)

As Morgensen points out, 'colonial principles set the legal standard for determining the nature or evidence of "harm" in research with indigenous people' (2012, p. 807). The ethical standard is likely to be of a qualitatively different nature. Data generation is by its nature extractive; the challenge is how to alleviate that burden as much as possible, to justify it in relation to the potential gain (to the researched rather than the researcher), or to decide that it is not in fact appropriate to embark on a piece of research tourism which may be desirable for personal or professional reasons.

The extractive colonial approach may also colour relations within data collection teams, not just between researchers and participants. One of the major crises facing the world today – and, therefore, education systems – is the plight of refugees and forced migrants fleeing war zones. As a result places such as Syria and their displaced populations have become a popular research topic in the West. Researchers rarely speak the language of their participants and often rely on local research assistance for data collection. These research assistants may then be written out of the research entirely, as reported by Sukarieh and Tannock (2019): 'While refugee research is framed in the UK as a noble project of helping the world's most vulnerable, these assistants speak critically of their sense of alienation, exploitation and disillusionment with the research they work on' (p. 664). They describe the phenomenon as 'subcontracted ghost production of overseas academic research' (2019, p. 665). They describe one powerful example from their interviews with these 'ghost' producers:

> 'I was sitting in the audience while [the principal investigator] was presenting our research', one Lebanese research assistant (RA) recalls: 'She presented as if it was her work, quoting Syrian refugees as if she had done the interviews herself, and we (myself and the other RA who did all the research) were just part of the audience, we did not exist'. 'At one point', the assistant says, 'she was reading from the paper that I had written and said that "one of the refugees told me" as if she was the one doing the interviews'. 'I was trying to swallow my anger and disgust', the assistant continues: 'The meeting ended, everyone celebrated and clapped for the great doctor on her great work, and I clapped along'. 'It wasn't the fact that I was angry at being plagiarised', the assistant reflects, 'I was angry because I was being ignored, even in my presence.' (Sukarieh and Tannock, 2019, p. 671)

Ethical thinking within research projects rarely extends to the exploitation of research assistance. Some journals, and some research groups, have protocols about who should be credited with authorship of work (see Chapter 9 for why citations matter), but it is not by any means universal. It is particularly problematic in research that claims to be 'noble' or especially ethical in other ways.

While thinking about research with Indigenous communities we should consider the case for regarding the environmental impact of research as part of ethical thinking. Climate change disproportionately impacts the communities who are least able to withstand its effects, particularly in developing countries (Thomas et al., 2019). That is to say, in contributing to global emissions by taking international flights, or travelling to remote locations for research purposes, researchers are contributing to inequality and social injustice, arguably to a greater extent than they are alleviating it via their research. The relational accountability discussed in Chapter 2 includes 'all our relations' including the water and air, a principle which urges us to think about the consequences of our research more widely (Steinhauer, 2002, p. 72).

After the declaration of the Covid-19 pandemic in 2020 many doctoral students switched to remote fieldwork as they were no longer able to access research sites or travel internationally. While some methodologies do not allow for this, there seems to be a good case for most interview studies, for example, to take place online in future. There are other advantages: if I want to conduct interviews with American teachers I can have a huge geographical spread if I do not have to cost in travelling to each of their locations. Although telephone and videoconferencing interviews have been part of educational research for a while, they have often been regarded as second-best to in-person interviews. The greater familiarity with online meetings engendered during the pandemic is likely to also alleviate some of the fears associated with remote data collection: a much greater proportion of the population is now comfortable with online communication. In addition such a move could provide greater integration of disabled researchers and participants into mainstream research.

8.1 Linda Tuhiwai Smith

Linda Tuhiwai Smith (1950–) is a professor of Indigenous education in New Zealand. She affiliates to the Ngāti Awa and Ngāti Porou iwi. (An iwi is the largest unit of Maori social organization – it is often translated as tribe but is more accurately nation.) Smith is one of the most influential Indigenous academics in the world. Her book *Decolonizing Methodologies* (1999) was ground-breaking in challenging knowledge production in the social sciences for the embedded colonial and imperial practices and values, and the ways in which social science research serves to reproduce colonial privilege.

Although Smith's research is embedded in the Maori context, she has noted how Indigenous communities around the world share many of the same concerns about education (2005). She has argued for the importance of Indigenous-led research and noted the differing questions asked by and about Indigenous people in reference to education: 'Indigenous communities often have a quite different set of questions that frames the key educational issue as being primarily about epistemic self-determination that includes language and culture and the challenges of generating schooling approaches from a different epistemological basis' (Smith, 2005, p. 94).

In 2019 Smith edited a book with Eve Tuck, *Indigenous and Decolonizing Studies in Education*, which draws together Indigenous educational researchers from all over the world, with works which apply the principles of *Decolonizing Methodologies*. She has also continued to be a vocal critic of the ways in which Maori people are discriminated against in New Zealand educational practices and institutions, including her own.

Thinking Ethically about Power Hierarchies

'The relationship [between researcher and researched] is predetermined based on the ethics review form. Rather than a transgression of the categories of powerful and powerless, privileged and vulnerable, this predetermination results in the maintenance of them' (Whetung and Wakefield, 2019, p. 149). That is to say, in codifying the vulnerabilities of certain participants the research ethics process reifies them and frames them in a particular way which has problems not only for ethical research (as opposed to procedures) but also for the rigour of that research, in that it predetermines how the researcher views the data generated from, by and about those participants. Whetung and Wakefield also suggest that rather than thinking in terms of 'benefits to the community' and 'minimizing harm' we should be thinking about responsibility and accountability to the communities which we research, which echoes the discussion above. This applies equally to all research participants.

Children in particular are codified in ethics procedures and codes (e.g. BERA, 2018; AERA, 2011) as being vulnerable and below a certain age incapable of giving consent; instead we talk of 'assent' in the context of children's agreement to take part in research (Richards, Clark and Boggis, 2015). As Richards, Clark and Boggis also point out, the social science model of ethics for researching with children is largely drawn from a medical model, and a model which deals with consent to medical treatment. It is for this reason that the concept of 'Gillick competence' is important in educational research. The term arises from a court case in the UK in the 1980s in which Victoria Gillick objected to the British National Health Service advice that doctors could prescribe contraception for minors under sixteen. The case was litigated at several levels, eventually ending up in the House of Lords, where the judgement of Lord Scarman has become known as the test for Gillick competence: 'As a matter of Law the parental right to determine whether or not their minor child below the age of sixteen will have medical treatment terminates if and when the child achieves sufficient understanding and intelligence to understand fully what is proposed' ('Gillick vs. West Norfolk and Wisbech AHA', 1985). This test has been widely applied outside the original context, although in very few contexts do researchers seek only consent from children without parental consent as well. This is a test developed to apply in a high-stakes and contentious situation (as it remains so even almost forty years later). Its use in social sciences serves to highlight the onus to prove that a child is competent rather than the other way round. While this is certainly important in preventing harm to children, it also frames them as largely incompetent, and diminishes the weight we place on their evidence. Mohanty (2003) notes the danger of any research which 'sets up its own authorial subjects as the implicit referent, that is, the yardstick by which to encode and represent cultural others' (p. 21).

The concept of the 'voiceless' participant is considered in the next chapter, but even as we attempt to elicit the views of some participants we are encouraged by our frameworks to dismiss their reliability as sources. It also casts as 'perpetually "inappropriate"' some topics as being too sensitive to discuss with children (Richards, Clark and Boggis, 2015, p. 17). This emphasizes the need to protect from risk (on the part of the researcher and their institution) rather than the ethical questions of the research per se. This construction by ethics frameworks echoes the construction of children through societal discourses in the West as vulnerable, dependent and irrational (Archard, 2014), creating a reinforcing circle. To contrast this, children in the Solomon Islands as young as three or four are sent to collect fire from other households by means of flaming branches: competence and responsibility are culturally defined attributes. One consequence of this construction is the creation of taboos around researching some topics with children and young people. Richards, Clark and Boggis (2015) raise the topic of sex and sexuality in children's lives as one such taboo: as a consequence we can research teenage pregnancy and its prevention, sexual exploitation and sexually transmitted disease, but there is a major lack of research on, for example, positive experiences or sex education which focuses on pleasure. This then has consequences for the knowledge which is available to train educators and those who work with young people, and therefore for the experiences which young people have.

The Complications of Anonymity

Anonymity is one of the main conventions of the ethics of research and yet, particularly in a hyper-connected twenty-first-century world, it has become rather complicated to maintain. It is a particular problem with highly individual cases which are studied for the very reason that they are so unusual, and indeed where much of the value of the research may come from identifying the site. A study of policy-making decisions in the US Department of Education gets its value from its location; a study of policy-making decisions in an education department in one of the US states would not need the location to be identified, but it is likely that it would be traceable if any details were given about the kinds of decisions being made, the context of the state politics and so on. Researchers may decide to institute anonymity at a particular level, so, for example, concealing the identity of the individual, but not other details. This may involve conflating or disguising some details if the study is in a highly identifiable site, to protect individuals.

In some cases, the researcher may illustrate findings with vignettes drawn from one particular participant who illuminates some aspect of the data particularly well. In others, the vignette may be a composite, drawing on elements of several participants, 'selecting representative elements from the data set and composing a new original which is not traceable back to the originals' (Markham, 2012, p. 342). The advantage is the creation of 'composite quotations and case studies, which conceal participants' identities and preserve their anonymity' (Philips and Kara, 2021, p. 2). (Quantitative-minded researchers who are drawing in their breath at this technique could consider its parallels to imputation – the process of replacing missing data with imputed values to avoid the problems of deleting data listwise.)

Where narratives form the data it can be hard to anonymize, particularly in the age of the internet. In an educational study, for example, a determined reader is likely to be able to trace at least the school which formed a research site, if not the specific member of staff who is quoted, and within that school it is likely that the speaker is easily identifiable. This brings responsibilities on the part of the researcher – more than once I have had to relinquish a particularly juicy quotation in order to prevent repercussions for a research participant – but may also lead us to question if anonymity in social research is to some extent a convenient fiction in the twenty-first century. A narrative may also be so individual that it is impossible to prevent it being recognizable. McDowell (2014) reports some of the data generated by incarcerated individuals during her study of how prison education enables participants to refigure their lives (and hence to avoid recidivism when they are released). The data were generated through a life-writing not-for-credit class as part of a prison education degree programme. Some of the participants did not understand why she was required to use their writing anonymously – nor did they want that anonymity; for them it was some of the best and most personal writing they had ever produced (McDowell, personal communication, 2011). Similar issues arise in research utilizing creative methods where poetry or art generated by participants is part of the data set and the participants wish (fairly) to be credited for their work and acknowledged as authors. In other contexts the identity of the interviewee may be part of the interest in what they have to say, as in the case of elite interviews, for example, but the ease of their identification may also be a factor in their willingness – or otherwise – to participate.

One particular challenge to anonymity in educational research is action or practitioner research where the researcher is engaged in researching their own practice or their immediate environment, and anonymity becomes very difficult very quickly. It is extremely easy to identify a research site from the researcher's name, and within that site, the identities of individual student participants could well become obvious to other teachers or other pupils within the context. If a practitioner research project is less closely tied to the classroom, instead focusing on an element of school life where other practitioners become the data source, then there is an extra risk attached of repercussions if the leadership team of the school do not like what has been said (made more complex by the fact that the senior leadership are likely to have acted as gatekeepers for the research (Brindley and Bowker, 2013) and may well have required some form of reporting to the school as part of access arrangements).

We should note that practitioner research has its own ethical challenges external to the question of anonymity. Research ethics are not always the same as, and indeed can be in tension with, practitioner ethics or what Mockler describes as 'everyday ethics' (2014, p. 146). Fancourt (2017) notes that this does not lead to an ethical dilemma where there are two clear but contradictory ethical guidelines, but to an ethical quandary where it is not clear which set of rules should be followed at all.

> A dilemma is akin to a sports team having to make decisions how to play the game together, whereas a quandary is as if there is disagreement within the team as to what game they are playing. Teachers may well have a different view to the researchers or government agencies of the ethical issues involved, how they are constructed and how they might be resolved. (Fancourt, 2017, p. 168)

A similar quandary can arise in any educational research in relation to the question of confidentiality – related to the principle of anonymity. While teachers are bound legally in the UK to pass on any information a child gives them that shows they are at risk of harm (such as disclosure about physical or sexual abuse), the principle of confidentiality means that researchers tend to promise not to discuss what an individual has said during data collection, except in the anonymous context of the research. If a child makes a disclosure the researcher must either break the promise, or fail to protect the child. When I first left teaching for the world of educational research I was appalled to be given this as an absolute guideline; the world has moved on somewhat since then and I think it is no longer controversial to suggest that when talking to children researchers should give the same disclaimer that teachers must – if the child discloses something to show they are at risk then that will have to be passed on to a suitable person, whether or not that restricts the information that they then give. Children do make disclosures to virtual strangers; they must have the right to decide whether to make that disclosure or not if it is going to be passed on, not least because of the harm caused by the breaking of trust with an already vulnerable young person. This mainly applies in school-based research where you do not have an ongoing relationship with the child; some researchers work in environments with young people for a long time. If you are conducting an ethnography in an inner-city community programme, for example, then you may well witness statements about under-age sex, drug use and commerce or weapons-based violence. Some young people might use such statements to test the trustworthiness of researchers. Blackman and Commane (2012) explore the concept of 'research friendship' where the bounds of the researcher-participant relationship are changed by long-standing contact. There are no easy answers or absolute guidelines, and many projects of this nature face later scrutiny of their intentions and ethics upon publications. One might, for example, look at Sudhir Venkatesh's *Gang Leader for a Day* (2009), which is a fascinating study of drug gang economics in Chicago but which raises a number of ethical issues based on his participant observation which became very participatory at some points. These issues can be further complicated by the overlap between some journalistic work and some social science research. Sieber and Tolich (2013) discuss some of these issues in a chapter named 'Journalist Ethics ≠ Social Scientist Ethics'. They recommend reading *Gang Leader for a Day* alongside Mitchell Duneier's *Sidewalk* (Duneier and Carter, 1999), which is an exemplary for ethical research, on a similar topic, and comparing the ethical decisions made by each.

Participatory action research (PAR) may have a particular difficulty with institutional requirements for anonymity. Empowerment is most commonly cited as the reason for using PAR with young people (Cooper, 2005; Cullen and Walsh, 2020), but Yanar, Fazli, Rahman and Farthing's (2016) young participants challenged how they would be able to claim their work and use it to create change if they were not acknowledged by name. PAR often involves the co-creation of research, which results in participants named as authors, rather than remaining anonymous within the data. Houghton (2015) argues that it is essential to involve young people who are survivors of abuse with policy making and in discussions about ethics for the researching of their lives: his young participants were concerned for confidentiality in order to avoid risk, but felt that imposing blanket anonymity was tantamount to allowing their former abusers to control their lives. The avoiding of risk for children is a major issue for educational researchers, particularly in relation to photographs or the ability to identify locations of certain types of young people. This might mean conflating or confusing locations in reports of research, or other tactics.

At the moment these challenges for anonymity do not mean that the convention has been abandoned in educational research. It does mean that in some instances anonymity is a convenient fiction, and that therefore when writing up research we must be more careful than ever what we attribute to individuals who might be identified. It may mean obfuscating the origin of particular comments, but in a small enough study that is not enough. I refer you here to the Agatha Christie crime novel *Ordeal by Innocence* – a small group of suspects exist for a murder but it cannot be proved to have been any one of them. All of them therefore are treated as potentially guilty. Where power relationships exist in research sites, and those in power know you have been researching in that site, and who you have talked to, then disguising *which* of your participants said something may not be enough to protect them. In other situations the identification of participants will not be easy even for those within the study. This is where the individual ethical judgement of the researcher comes in, as to what it is and it is not ethical to make public, even though your participants have given their informed consent.

This is one of the advantages of large-scale quantitative data, in that individuals are subsumed within statistical analyses. Even in the generating of such data participants feel the freedom of the large-scale survey, and the anonymity of the internet which frees them from the need to appear socially acceptable to the researcher. This may generate more accurate data, although it also may not: we received hundreds of responses to a survey explicitly aimed at school teachers in England (reported in Elliott et al., 2020) from university lecturers in the United States, which were easily identified because we asked for a postal code of school location in order to identify clusters in the data. We did not expect to have to use it as a validating question to ensure eligibility for the survey and relevance to the research questions!

'Informed' Consent?

Informed consent is another of the fundamental concepts of the ethics of research: the principle that participants have sufficient information to be able to make a decision about whether or not to participate, based on the burden on them, the topic of the study, the conditions under which and the purpose for which their data will be used.

There are one or two classic studies in social science which are used to illustrate the principle of consent, particularly because they would be unlikely to gain ethical clearance now. One is the Milgram experiment (or in fact a series of experiments, gathered together in Milgram (1974)) in which participants were told that they had been selected at random out of a pair to be the 'teacher' while the other person was the 'learner'. In fact the learner was always a member of the research team. The learner was connected to some 'electrodes' and the teacher had a machine labelled with different voltages of electricity with increasing levels of shock (including the word 'Danger'). The learner had allegedly learned a list of paired words: the task was to recall the pair for the word given by the prompter. The teacher was told to shock the learner each time he made a mistake, and to increase the intensity of the shock each time. The study is ostensibly a study of learning but is in fact a study of how far obedience to an authority figure will make the 'teacher' go in harming the 'learner' (although the participants *had* been assured no lasting damage would be done). The learner in fact faked his reaction to the 'shocks' but behaved with increasing distress. If the teacher refused to go on, a series of reminders were given: Please continue; the experiment requires you to continue; it is absolutely essential that you continue; you have no other choice but to continue. The majority of the participants continued up to giving a shock of 450 volts, despite displaying increased signs of distress and unhappiness at their own actions.

These studies prompted a review of some of the ethical standards of psychological research. Baumrind (1964) argued that even though the participants had given consent to a study in which they knew they could be giving (or in theory receiving) an electric shock, the researchers had a duty of care to the participants and should have halted the experiment when they saw the extent of the distress caused. Participants had not given – and could not give – consent to the distress caused by the deception: so was it informed consent? Explicit deception of this nature – or of any nature – is rarely given permission in modern research, and one outcome of the Milgram experiments has been an insistence on thorough debriefing of participants if deception does occur. Avoiding explicit deception does not give the researcher a get-out-of-ethics-jail free card, however; Newkirk (1996) talks of 'seduction and betrayal' in which the framing of the project is benign, but the representation of participants is not.

Another study which is often used for a case study in discussing consent is *Tearoom Trade: Impersonal Sex in Public Places* (Humphreys, 1970). As part of his study, Humphreys noted car registration plates outside places which were known locations for anonymous male homosexual sex in public toilets (known as 'cottaging' in the UK and 'tea-rooming' in the United States, hence the name). He utilized these number plates to track down men who were participating in these activities and posed as a health researcher to interview them without revealing why he was recruiting them to his study. The book had a revolutionary effect on the way that gay sex was considered, and participants in cottaging, as many of his participants (or perhaps we should use the term 'subjects' here since their 'participation' was not under fully informed consent) were married men who lived otherwise respectable lives (a value judgement of the time, not mine). Was the deceit harmless? Interviewees were not identifiable in any way in the final research. Nevertheless it is highly unlikely that these men would have consented had they known the full truth about the research. Humphreys did collect other data in a more traditionally ethnographic way, by spending time at the cottaging locations and talking to men, but not always revealing his identity as a researcher. (If you are interested in 'undercover' research of these kinds, then Calvey's *Covert Research* (2017) deals with the methods, ethics and debates in depth. Boeri and Shukla's *Inside Ethnography* (2019) considers hidden populations and the difficulty of reaching them.)

A third classic study used for considering research ethics (but not consent as such) is the Stanford Prison Experiment (Haney, Banks and Zimbardo, 1973), in which a simulation of a prison was created with participants assigned randomly to be prisoners and guards. The intent was to investigate the effects of power in the prison environment, and the guards were recorded as descending into psychological torture and abuse of prisoners, despite the knowledge that they were all participants in the simulation. More recently the validity of the findings has been strongly challenged, with allegations that the lead researcher provoked the behaviour of the guards deliberately.

However, the study has entered the public imagination in a way that is true of few pieces of social science research.

One question in relation to consent is whether it must be written or if spoken consent is sufficient. I noted earlier in the chapter the idea that institutional ethics procedures are intended to codify decisions and create written 'ethics insurance' for the research and the institution (Whetung and Wakefield, 2019). For this reason written consent is seen as the gold standard. There are situations in educational research, however, in which insisting on written consent may detract from the real ethical issues, and potentially be a source of bias for the research. Bhutta (2004) noted that in international contexts and particularly in developing countries researchers can emphasize the need for a signature on a consent form over and above the need to actually ensure that participants fully understand what it is they are consenting to. This is symptomatic of a wider issue which considers consent to be an event, a ticking of a box, rather than an ongoing process during the research: participants have the right to withdraw at any time, and to refuse to answer any question. In some contexts there might be a risk attached, or perceived to be attached, to having your name written on a piece of paper in the possession of the researcher (imagine collecting data in an authoritarian regime); in others the participant may simply not be comfortable signing something they cannot read, if they are illiterate, for example. Persisting in requiring a written signature in such contexts can have two effects: one, it can bring harm to the participants if they sign despite their lack of comfort with that particular aspect of the process, whether emotional or physical; and two, it can systematically bias your data by excluding that group if they decide not to sign and therefore do not take part in the research.

Returning to practitioner research Homan (2001) also highlights the difficulty of truly free consent from students: 'while students are formally free to withhold consent, the psychological and emotional reality is that freedom is compromised' (p. 366). In many cases the need for consent is considered moot if the changes are within the normal range of decisions that a classroom practitioner could make anyway, and since they have normal access to attainment data to evaluate the effect of those changes (reasoning that has also been used in terms of enabling headteachers to give consent for pupils to take part in RCTs sponsored by the Department for Education in the UK (Fancourt, 2017)). Similarly, the National Pupil Database is a large data set owned by the UK government, which researchers can apply for access to in order to carry out specific analyses. No parent of any child has the right to withdraw their data from that database, and the consent is given for its use by agents of the government, not the schools, children or parents of children represented within it. Each child is identified by a specific number which allows tracking of attainment throughout school, and linking of other characteristics such as eligibility for free school meals or special educational needs. However, it is impossible for researchers to convert those identity numbers to names or actual identities. Most other large-scale data sets take informed consent at the point of data collection.

If access takes place through gatekeepers it can involve going through several layers of authority before you reach your 'real' participants, and they may no longer feel able to refuse consent if (for example) the principal of their school and the head of their department have already consented to their participation on their behalf. There is a balance to be struck between access, particularly if access is required to students as well as staff, in which case access has to go through senior management, and freedom to consent on the part of the participants, where it might be more considerate to gain a teacher's agreement to participate first, before then seeking access via the school hierarchy (perhaps sponsored by the teacher in question).

It has been mentioned above that children are generally asked for 'assent' rather than 'consent' and that the true power to allow their participation lies elsewhere. Many researchers with children still choose to gain fully informed consent from the child as well as their parent or a teacher in loco parentis. This can be aligned to the purpose of the research, as studying children's views is likely to be part of a wider commitment to their having an input into their education and into educational research. It is also true that getting a child to participate in research who is truly determined not to, whatever their parent or teacher says, is unlikely to be successful.

Rapport – an Aspect of Ongoing Consent

If we consider that consent is an ongoing process, it creates more jeopardy for the researcher in relation to the question of rapport. Rapport refers to the positive relationship generated between a researcher and their participant, and is particularly important for the interview as a research method, where the researcher may only have a short time to generate the best data possible from their interlocutor. (Mann (2016), in a book on *The Research Interview* has no fewer than twenty-one entries for 'rapport' in the index.) Generating rapport also means that your interviewee will continue to give their consent for the interview and continue to answer your questions. It often means finding common ground (and the physical effect of the individual researcher is discussed in Chapter 6); so, for example, when I interview teachers I will often use my history as a teacher to introduce myself, with the implication of some fellow feeling.

One question which arises is, what is ethical to share with your participants? Some researchers would argue for a complete one-way relationship where no personal information about the researcher should be revealed to the participant. For the researcher who is particularly aware of the power dynamics of research, discussed above, this may not be acceptable, and some return of personal information may be necessary to redress a power imbalance. With some participants, such as small children, some degree of sharing is inevitable to build rapport, but is unlikely to be of such import as to bias the resulting data. It may also be impractical to retain a completely one-way flow of information for various reasons. With participants who have reason to distrust the academy or researchers who appear to be in positions of authority, some positioning of the self as an ally may be required, or revelation of information that makes them feel safe. It might be argued that to insist on the rehearsing of vulnerability for data collection, as, for example, with child refugees, without offering a vulnerability on the researcher's part in return, is itself unethical. On the other hand, too much personal information leads to a greater risk of leading the interviewee in their responses and reducing the reliability and validity of the data.

When discussing good interview technique, researchers are often told to maintain a good listener pose – slightly forward, making eye contact (although it is important to note that this is not a universal cultural norm, so may be inappropriate and may cause discomfort to some people for other reasons), nodding and often making small noises to encourage continuation or indicate agreement (and therefore encourage continuation). Now imagine you are interviewing a teacher and they make a clearly racist comment. Do you maintain your good listener pose and give them the comfort of social acceptability? Or do you indicate by speech or gesture that you disagree with what they have just said (or are disgusted by it) and risk the interviewee withdrawing consent and ending the interview, or simply just reducing the quality of the data that are being generated? Which is the greater good: showing that individual that their views are not acceptable or generating a piece of research which shows that there are racist views among teachers and that therefore more general action needs to be taken?

You may be interested in racist views and have come prepared for them, and be ready to hold a neutral pose. You may not have and have been unable to disguise your natural reaction. You may be shocked and unable to believe what you have heard. When I raise this hypothetical with students we usually come to the conclusion that we might wait until the end of the interview before saying 'by the way, I don't think what you said about x was appropriate' or some equivalent phrase. In this particular case, there is also an issue in that the teacher is in a position to cause harm by virtue of their racist views, but what if the interviewee were a student being interviewed about their experiences at business school? What action might be appropriate then? By extension, what if you are conducting participant observation in a school and a child makes a homophobic comment to you – or to another child which you overhear? To take an opposite example, Pacheco-Vega and Parizeau (2018) raise the question of stigmatized behaviours, using the example of their research with informal waste-pickers in Argentina and Mexico, who will eat food from the waste stream as well as using it for other purposes. They raise this in relation to the representation of these behaviours but it is equally a question of how the researcher reacts to something which is culturally undesirable to them but which is a normal part of life for others, particularly if those others are aware of the stigmatization. Nicklin (2020) conducting ethnographic research with young offenders who had been 'sentenced to Shakespeare' in the United States deliberately avoided finding out what her participants had been convicted of, a common stance among researchers in prison education; however, it is not always possible to avoid finding out, which may colour not only relationships in the field but also attitudes in data analysis.

Conclusion

The main point of this chapter, as well as introducing some key concepts and classic studies with which it is essential to be familiar, has been to show that ethics in research is never a matter of one-time decision-making and form filling; it is an ongoing thought process which can be challenged and challenging at every step. Although there are some non-negotiables, there are many areas of ethics in research which are not easily entered into a flow chart to come out with the most ethical outcome: it is possible to prepare by thinking out some of the most likely scenarios, and considering what has been written about the ethics of researching in your particular context, it is also extremely likely that ethical decisions will need to be made during every part of the data generation, analysis and writing-up processes.

> ## 8.2 bell hooks
>
> bell hooks (1952–2021) was a feminist and social activist writer, whose academic discipline was English literature. She wrote extensively about the intersectionality of race, gender and other characteristics, particularly in relation to white supremacist capitalism. *Ain't I a Woman?: Black Women and Feminism* (1981), named after a speech by the African American abolitionist and formerly enslaved woman Sojourner Truth, is considered a major work in feminist thought.
>
> hooks also wrote three specifically educational works: *Teaching to Transgress: Education as the Practice of Freedom* (1994), *Teaching Community: A Pedagogy of Hope* (2004) and *Teaching Critical Thinking: Practical Wisdom* (2010). *Teaching Community* deliberately references Paulo Freire's work, and hooks has named him as an influence. Her earlier two books focus on the achievement of freedom through education, through resisting (and 'transgressing') boundaries imposed on racial, gender or class lines. They combine feminist theory with critical pedagogy, challenging educational norms which figure teachers as authority and control figures, which condemn 'each pupil to a rote, assembly-line approach to learning' (hooks, 1994, p. 12). However, her work is not limited to critique, instead offering a vision of 'hope' based around collaboration between student and teacher, in which individuals utilize learning to change themselves and their environments. Another aspect of her work is the use of autobiographical material in teaching to encourage emotional connection which fosters the collaboration between teacher and student.
>
> hooks was one of a number of educational thinkers who have challenged and continue to challenge a neoliberal model of education, particularly as they see it failing to provide equity for youth marginalized by race or socio-economic status, serving rather to reproduce social injustice. Carolissen et al. (2011) consider that her work adds a welcome dimension of emotion to Freire's earlier work, which is perhaps what makes hooks's work unique.

9

Research as a Political Practice

This chapter starts from the principle that education is a political practice. By this I do not mean partisan, that is, party political, but political in that it relates to the way that power is achieved and used in societies and countries across the globe, on a micro, meso and macro level. What we teach and how we teach it are political decisions that serve to reinforce or challenge the status quo. How individuals are assessed and how that is used to discipline them or the institutions in which they study or the people who teach them are all political matters. Those who say that education is not political or that it should not be political are likely to be those who are privileged, that is, for whom the status quo offers some measure of protection, and unaware that education is already political.

Recent controversies in both the United States and the UK exemplify how schooling forms a site of political contestation. In late 2020 the UK government issued guidance about health, sex and relationships education which banned the use of materials produced by organizations which take 'extreme political stances'; an example of which might be 'a publicly stated desire to abolish or overthrow democracy, capitalism, or to end free and fair elections' (Department for Education, 2020, n.p.) – where capitalism is equated with democracy – a stance which verges on the partisan, not just the political. It also banned promoting 'divisive or victim narratives that are harmful to British society' (ibid) which was widely seen as a reference to Black Lives Matter and the wider publicity of racism in British society and history which had been emerging since demonstrations earlier in 2020. In the United States we might point to the 1619 project, named for the year that enslaved African people were first brought to the American colonies, and seeking to centre slavery and the contributions of Black Americans in the history of the United States. Then-President Trump spoke against the project on Fox News while the resources, which were produced by *The New York Times*, won a Pulitzer Prize (Swalwell and Sinclair, 2020). These resources are part of a long tradition of state-mandated textbooks and their use to ensure particular versions of history or science are taught. Swalwell and Sinclair (2020) note that both Texas and Oklahoma state school-boards attempted to prevent schools from teaching a revised A.P. US history syllabus because of its alleged 'anti-American bias', among a raft of other examples of states' political apparatuses taking notice of (particularly history) curriculum content. Political use of textbooks to teach specific national narratives is a phenomenon widely noted in the literature, including in South Korea (Kim and Kim, 2019), Japan (e.g. Takayama, 2009), Pakistan (Ali, 2008) and Germany, among others (Hein and Selden, 2000). We might also point to the banning of Mexican-American studies in Arizona as being divisive, despite later research demonstrating the courses were beneficial to the overall academic attainment of students who took them, particularly those of Mexican heritage (Cabrera, Milem, Jaquette and Marx, 2014).

In these cases the politicization is often quite obvious, but the political nature of education is not limited to such materials. Within whatever is taught is also found the 'hidden curriculum' (Apple, 2004), a name for the normalization of hierarchies of race, gender, class, wealth, sexuality and other power dimensions. The hidden curriculum is coherent with Gramsci's theory of cultural hegemony (see *Antonio Gramsci* textbox), which essentially argues that the ruling classes maintain their hegemony by creating a system in which their knowledge and cultural tastes are valued, and others are not. A good example of this in education is the refusal to allow non-standard English such as African American Vernacular English (AAVE) in the classroom, or the insistence on Standard English in classrooms in England. This is framed as concern for the students – that they need to speak 'properly' in order to get ahead (Cushing, 2020). However, by creating this insistence, and therefore emphasizing the hierarchy of language use, the education system and those who drive it are in fact reproducing the inequality of the language hierarchy and maintaining the cultural hegemony of the ruling classes, which is used as justification for ongoing inequality. One of the challenges to the educational research which seeks to explain inequalities of outcome is that it can seek to excuse rather than challenge that inequality. Sarah Saini argues, for example,

> It's difficult to avoid concluding that the reason anyone pursued the scientific idea of race was not so much to understand the differences in our bodies, but to try to justify why we lead such different lives. Why else? Why would something as superficial as skin colour or body shape matter otherwise? What the scientists really wanted to know was why some people are enslaved and others free, why some prosper while others are poor, and why some civilisations have thrived while others haven't. Imagining themselves to be looking objectively at human variation, they sought answers in our bodes to questions that existed far outside them. (Saini, 2019, pp. 60–1)

Similarly the concept of meritocracy as the basis of society seeks to explain inequality of outcome by reference to individual factors even where it is clear structural factors exist (see, e.g. Sandel, 2020). The same could be said of a wide range of inequalities: although there is plenty of research to demonstrate that socio-economic disadvantage is strongly associated with lower academic outcomes (e.g. Strand, 2014; Perry and McConney, 2010) the attempts to rectify this are at the school level, rather than, for example, ensuring that no child is born into or grows up in poverty. (This returns us to the discussion in the previous chapter of the discourses which locate the responsibility for solving social injustice with teachers and schools rather than in fundamental changes to the (re)allocation of resources in society. This is a firmly political framing of the responsibilities and possibilities of education.)

If education is unavoidably political, therefore, so is education research. Indeed,

> In social science, it is impossible to say anything of social significance without having some implications for the formation of society – social science is notoriously and inevitably political. Neither the researcher nor the other actors involved in influencing a research process and its outcome (research foundations, research leaders, editors and reviewers, the people studied and the mass media, and others who would guide them in how to think and how to express themselves) can exist in an ideological vacuum. (Alvesson and Kärreman, 2011, p. 6)

Kettley (2010) has suggested it is partly the priorities of the funders that mean that educational research does not produce educational theory that can create systemic change – in other words they have a vested interest in the status quo. The charge of 'identity politics' is one which has become a frequent feature of discourse in both the United States and the UK. It is typically levelled at those who want to highlight power differences where the dominant group gains privilege at the expense of the less dominant one.

As has been pointed out by others, it is often used by members of the white hegemony to attempt to shut down protest (and indeed to create divisions rather than solidarity between different non-dominant groups). (For a nuanced discussion of identity politics see Younge, 2020.) Educational research is often concerned with social justice in some shape or form, and those in the field often entered driven by such concerns, so raising issues of structural inequality and the political nature of education can feel like a personal challenge when it is something you yourself have benefited from. As the personal is political, so the political is personal. This means that we often have to consider our knee-jerk defensive positions and take a moment to get past that defensiveness (e.g. 'I'm not racist!') in order to allow ourselves to engage critically with the concepts.

I am discussing this because it may impact how you interact with this chapter. In the next section I discuss the particular stance which informs my work and how I consider research. It is a stance which has taken me a while to come to and which I am still working on enacting in my everyday life. I still have to take time and get through my defensiveness sometimes. To get the most out of this chapter you do not have to follow the same stance as I do. Instead I would suggest you think carefully about what matters to you in terms of change and how it can be achieved.

> [Education] is a field that, when it is at its best, embraces and anticipates change. Change, the likelihood of change, the certainty of change with uncertain outcomes, are foundational to questions of education and learning. The whole field pivots on how change happens and how our efforts as humans can bring about the changes we want to see. (Tuck, 2019b, p. 8)

Your stance affects how you interact with research, and how you design it, how you react to education policy and how you interact with others around you and the system in which you work.

Taking a Stance

I adopt a particular stance in the ways I think about and analyse policy, research and discourse. It stems from Ibram X. Kendi's definition of anti-racism:

> A racist policy is any measure that produces or sustains racial inequity between racial groups. An antiracist policy is any measure that produces or

sustains racial equity between racial groups. By policy, I mean written and unwritten laws, rules, procedures, processes, regulations and guidelines that govern people. There is no such thing as a nonracist or race-neutral policy. (Kendi, 2019, p. 18)

I would extend that to thinking about a variety of inequalities, including between groups of different genders, sexuality, socio-economic statuses, countries of origin and so on. If a policy (or by extension an action) is not contributing to lessening inequality, but simply upholds the status quo, then that policy or action is sustaining inequality. Being 'apolitical' is a luxury (what is often called white privilege or male privilege) not afforded to those whose bodies are politicized automatically, that is, women, transgender people, people of the Global Ethnic Majority in Western countries and disabled people, among others. I am aware that this is a strong stance and that it may be off-putting. Although this stance informs what I have written in this chapter (and in the book as a whole), I think that there are options for you as readers, students and researchers. You may choose to be consciously and deliberately political, or you may simply be aware of the possible political implications. Awareness may cause you to choose differently in the future or enable a more critical reading of research or of educational problems.

9.1 Judith Butler

Judith Butler (1956–) is principally known for her work as a gender theorist. Her major book on the subject, *Gender Trouble*, was published in 1990. Butler's work has been influential in two major ways: the concept of performativity, and specifically gender as performative identity; and in critiquing the normative heterosexual hegemony and its function in controlling and determining identity.

'Gender as performance' is sometimes misunderstood: Butler's argument is that it is through performance that identity is created. This is in contrast to being 'expressive' – that is, there is not a core gender which is being expressed via acts, but gender is instead performed, that is, constituted via acts. She also construes gender as a social construct: 'Gender reality is performative which means, quite simply, that it is real only to the extent that it is performed' (Butler, 1988, p. 528). Butler is evidently extremely relevant not only in relation to thinking about transgender identities but also in terms of the ways in which boys and girls develop gender identities and how that interacts with the ways they engage with education.

Butler also argues that gender is performed in relation to a hegemonic heterosexual matrix, which is strongly normative. To exemplify this, Renold (2006) uses this matrix as an analytical framework to consider her data from a one-year ethnographic study of children in their last year of primary school. Boy–girl friendships and play were strongly regulated through the roles of 'boyfriend' and 'girlfriend' and normative romantic discourses, and individuals were coerced into their roles by the prevailing norms, with exceptions provided for escape by allowable alternative identities such as 'tomboy'. It is this framework that has made Butler an important figure in Queer Theory, which considers the power dynamic of heterosexual norms implied in the matrix. 'Tomboy' is a queer identity, not because it implies homosexuality on the part of the individual but because it 'queers' heterosexual norms.

Citation as a Political Practice

Sara Ahmed in her text *Living a Feminist Life* makes a decision not to cite any 'white men'. She explains,

> This is a very blunt citational policy (and I might need to add cis, straight, and able-bodied to the general body I am evoking). Perhaps you need to form a blunt policy in order to break a long-standing habit. This policy is blunt rather than precise because I understand white men as a cumulative effect rather than a way of grouping together persons who share a common attribute ... I am quite aware that in specific instances we could have a debate as to whether such-and-such individual is or should be regarded as part of the institutional apparatus of white men. (Ahmed, 2017, p. 270)

In other words, she is using 'white men' as a phrase to represent the institutional status quo and the long-standing embedded hierarchy of theory and academia. It can feel heavy-handed and alienating (particularly if you are indeed a white man, particularly one who is cis, straight and able-bodied). However, if a piece cited nothing *but* white men it would be completely unremarkable.

One of the issues with the politics of citation is that researchers are expected to demonstrate familiarity with the history of their discipline (or of social science theory more generally). This leads to the need to cite canonical work, typically by white men, partly to show your credentials, or even if you are building an argument to dismantle their work. Padilla Peralta (2020) has pointed out that some researchers take a 'smash and grab' approach to citation of some theorists in order to establish their credentials despite having little or no engagement with the work of those theorists. Citation is seen as a measure of influence and significance of a particular piece of work or an individual researcher. We might trace this idea back to Westbrook (1960) who suggested the number of citations a paper received formed a sort of 'natural selection' (p. 1229) to identify those of significance, but it has been wholeheartedly taken up by the neoliberal academy in terms of evaluating academic work, from that of the individual (in early 2021 the University of Liverpool proposed making a series of redundancies based on two metrics: grant capture and citation scores (McKie, 2021)) to whole journals which proudly promote their 'impact' scores based on the number of citations their articles have received. For an exploration of the appropriateness of citation metrics for researchers in education, and the potential for unscrupulous manipulation of such metrics, see Merga, Mat Roni and Mason (2020). To talk in Bourdieuan terms (see *Pierre Bourdieu* textbox), we might consider citation scores to be a form of academic capital. The conjoining of the need to cite certain things to demonstrate your credentials and the significance attached to citation serves to reproduce privilege and canon within social theory (see, e.g. Mott and Cockayne, 2017). Smith and Garrett-Scott (2021) demonstrate the systematic undercitation of Black women anthropologists relative to their contribution to the field, and particularly in top-tier journals where in the rare instances they are cited, they are cited by other Black anthropologists. A study of Google Scholar's citation data in 2016 revealed only one woman author within the top twenty-five cited books in social sciences – Jean Lave (Green, 2016) (see *Lave and Wenger* textbox). This leads to situations where not citing white men is seen as a weakness in a research paper. Canadian political scientist Megan Gaucher tweeted about her experience of the review process in which one of her reviewers commented,

> I noticed you don't reference any male citizenship scholars in this manuscript, so have provided a list. While their work doesn't speak specifically to your topic, it might help you become more well-rounded in the field. (Gaucher, 2019)

Even if they are not relevant, men are considered central. (This also points to the important political role of gatekeepers in academic peer review processes.)

Ahmed (2017) notes the dangers, therefore, in conflating the history of ideas with white men, and in doing so notes that 'we are being taught where ideas are assumed to originate' (p. 16). However, these assumptions are not always valid, as Michael Hames-Garcia has demonstrated. In his chapter 'Queer Theory Revisited' in the *Gay Latino Studies Reader* (2011) he demonstrates that the white theorists generally cited on gender and sexuality actually come after theorists of colour, and the chronology is largely ignored in favour of white people citing white people (and leaving race out of the intersectional discussion). Foucault's *History of Sexuality* is at best contemporaneous with works of Audre Lorde and Barbara Smith which not only considered sexuality and gender but also integrated them with race. That is to say, intersectionality was largely written out of theory on gender and sexuality for many years because of white citation practices.

We might also see 'white men' as representative of the intellectual tradition of the Global North; many journals require authors from the Global South or Indigenous authors to engage with the canon of the Global North as a reference point, thus reinforcing a hierarchy and doubling down. This might result in the (literal) marginalizing of some voices: 'Once, when I was still a graduate student, Linda [Tuhiwai Smith] and I talked about the idea that Indigenous women and non-binary people are always writing to each other in our footnotes' (Tuck, 2019a, p. 5). It can also result in a situation where the hurdles for researchers in some traditions and from some geographical locations are higher, making it harder for them to disseminate their work.

For this reason, there is also a political dimension to debates over what type of sources are appropriate to cite, in that non-traditional academic sources can provide a forum for such discussions and discussants. The intellectual tradition has always been one of discussion and communal thought which prompts and results in individual (or group) achievement. Mohanty (2003) is unusual in her explicit acknowledgement of this:

> While many of the ideas I explore here are viewed through my own particular lenses, all the ideas belong collectively to the various feminist, antiracist, and anti-imperialist communities in which I have been privileged to be involved. In the end, I think and write in conversation with scholars, teachers, and activities involved in social justice struggles. My search for emancipatory knowledge over the years has made me realize that ideas are always communally wrought, not privately owned. (Mohanty, 2003, p. 1)

Informal intellectual discussion now takes place not just within the university or the conference space but in a much wider range of individuals via the internet. As you have seen I have cited tweets in this chapter, something which I am happy to do throughout my work.[1] There can be nervousness about citing what are seen as informal sources, but citation is an important way of giving credit to the source of ideas, in particular when that source comes from a demographic whose labour has historically gone unrecognized or been straight out stolen. However, 'Citational ethics is never just about giving credit, although that in and of itself is important, especially when it comes to Black women's labour. It's also about creating new possibilities that don't reproduce colonial, hyper-consumptive logics. Who and how you cite is political' (Bentil, 2020). One exercise which can be revealing of your own work, and also that of others, is to code an article's or essay's list of references for the authors' gender, race, country of origin and so on. This demonstrates any bias in the reading (and therefore that there might be perspectives that you or the author of the article is missing). Identifying such a lacuna can be the first step in rectifying it.

> Citation is feminist memory. Citation is how we acknowledge our debt to those who came before; those who helped us find our way when the way was obscured because we deviated from the paths we were told to follow. (Ahmed, 2017, pp. 15–16)

The idea of citation as acknowledging a debt then raises corresponding questions. What if one of the major researchers in your field is a known abuser or a racist? To what extent is it possible or desirable to separate the person from their work? Or, on a more intellectual level, what if the author has some work which you wish to cite and think makes good points, but has also written work which calls for the infanticide of disabled babies? (This is not a hypothetical – imagine being a disabled student and finding his work on your core reading list.) To refuse to cite someone might leave you in an awkward position with reviewers who do not know the record of this person but do know of their work. It might make you look like you are unaware of some foundational work in your field. It is also a principle that leaves a researcher open to being accused of 'cancel culture', while on the other hand, citing the person in question admiringly may cause others to discount your work. On a personal level you may not wish to cause academic

---

[1] It is important to point out the dangers of this practice as well: two of the tweets I wanted to use for this chapter in quick succession are no longer on the internet because of deleted accounts. Transient materials require careful recording, even more so than traditional sources. This is ironic, because many paper-only publications are also very difficult to access and cite now.

capital to accrue to someone who holds these views or acts in these way, via the medium of citation. However, it is the effect not just on the writer but also on their readers. If I cite admiringly a known homophobe, then I am potentially causing harm through the message that sends to any gay readers of my work.

This is the academic corollary of a much wider issue in modern culture, in the wake of #metoo and greater knowledge of individuals' beliefs and actions largely through the connectedness of social media. It is the same question whether you are asking: Do we as a government trade with countries perpetrating human rights abuses? Do we as individuals buy the books of someone who has revealed themselves to be an abuser? Do we watch films featuring racist actors? Do we pass on to our children much loved books of our own childhood which espouse views we would not find acceptable in new work? Do we continue to be friends with someone who has shown themselves to have abhorrent views? 'Silence gives consent' according to Plato – in other words, if you are not calling out injustice and its perpetrators, you are condoning it.

Guth (2018) talks of the concept of 'moral injury' in relation to tainted legacies of particular individuals or institutions. Moral injury results from 'perpetrating, failing to prevent, or bearing witness to acts that transgress deeply held moral beliefs and expectations' (Litz et al., 2009, p. 695). It is a concept which comes from an exploration of the emotional damage suffered by soldiers which is not covered by traditional diagnoses of PTSD. If it seems a stretch to apply this concept to research, then perhaps it is worthwhile instead drawing on the concept of cognitive dissonance (Festinger, 1957), which argues that if someone holds two contradictory cognitions (e.g. thoughts, feelings or ideas) they will experience *dissonance* – a drive to reconcile them through changing themselves or their beliefs. If one of the beliefs is 'my fundamental belief that I am a good person' then the action or thought which contradicts that will have to be either eradicated or refigured as being that of a good person (for the vast majority of people). Thus a teacher who is challenged by her class for saying the n-word defends herself by believing, and stating to the class, that it is not unacceptable. This could also be applied to the defensiveness discussed earlier in this chapter. For a researcher, it can cause an ethical dilemma about whether or not to cite an abuser, to return to our original question. It might be key to the political alignment (remembering we are discussing the relations of power within society and not partisanship) of an individual not to support abusers; but it might also be a statement or position that causes their work to become a target, distracts from their main point or leaves them open to personal abuse which they do not feel equipped to handle.

I am also aware that for the vast majority of people whom I cite, I have very little or no knowledge of them beyond the particular book or article which I am reading. I might make a principled decision to omit a particular person while citing another who has done similar or worse things. This aspect of citational politics is a tricky one and ultimately a personal decision. The key point is that citation is political, as well as a necessary part of academic life.

The Politics of Theory

Extending from the politics of citation, some researchers make the choice to frame their work within a particular theorist for political reasons. A researcher studying Black experiences at Ivy League schools, for example, might choose to only utilize theory and concepts from Black theorists. A feminist researcher might choose to only use women theorists. This is particularly applicable when following a critical theoretical approach, as there is often a choice of people who have written about any given grand theory. If such an approach seems jarring to you, reflect on the fact that if a project drew only on white male theorists it would be completely unsurprising.

One theorist whose use is often explicitly political is Paulo Freire. Freire's *Pedagogy of the Oppressed* was the most cited book in education according to Green's analysis of Google Scholar data in 2016 (and third overall in social sciences).[2] Freire's biographer, Daniel Schugurensky, claims that Freire has had the greatest impact of any scholar from the Global South internationally (2014). (See *Freire* textbox for information about critical pedagogy and *The Pedagogy of the Oppressed*.) Freire is frequently drawn on as a theorist by education researchers considering power explicitly in their work (and educators seeking to dismantle hierarchies); using Freire's work as a theoretical framework is a clear signal of a particular political motivation for a piece of research, namely one critical of existing class, race and wealth power structures. More than that, critical pedagogy seeks to free the oppressed. Yet,

---

[2] Green's analysis is found in a short but interesting blogpost which shows all twenty-five of the most cited works in social science. The most recent publication on it is Etienne Wenger's *Communities of Practice* (1999) which slides in at number twenty-two. Many of the names on the list can be found in the theorist textboxes in this book.

to some minds these are dangerous ambitions, and Freire himself was exiled from Brazil following a military coup. In Brazil the current president, Jair Bolsonaro, declared on the campaign trail that he would 'enter the education ministry with a flamethrower to remove Paulo Freire' (Osborne, 2019), and showing yourself to be an adherent to his ideas or associated with critical pedagogy can be a risk in Brazil's current environment, not least because of the memory of the violence of the military coup which fell on the left-wing educators associated with Freire. International researchers might think Freire an ideal theorist to draw on if studying Brazil: they might then find themselves lacking participants as the memory of reprisals against left-wing educators has not faded.[3]

In contrast, researchers from and in former colonies often utilize postcolonial theorists (see, e.g. the textbox on *Gayatri Spivak*) as a frame for their research or to direct the kinds of questions which they ask. Frantz Fanon declared that 'Imperialism ... leaves in its wake here and there tinctures of decay which we must search out and mercilessly expel from our land and from our spirits' ([1961] 2001, p. 200). Utilizing certain theorists is one way to ensure that these 'tinctures of decay' are not embedded in the research being carried out in these contexts. I would argue, however, that postcolonial theory is of use not only to inform educational research in countries which have been colonized but also in those that have done the colonizing. The history of Empire has left a long shadow over the English curriculum in the UK, for example (Elliott, 2020), which has implications both for ethnic minorities and for white students of low socio-economic status. As discussed above, theorists are considered to be explicitly political when they challenge the status quo: modern researchers utilizing critical theory, such as postcolonial, feminist, queer or intersectional approaches to research, may well find such use challenged for being 'fashionable' or 'woke' (at the risk of dating this book!).

9.2 Kimberlé Williams Crenshaw

Kimberlé Williams Crenshaw (1959–) is a leading American scholar of Critical Race Theory and a lawyer as well as a civil rights advocate. She coined the term 'intersectionality', drawing on the work of a number

---

[3] I am indebted to discussions with Christine Paget for this point.

of earlier scholars, particularly women of colour, which proposed that in analysing oppression, it is important to consider the *intersection* of characteristics. A Black woman experiences a different set of oppressive experiences than a white woman, and it is important to see both the experiences that are due to race, and to gender and to the combined effects of race and gender. This is true by extension of other characteristics including sexuality, gender identity, caste, religion, disability and so on.

Critical Race Theory, the framework within which Crenshaw cites much of her work, is specifically a means to critically examine the law (broadly constituted so including the governmental structures of a country) as it affects the lives of people of colour. It acknowledges the existence of white supremacy and the social and institutional factors that contribute to the oppression of those who are socially constructed as racialized, rather than considering these to be due to individual factors. Race is a social construct, not a biological one. Critical Race Theory is not attributable to a single individual but is espoused and theorized by a number of scholars.

Research with an Explicitly Political Intention

Echoing the stance outlined by Kendi above, Barnes (1996) argued that you cannot be independent when researching oppression; you are either on the side of the oppressors or the oppressed. Emancipatory researchers would argue that insisting on preserving 'objectivity' in the name of validity is neither possible nor ethical (Oliver, 1997). The development of the emancipatory paradigm

> stems from the gradual rejection of the positivist view of social research as the pursuit of absolute knowledge through the scientific method and the gradual disillusionment with the interpretive view of such research as the generation of socially useful knowledge within particular historical and social contexts. The emancipatory paradigm, as the name implies. is about the facilitating of a politics of the possible by confronting social oppression at whatever levels it occurs. (Oliver, 1992, p. 110)

Emancipatory research therefore is politically motivated research which deals with participants who are oppressed by social relations. Oliver, quoted above, researches with and for disabled people; emancipatory research might equally be driven by feminist or anti-racist concerns, or be the approach adopted for work with young people living in poverty or who have been excluded from the educational environment. An important element is that emancipatory research is not something that is done to people or on their behalf but in partnership with and in support of them.

> The issue then for the emancipatory research paradigm is not how to empower people but, once people have decided to empower themselves, precisely what research can then do to facilitate this process. This does then mean that the social relations of research production do have to be fundamentally changed; researchers have to learn how to put their knowledge and skills at the disposal of their research subjects, for them to use in whatever ways they choose. (Oliver, 1992, p. 111)

This recalls our discussions of the ethical responsibilities of those working with Indigenous communities who are not themselves Indigenous in the previous chapter. In education it particularly resonates with calls to let teachers' concerns drive educational research questions. Challenges have been issued to this model of research, however, in particular the suggestion that as a paradigm it undermines the 'generation of knowledge' that can be used by the target community for self-emancipation (Danieli and Woodhams, 2005, p. 281). White (2013) rehearses some of the arguments which challenge whether emancipatory research is compatible with truly question-led curiosity-driven research, primarily claims that emancipatory researchers privilege their political views above knowledge production (e.g. Hammersley, 1995; Walford, 2001). This argument, however, presumes that there is such a thing as objectivity – if we agree that one can be either on the side of the oppressed or of the oppressors, then 'objective knowledge production' cannot exist and it is likely instead to be ignoring important factors at work in the name of neutrality.

The critiques recall some of the debates about participant or member checking that were discussed in Chapter 7, and raise questions of rigour and, again, objectivity, when participant concerns are centred in research. Ultimately there is probably a place for both sorts of research in the world, but there is a particular value in listening to and centring participant voices from oppressed groups to which a researcher does not belong, simply because their lived experiences can illuminate and even transform the understanding of a problem and lead to stronger and more pointful lines of inquiry. Whichever route is taken, however, it is important not to situate the participants within a frame of patronage, and there is a phrase that evokes this in particular.

That phrase is an aspiration which has been frequently claimed for research – its ability to 'give a voice to the voiceless'. On the face of it, this seems like a positive, good intention for the purpose of research. The problems with this aspiration are neatly summarized:

> The use of the expression 'give people a voice' is the perfect example: if we give it to them, we assume that they do not have a voice until we give it to them, that they cannot speak for themselves until we allow them to. But isn't it true that people have a voice even if we don't listen? Isn't it ridiculous to think that we have the power to give people a voice, as if our inability to listen defines their ability to speak? (Iacucci, 2017, n.p.)

In other words, research that aims to give a voice to the voiceless is inadvertently part of the problem, in presuming the right to speak for the research participants, and the authority to give that voice. However well-intentioned it may be, it reinforces the existing power relationships rather than disrupting them and smacks of white saviourism. The researcher may well be part of the Western academic knowledge-production 'monolith' and thus complicit in extractive knowledge processes, including asking participants to take part in research whose focus and trajectory is determined by the researcher according to their priority, not by the participants in accordance with theirs. There is also the question if the creation of research reports published in academic journals, probably behind paywalls,[4] is in any way giving a voice that might be heard. bell hooks writes eloquently, in the voice of the colonizer:

> *No need to hear your voice when I can talk about you better than you can speak about yourself. No need to hear your voice. Only tell me about your pain. I want to know your story. And then I will tell it back to you in a new way. Tell it back to you in such a way that it has become mine, my own. Re-writing you I write myself anew. I am still author, authority. I am still colonizer, the speaking subject and you are now at the center of my talk.* (1990, p. 343)

---

[4]Some researchers deliberately only publish in open access venues for political reasons, namely factors associated with the public ownership of knowledge or the democratization of the academy. There are movements in Europe and the United States to encourage open access publishing. However, the politics of citation also means that since some of the most prestigious journals can only be open access on payment of large publication fees, which are not sustainable for many authors, but academics need to publish in high-prestige journals for their career, ethical – or political – dilemmas arise in this area.

There is much to be unpicked here, thinking about who we research, how we research and how we pursue explicitly politically oriented research, ensuring that it does not verge on voyeurism. To back away from this power dynamic, Campbell, Gilroy and McNamara (2009) suggest research being a 'microphone' for participants, with the idea of amplification as opposed to a voice being within the researcher's gift. It is also possible to *privilege* the voices of participants, which might mean a commitment to certain methodologies, such as phenomenology, for example, or smaller actions such as using 'in vivo' code names (where quotations 'from life' are lifted to name codes). Creswell calls these the 'best' code labels because 'you start to build codes and later themes that resonate with your participants' (2015, p. 160). (For a full discussion, see Chapter 7.)

The concept of the 'voiceless' also raises the question of hierarchical relations in the research process. Ethical procedures, as suggested in the previous chapter, largely claim the hierarchical relationship with participants lies in one direction, with the power resting with the researcher. Elite participants are sometimes considered to be an exception to that in that they are elite by virtue of possessing power, and the researcher acts effectively as supplicant, although others have argued (e.g. Walford, 2012) that power relationships in elite interviewing are largely the same as in other interviews. Research approaches that draw on an emancipatory paradigm, or use critical theoretical frameworks, will attempt to disrupt these power hierarchies and may feature co-creation of research, or participant-led non-directive methods.

So far our consideration of politically motivated research has largely been situated within deep engagement with participants and reflected concerns which are mostly likely to arise within qualitative methods. However, political motives are equally possible with large-scale quantitative research and secondary data analysis, and some researchers might say that they choose these methods specifically because of their political power.

The 'Gold Standard' of Research

One of the themes throughout this book has been the plurality of what educational research looks like, draws on, is and does, but in Chapter 4 we discussed the idea of a particular type of evidence being the 'gold standard' of educational research. Worldwide the countries of the Global North play a neocolonial role in promoting a certain type of research as 'gold standard', drawing on 'the assumed universality in modernity' couched in the 'the idea of development based on science as the only reliable truth and "harbinger of progress"' (Escobar and Harcourt, 2018, p. 7). There are perhaps three main routes by which this neocolonial role is achieved: research training; research funding; and publication practices. In terms of research training, there is a perceived cachet attached to studying at certain universities, particularly in the United States and the UK, which have globally recognized names (e.g. Mpinganjira, 2009). Various scholarship schemes provide funding for students from the Global South to attend these universities, often with the intention of promoting their recipients as future leaders in their home countries, whether in political or academic positions. Either way the internalization of the approaches, norms and standards of the Global North, often required in order to find a way successfully through a research training programme, then affects the standards held by returning students. Research funding, on the other hand, when targeted at the Global South as part of overseas development aid, will usually come with strings firmly attached in terms of what kinds of activities are allowable, and what kinds of 'development' of local researchers will occur. Journals hosted in the Global North, which rely on the service of scholars in academic posts as reviewers and editors, face the difficulty of multiple gatekeepers defending their discipline as they see best, from the breadth – or narrowness – of their own experience. This gatekeeping presents problems even for qualitative researchers from the Global North (e.g. Pratt, 2008), let alone those working from still less familiar (to the gatekeepers) paradigms. As we saw above, citational politics and practices can affect the ways in which scholars from the Global South and Indigenous researchers are permitted to enter the academy and interact with it in terms of written documents.

The engagement with the work of scholars of the Global South and of Indigenous authors by academics from the Global North also presents difficulties for incorporation of differing perspectives. Tuck (2019c) highlights the problem of 'settler reading', that is, reading 'extractively' (p. 15) from Indigenous authors (a problem more widespread in academe, where an emphasis on productivity and speed produces ethical and methodological dilemmas associated with extractive reading of everything): 'for particular content to be removed for future use. The reading is like panning for gold, sorting through work that may not have been intended for a particular reader, sorting it by what is useful and what is discardable' (Tuck, 2019c, p. 15). This type of reading discards the overall source apart from the nuggets and is associated with the concept of the voiceless – voiceless because of the deaf ear that is turned. Extractive reading takes argument and information out of context and risks misrepresentation of sources, posing a danger for the reader and their writing. It astonishes me how frequently when you follow up a quotation in a published work to its source that even the juxtaposed sentences demonstrate the author intended a meaning directly opposite to that which has been claimed by the quoter.

Conclusion

Educational research is a complex and fascinating field, drawing as it does on so many disciplines and topics, and being the study of something which is fundamental to the life of every human being on this planet. Politics – with a small p – is universal wherever we find people, and the field of educational research is no different. This chapter has argued that education and by extension educational research is always political, even when it claims not to be. There is a consequence to accepting this: in any piece of research design the researcher must always consider where they stand in relation to the power hierarchies involved in the research and acknowledge the implications for their findings.

This book has sought to establish the foundations of educational research – the terminology, the concepts and the theorists that any student of education may be faced with in their encounters with the discipline. In doing so, my intention has been to demystify the field and the large range of referents within it. It has also been my intention to ensure that the 'foundations' cover not just the historic white males of the discipline but the much broader set of foundations on which educational research now rests worldwide. This in itself is a political intent – as utilizing the concepts in this chapter to reflect on the contents of the book will show.

References

Abbas, J. (2020). Service quality in higher education institutions: Qualitative evidence from the students' perspectives using Maslow hierarchy of needs. *International Journal of Quality and Service Sciences*, *12*(3), 371–84.

AERA (2011). *Code of Ethics American Educational Research Association*. Available from https://www.aera.net/Portals/38/docs/About_AERA/CodeOfEthics(1).pdf. Accessed 26 April 2022.

Ahmed, S. (2017). *Living a Feminist Life*. Durham, NC: Duke University Press.

Ali, N. (2008). Outrageous state, sectarianized citizens: Deconstructing the 'textbook controversy' in the Northern Areas, Pakistan. *South Asia Multidisciplinary Academic Journal*, *2*, 1–21.

Alise, M. A., and Teddlie, C. (2010). A continuation of the paradigm wars? Prevalence rates of methodological approaches across the social/behavioral sciences. *Journal of Mixed Methods Research*, *4*(2), 103–26.

Alvesson, M., and Kärreman, D. (2011). *Qualitative Research and Theory Development: Mystery as Method*. London: Sage.

Anderson, L. (ed.) (2006). *Creative Writing: A Workbook with Readings*. Abingdon: Routledge.

Anfara, V. A., Jr., and Mertz, N. T. (eds) (2006). *Theoretical Frameworks in Qualitative Research*. London: Sage.

Anzaldúa, G. (2002). Now let us shift … The path of conocimiento … Inner work, public acts. In G. Anzaldúa and A. Keating (eds), *This Bridge We Call Home: Radical Visions for Transformation* (pp. 540–78). New York: Routledge.

Apple, M. (2004). *Ideology and Curriculum*. New York: Routledge Falmer.

Archard, D. (2014). *Children: Rights and Childhood*. Abingdon: Routledge.

Atkinson, P., and Coffey, A. (2010). Analysing documentary realities. In D. Silverman (ed.), *Qualitative Research* (3rd edn) (pp. 56–75). London: Sage.

Bacher-Hicks, A., Goodman, J. and Mulhern, C. (2021). Inequality in household adaptation to schooling shocks: Covid-induced online learning engagement in real time. *Journal of Public Economics*, *193*, 104345, 1–17.

Bagley, C., and Castro-Salazar, R. (2012). Critical arts-based research in education: Performing undocumented historias. *British Educational Research Journal*, *38*(2), 239–60.

Bain, A. (1879). *Education as a Science*. New York: D. Appleton.

Baird, J. A., and Elliott, V. (2018). Metrics in education – control and corruption. *Oxford Review of Education*, *44*(5), 533–44.

Ball, S. J. (1995). Intellectuals or technicians? The urgent role of theory in educational studies. *British Journal of Educational Studies*, *43*(3), 255–71.

Barnes, C. (1996). Disability and the myth of the independent researcher. *Disability and Society*, *11*(1), 107–12.

Batz, G. (2019). The Ixil University and the decolonization of knowledge. In L. Tuhiwai Smith, E. Tuck and K. W. Yang (eds), *Indigenous and Decolonizing Studies in Education* (pp. 103–15). Abingdon: Routledge.

Baumrind, D. (1964). Some thoughts on ethics of research: After reading Milgram's 'Behavioral study of obedience'. *American Psychologist*, *19*(6), 421.

Bayley, S. (2016). *The Private Life of the Diary*. London: William Collins.

Bazzul, J. (2014). Critical discourse analysis and science education texts: Employing Foucauldian notions of discourse and subjectivity. *Review of Education, Pedagogy, and Cultural Studies*, *36*(5), 422–37.

Becker, H. S. (2007). *Writing for Social Scientists: How to Start and Finish Your Thesis, Book, or Article*. Chicago: University of Chicago Press.

Bentil, J. [@divanificent] (2020, 27 May). Citational ethics is never just about giving credit, although that in and of itself is important, especially when it comes to Black women's labour. It's also about creating new possibilities that don't reproduce colonial, hyper-consumptive logics. Who and how you cite is political. [Tweet]

BERA (2018). *Ethical Guidelines for Educational Research* (4th edn). Available from https://www.bera.ac.uk/publication/ethical-guidelines-for-educatio nal-research-2018. Accessed 10 March 2022.

Berger, R. (2015). Now I see it, now I don't: Researcher's position and reflexivity in qualitative research. *Qualitative Research*, *15*(2), 219–34.

Bhutta, Z. A. (2004). Beyond informed consent. *Bulletin of the World Health Organization*, *82*, 771–7.

Biddle, C., and Schafft, K. A. (2015). Axiology and anomaly in the practice of mixed methods work: Pragmatism, valuation, and the transformative paradigm. *Journal of Mixed Methods Research*, *9*(4), 320–34.

Biele, G., Gustavson, K., Czajkowski, N. O., Nilsen, R. M., Reichborn-Kjennerud, T., Magnus ... and Aase, H. (2019). Bias from self-selection and loss to follow-up in prospective cohort studies. *European Journal of Epidemiology*, *34*(10), 927–38.

Biesta, G. (2010). Pragmatism and the philosophical foundations of mixed methods research. *Sage Handbook of Mixed Methods in Social and Behavioral Research*, *2*, 95–118.

Biesta, G. (2015). On the two cultures of educational research, and how we might move ahead: Reconsidering the ontology, axiology and praxeology of education. *European Educational Research Journal*, *14*(1), 11–22.

Biesta, G. (2020). *Educational Research: An Unorthodox Introduction*. London: Bloomsbury.
Binet, A. (1908). La consommation du pain pendant une annee scolaire. *Annee Psychologique, 4*, 337.
Birt, L., Scott, S., Cavers, D., Campbell, C. and Walter, F. (2016). Member checking: A tool to enhance trustworthiness or merely a nod to validation? *Qualitative Health Research, 26*(13), 1802–11.
Blackman, S., and Commane, G. (2012). Double reflexivity: The politics of friendship, fieldwork and representation within ethnographic studies of young people. In S. Heath and C. Walker (eds), *Innovations in Youth Research* (pp. 229–47). London: Palgrave Macmillan.
Blaikie, N. (2000). *Designing Social Research*. Cambridge: Polity.
Bloom, B. S., Engelhart, M. D., Furst, E. J., Hill, W. H. and Krathwohl, D. R. (1956). *Handbook I: Cognitive Domain*. New York: David McKay.
Blum-Ross, Alicia (2013). Authentic representations? Ethical quandaries in participatory filmmaking with young people. In Kitty te Riele and Rachel Brooks (eds), *Negotiating Ethical Challenges in Youth Research* (pp. 55–68). London: Routledge.
Boeri, M., and Shukla, R. K. (eds) (2019). *Inside Ethnography: Researchers Reflect on the Challenges of Reaching Hidden Populations*. Berkeley: University of California Press.
Botvinik-Nezer, R., Holzmeister, F., Camerer, C. F., Dreber, A., Huber, J., Johannesson, M. ... and Rieck, J. R. (2020). Variability in the analysis of a single neuroimaging dataset by many teams. *Nature, 582*(7810), 84–8.
Bourdieu, P. (1977). Cultural reproduction and social reproduction. In J. Karabel and A. H. Halsey (eds), *Power and Ideology in Education* (pp. 487–511). New York: Oxford University Press.
Bourdieu, P., and Wacquant, L. (1992). *An Invitation to Reflexive Sociology*. Chicago: University of Chicago Press.
Bracht, G. H., and Glass, G. V. (1968). The external validity of experiments. *American Educational Research Journal, 5*(4), 437–74.
Brindley, S., and Bowker, A. (2013). Ethics and school based practitioner research. *Educational Action Research, 21*(3), 289–306.
Bronfenbrenner, U. (1977). Toward an experimental ecology of human development. *American Psychologist, 32*(7), 513.
Bronfenbrenner, U., and Ceci, S. J. (1994). Nature-nurture reconceptualised: A bio-ecological model. *Psychological Review, 10*(4), 568–86.
Bruner, J. (1987). Life as narrative. *Social Research, 54*(1), 11–32.
Bryman, A. (2001). *Social Research Methods*. Oxford: Oxford University Press.
Bukve, O. (2019). *Designing Social Science Research*. London: Palgrave Macmillan.

Burman, E. (2018). *Fanon, Education, Action: Child as Method.* London: Routledge.
Butler, J. (1988). Performative acts and gender constitution: An essay in phenomenology and feminist theory. *Theatre Journal, 40*(4), 519–31.
Butler, J. (1990). *Gender Trouble: Feminism and the Subversion of Identity.* London: Routledge.
Cabrera, N. L., Milem, J. F., Jaquette, O. and Marx, R. W. (2014). Missing the (student achievement) forest for all the (political) trees empiricism and the Mexican American studies controversy in Tucson. *American Educational Research Journal, 51*(6), 1084–118.
Cahill, C. (2007). Including excluded perspectives in participatory action research. *Design Studies, 28*(3), 325–40.
Calvey, D. (2017). *Covert Research: The Art, Politics and Ethics of Undercover Fieldwork.* London: Sage.
Campbell, A., Gilroy, P. and McNamara, O. (2009). *Practitioner Research and Professional Development in Education.* London: Sage.
Campbell, D. T. (1957). Factors relevant to the validity of experiments in social settings. *Psychological Bulletin, 54*(4), 297.
Candela, A. G. (2019). Exploring the function of member checking. *Qualitative Report, 24*(3), 619–28.
Carolissen, R., Leibowitz, B., Swartz, L., Bozalek, V., Nicholls, L. and Rohleder, P. (2011). bell hooks and the enactment of emotion in teaching and learning across boundaries: A pedagogy of hope? *South African Journal of Higher Education, 25*(1), 157–67.
Carter, J. (2020). The assessment has become the curriculum: Teachers' views on the Phonics Screening Check in England. *British Educational Research Journal, 46*(3), 593–609.
Chávez, K., and Mitchell, K. M. (2020). Exploring bias in student evaluations: Gender, race, and ethnicity. *PS: Political Science and Politics, 53*(2), 270–4.
Chilisa, B. (2020). *Indigenous Research Methodologies.* London: Sage.
Chong, P. W., and Graham, L. J. (2013). The 'Russian doll' approach: Developing nested case-studies to support international comparative research in education. *International Journal of Research and Method in Education, 36*(1), 23–32.
Chu, M., and Kita, S. (2011). The nature of gestures' beneficial role in spatial problem solving. *Journal of Experimental Psychology: General, 140*(1), 102.
Claparede, E. (1911). *Experimental Pedagogy and the Psychology of the Child* (4th edn) [English translation]. London: Edward Arnold.
Clark, J. S. B., and Dervin, F. (eds) (2014). *Reflexivity in Language and Intercultural Education: Rethinking Multilingualism and Interculturality.* London: Routledge.

Clark, T. (2010). On 'being researched': Why do people engage with qualitative research? *Qualitative Research, 10*(4), 399–419.

Collier, A. (1994). *Critical Realism: An Introduction to Roy Bhaskar's Philosophy*. London: Verso.

Collins, K. (2021). Migrants like these. In R. Philips and H. Kara (eds), *Creative Writing for Social Research* (pp. 133–6). Bristol: Policy Press.

Connell, R. (2007). *Southern Theory*. Cambridge: Polity.

Convery, I., and Cox, D. (2012). A review of research ethics in internet-based research. *Practitioner Research in Higher Education, 6*(1), 50–7.

Cook, B. G. (2014). A call for examining replication and bias in special education research. *Remedial and Special Education, 35*(4), 233–46.

Cooley, C. H. (1930). *Sociological theory and social research: Being selected papers of Charles Horton Cooley*. New York: Augustus M Kelley.

Cooper, E. (2005). What do we know about out-of-school youths? How participatory action research can work for young refugees in camps. *Compare: A Journal of Comparative Education, 35*(4), 463–77.

Cormier, G. (2018). The language variable in educational research: An exploration of researcher positionality, translation, and interpretation. *International Journal of Research and Method in Education, 41*(3), 328–41.

Crandall, A., Powell, E. A., Bradford, G. C., Magnusson, B. M., Hanson, C. L., Barnes, M. D. ... and Bean, R. A. (2020). Maslow's hierarchy of needs as a framework for understanding adolescent depressive symptoms over time. *Journal of Child and Family Studies, 29*(2), 273–81.

Crenshaw, K. (1989). Demarginalizing the intersection of race and sex: A black feminist critique of antidiscrimination doctrine, feminist theory and antiracist politics. *University of Chicago Legal Forum*, 139–68.

Creswell, J. (2013). *Qualitative Inquiry and Research Design: Choosing among Five Approaches*. Los Angeles: Sage.

Creswell, J. (2015). *30 Essential Skills for the Qualitative Researcher*. Los Angeles: Sage.

Cruess, R. L., Cruess, S. R. and Steinert, Y. (2018). Medicine as a community of practice: Implications for medical education. *Academic Medicine, 93*(2), 185–91.

Cullen, O., and Walsh, C. A. (2020). A narrative review of ethical issues in participatory research with young people. *Young, 28*(4), 363–86.

Cunningham, C. (2020). 8 beliefs about 'Good English' in schools. In C. Hall and R. Wicaksono (eds) *Ontologies of English: Conceptualising the Language for Learning, Teaching, and Assessment* (pp. 142–62). Cambridge: Cambridge University Press.

Cushing, I. (2020). The policy and policing of language in schools. *Language in Society, 49*(3), 425–50.

Danieli, A., and Woodhams, C. (2005). Emancipatory research methodology and disability: A critique. *International Journal of Social Research Methodology*, 8(4), 281–96.

Daniels, H. (2009). Situating pedagogy: Moving beyond an interactional account. *Pedagogies: An International Journal*, 5(1), 27–36.

Davies, P. (1999). What is evidence-based education?. *British Journal of Educational Studies*, 47(2), 108–121.

Denzin, N. K. (1999). Interpretive ethnography for the next century. *Journal of Contemporary Ethnography*, 28(5), 510–19.

Denzin, N. K. (2012). Triangulation 2.0. *Journal of Mixed Methods Research*, 6(2), 80–8.

Department for Education (2020). *Guidance: Plan Your Relationships, Sex and Health Curriculum*. London: UK Government. Available from https://www.gov.uk/guidance/plan-your-relationships-sex-and-health-curriculum. Accessed 15 March 2021.

de Souza, F., Neri, D. C. and Costa, A. P. (2016). Asking questions in the qualitative research context. *Qualitative Report*, 21(13), 6–18.

Dingwall, N. (2020). Thinking outside four walls: The case for reconfiguring traditional classrooms. *Emotional and Behavioural Difficulties*, 25(1), 59–67.

Drew, P. E., Raymond, G. E. and Weinberg, D. E. (2006). *Talk and Interaction in Social Research Methods*. London: Sage.

Du Bois, W. E. B. (1898). The study of the Negro problems. *Annals of the American Academy of Political and Social Science*, 11 (January), 1–23.

Du Bois, W. E. B. ([1903] 2007). *The Souls of Black Folk*. Oxford: Oxford University Press.

Duneier, M., and Carter, O. (1999). *Sidewalk*. New York: Farrar, Straus and Giroux.

Durkheim, E. (1897). *Suicide*. London: Routledge and Keegan Paul.

Durrheim, K. (2006). Research design. *Research in Practice: Applied Methods for the Social Sciences*, 2, 33–59.

Dwan, K., Altman, D. G., Arnaiz, J. A., Bloom, J., Chan, A., Cronin, E. and Williamson, P. R. (2008). Systematic review of the empirical evidence of study publication bias and outcome reporting bias. *PLoS ONE*, 3(8), e3081.

Dweck, C. (2016). What having a 'growth mindset' actually means. *Harvard Business Review*, 13, Available from https://hbr.org/2016/01/what-having-a-growth-mindset-actually-means. Accessed 26 April 2022.

Dweck, C. S. (2006). *Mindset: The New Psychology of Success*. New York: Random House.

Edge, J. (2011). *The Reflexive Teacher Educator in TESOL: Roots and Wings*. London: Routledge.

Edmiston, B., and Sobjack, L. (2017). Becoming warriors: Dramatic inquiry with 11-to 12-year-olds in an EBD classroom. *Emotional and Behavioural Difficulties, 22*(1), 50–65.

Ehrlich, S. B., Levine, S. C. and Goldin-Meadow, S. (2006). The importance of gesture in children's spatial reasoning. *Developmental Psychology, 42*(6), 1259.

Eisenhardt, K. M. (1989). Building theories from case study research. *Academy of Management Review, 14*(4), 532–50.

Eliot, T. S. (1921, 31 March). Andrew Marvell. *Times Literary Supplement*, 10021.

Elliott, V. (2013). Empathetic projections and affect reactions in examiners of 'A' level English and History. *Assessment in Education: Principles, Policy and Practice, 20*(3), 266–80.

Elliott, V. (2018). Thinking about the coding process in qualitative data analysis. *Qualitative Report, 23*(11), 2850–61.

Elliott, V. (2020). *Knowledge in English: Canon, Curriculum and Cultural Literacy*. Abingdon: Routledge.

Elliott, V., and Dingwall, N. (2017). Roles as a route to being 'other': Drama-based interventions with at-risk students. *Emotional and Behavioural Difficulties, 22*(1), 66–78.

Elliott, V., Randhawa, A., Ingram, J., Nelson-Addy, L., Griffin, C. and Baird, J.-A. (2020). *Feedback in Action: A Review of Practice in English Schools*. London: Education Endowment Foundation.

El Masri, Y. H., Baird, J. A. and Graesser, A. (2016). Language effects in international testing: The case of PISA 2006 science items. *Assessment in Education: Principles, Policy and Practice, 23*(4), 427–55.

Emerson, R. M., Fretz, R. I. and Shaw, L. L. (2011). *Writing Ethnographic Fieldnotes*. Chicago: University of Chicago Press.

English, A. R. (2016). John Dewey and the role of the teacher in a globalized world: Imagination, empathy, and 'third voice'. *Educational Philosophy and Theory, 48*(10), 1046–64.

Erickson, F., and Gutierrez, K. (2002). Comment: Culture, rigor, and science in educational research. *Educational Researcher, 31*(8), 21–4.

Ericsson, K. A., Krampe, R. T. and Tesch-Römer, C. (1993). The role of deliberate practice in the acquisition of expert performance. *Psychological Review, 100*(3), 363.

Escobar, A., and Harcourt, W. (2018). Post-development possibilities: A conversation. *Development, 61*(1), 6–8.

Estrada, M., Hernandez, P. R. and Schultz, P. W. (2018). A longitudinal study of how quality mentorship and research experience integrate underrepresented minorities into STEM careers. *CBE – Life Sciences Education, 17*(1), 1–13.

Etherington, K. (2004). *Becoming a Reflexive Researcher: Using Our Selves in Research*. Jessica Kingsley.

Fancourt, N. (2017). Research ethics in Closing the Gap. In A. Childs and I. Menter (eds), *Mobilising Teacher Researchers: Challenging Educational Inequality* (pp. 159–74). London: Routledge.

Fanon, F. (1967). *Black Skin, White Masks*. New York: Grove Press.

Festinger, L. (1957). *A Theory of Cognitive Dissonance*. Stanford, CA: Stanford University Press.

Finlay, L. (2002). 'Outing' the researcher: The provenance, process, and practice of reflexivity. *Qualitative Health Research*, *12*(4), 531–45.

Finley, S. (2005). Arts-based inquiry: Performing revolutionary pedagogy. In N. Denzin and Y. Lincoln (eds), *The Sage Handbook of Qualitative Research* (3rd edn) (pp. 681–94). Thousand Oaks: Sage.

Fish, J., and Syed, M. (2018). Native Americans in higher education: An ecological systems perspective. *Journal of College Student Development*, *59*(4), 387–403.

Fleer, M. (2003). Early childhood education as an evolving 'community of practice' or as lived 'social reproduction': Researching the 'taken-for-granted'. *Contemporary Issues in Early Childhood*, *4*(1), 64–79.

Flood, G. (1995). *Beyond Phenomenology: Rethinking the Study of Religion*. Edinburgh: A&C Black.

Foucault, M. (1977). *Discipline and Punish: The Birth of the Prison* (A. Sheridan, Trans.). London: Allen Lane, Penguin. First published in French as Surveiller et punir, Gallimard, Paris, 1975.

Foucault, M. (1990). *The History of Sexuality: Volume 1, an Introduction* (R. Hurley, Trans.). New York: Vintage Books.

Fox, K. (2021). 'A funny turn'. In R. Philips and H. Kara (eds), *Creative Writing for Social Research* (pp. 159–63). Bristol: Policy Press.

Furlong, J. (2013). *Education – An Anatomy of the Discipline: Rescuing the University Project?*. Abingdon: Routledge.

Gabriel, Y., and Connell, N. A. D. (2010). Co-creating stories: Collaborative experiments in storytelling. *Management Learning*, *41*(5), 507–23.

Galdas, P. (2017). Revisiting bias in qualitative research: Reflections on its relationship with funding and impact. *International Journal of Qualitative Methods*, *16*(1), 1–2.

Galuvao, A. S. A. (2018). In search of Samoan research approaches to education: Tofā'a'anolasi and the Foucauldian tool box. *Educational Philosophy and Theory*, *50*(8), 747–57.

Gardner, H. (1995). Reflections on multiple intelligences: Myths and messages. *Phi Delta Kappan*, *77*, 200–3, 206–9

Gaucher, M. [@MegGowcher]. (2019, 2 October). Reviewer: 'I noticed you don't reference any male citizenship scholars in this manuscript, so have provided a list. While their work doesn't speak specifically to your topic, it might help you become more well-rounded in the field of Canadian citizenship politics.' #sorrynotsorry [Tweet].

Gee, J. P. (2001). Identity as an Analytic Lens for Research in Education. In W. G. Secada (ed.), *Review of Research in Education* (pp. 99–126). Vol. 25. Washington, DC: American Educational Research Association.

Giddings, L. S. (2006). Mixed-methods research: Positivism dressed in drag? *Journal of Research in Nursing*, 11(3), 195–203.

'Gillick v West Norfolk and Wisbech AHA [1985] UKHL 7'. *British and Irish Legal Information Institute*. 1985. Available from http://www.bailii.org/uk/cases/UKHL/1985/7.html. Accessed 10 March 2021.

Given, L. M. (2008). *The SAGE Encyclopedia of Qualitative Research Methods* (Vols. 1-0). Thousand Oaks, CA: Sage.

Glaser, B. G., and Strauss A. L. (1967). *The Discovery of Grounded Theory: Strategies for Qualitative Research*. New York: Adline de Gruyter.

Goitom, M. (2020). Multilingual research: Reflections on translating qualitative data. *British Journal of Social Work*, 50(2), 548–64.

Goldacre, B. (2013). *Building Evidence into Education*. London: HMSO.

Goodwin, C. (1994). Professional vision. *American Anthropologist*, 96(3), 606–33.

Gordon, L. (1984). Paul Willis – Education, cultural production and social reproduction. *British Journal of Sociology of Education*, 5(2), 105–15.

Gramsci, A. (1971). *Selection from the Prison Notebooks* (Q. Hoare and G. N. Smith, eds and Trans.). London: Lawrence and Wishart.

Green, E. (2016). What are the most-cited publications in the social sciences (according to Google Scholar)? Blogpost. https://blogs.lse.ac.uk/impactofsocialsciences/2016/05/12/what-are-the-most-cited-publications-in-the-social-sciences-according-to-google-scholar/. Accessed 15 March 2021.

Green, E. H. (2009). Speaking in parables: The responses of students to a Bible-based ethos in a Christian City Technology College. *Cambridge Journal of Education*, 39(4), 443–56.

Greenwood, J. (2012). Arts-based research: Weaving magic and meaning. *International Journal of Education and the Arts*, 13 (Interlude 1).

Grix, J. (2002). Introducing students to the generic terminology of social research. *Politics*, 22(3), 175–86.

Guilfoyle, L., McCormack, O. and Erduran, S. (2020). The 'tipping point' for educational research: The role of pre-service science teachers' epistemic beliefs in evaluating the professional utility of educational research. *Teaching and Teacher Education*, 90, 103033, 1–15.

Guth, K. V. (2018). Moral injury, feminist and womanist ethics, and tainted legacies. *Journal of the Society of Christian Ethics*, 38(1) 167–86.

Halai, N. (2007). Making use of bilingual interview data: Some experiences from the field. *Qualitative Report, 12*(3), 344.

Halling, S., and Goldfarb, M. (1991). Grounding truth in the body: Therapy and research renewed. *Humanistic Psychologist, 19*(3), 313–30.

Hallion Bres, Sandrine. (2006). Similarités morphosyntaxiques des parlers français de l'Ouest canadien. *Revue de l'Université de Moncton, 37*(2), 111.

Hames-García, M. (2011). Queer theory revisited. In M. Hames-García and E. J. Martínez (eds.) *Gay Latino Studies: A Critical Reader* (pp. 19–45). Durham, NC: Duke University Press.

Hammersley, M. (1995). *The Politics of Social Research*. London: Sage.

Hammersley, M. (2008). Paradigm war revived? On the diagnosis of resistance to randomized controlled trials and systematic review in education. *International Journal of Research and Method in Education, 31*(1): 3–10.

Haney, C., Banks, W. C. and Zimbardo, P. G. (1973). A study of prisoners and guards in a simulated prison. *Naval Research Reviews, 26*(9), 1–17.

Harding, J. (2013). *Qualitative Data Analysis from Start to Finish*. London: Sage.

Harper, G. (2019). *Critical Approaches to Creative Writing*. Abingdon: Routledge.

Harris, A., and Jones, M. (2018). Why context matters: A comparative perspective on education reform and policy implementation. *Educational Research for Policy and Practice, 17*(3), 195–207.

Haynes, L., Service, O., Goldacre, B. and Torgerson, D. (2012). *Test, Learn, Adapt: Developing Public Policy with Randomised Controlled Trials*. London: Cabinet Office.

Hedges, L. V. (2013). Recommendations for practice: Justifying claims of generalizability. *Educational Psychology Review, 25*(3), 331–7.

Hein, L. E., and Selden, M. (2000). *Censoring History: Citizenship and Memory in Japan, Germany, and the United States*. Armonk, NY: ME Sharpe.

Hertz, R. (ed.) (1997). *Reflexivity and Voice*. London: Sage.

Hirsch, E. D. (1987). *Cultural Literacy: What Every American Needs to Know*. Boston, MA: Houghton Mifflin.

Hodges, C., Moore, S., Lockee, B., Trust, T. and Bond, A. (2020). The difference between emergency remote teaching and online learning. *Educause Review, 27*, 1–12.

Hofer, B. K., and Pintrich, P. R. (1997). The development of epistemological theories: Beliefs about knowledge and knowing and their relation to learning. *Review of Educational Research, 67*(1), 88–140.

Hoffmann, S., Schönbrodt, F., Elsas, R., Wilson, R., Strasser, U. and Boulesteix, A.-L. (2021). The multiplicity of analysis strategies jeopardizes replicability: Lessons learned across disciplines. *Royal Society Open Science, 8*(4), 1–13.

Holland, D., Lachicotte, W. Jr., Skinner, D. and Cain, C. (1998). *Identity and Agency in Cultural Worlds*. Cambridge, MA: Harvard University Press.

Hollway, W. (1983). Heterosexual sex: Power and desire for the other. In S. Cartledge and J. Ryan (eds), *Sex and Love: New Thoughts on Old Contradictions* (pp. 124–40). London: Women's Press.

Homan, R. (2001). The principle of assumed consent: The ethics of gatekeeping. *Journal of the Philosophy of Education, 35*(3): 329–43.

hooks, b. (1990). Marginality as a site of resistance. In R. Ferguson, M. Gever, T. T. Minh-ha and C. West (eds), *Out There: Marginalization and Contemporary Cultures* (pp. 341–3). Cambridge, MA: MIT Press.

hooks, b. (1994). *Teaching to Transgress: Education as the Practice of Freedom*. New York: Routledge.

Houghton, C. (2015). Young people's perspectives on participatory ethics: Agency, power and impact in domestic abuse research and policy-making. *Child Abuse Review, 24*(4), 235–48.

Huber, L. P., and Cueva, B. M. (2012). Chicana/Latina testimonios on effects and responses to microaggressions. *Equity and Excellence in Education, 45*(3), 392–410.

Hudson, J. M., and Bruckman, A. (2004). 'Go away': Participant objections to being studied and the ethics of chatroom research. *Information Society, 20*(2), 127–39.

Hudson, J. M., and Bruckman, A. (2005). Using empirical data to reason about internet research ethics. In H. Gellersen, K. Schmidt, M. Beaudouin-Lafon and W. Mackay (eds), ECSCW'05 Paris, France 18–22 September 2005, *Proceedings of the 9th European Conference on Computer Supported Cooperative Work*. The Netherlands: Springer, 289:306.

Humphreys, L. (1970). *Tearoom Trade: Impersonal Sex in Public Places*. London: Duckworth.

Iacucci, A. A. (2017). Stop saying you want to give voice to the voiceless! Anahiayala.com Available from https://anahiayala.com/2017/03/06/stop-saying-you-want-to-give-voice-to-the-voiceless/. Accessed 10 February 2021.

Ingram, J., and Elliott, V. (2016). A critical analysis of the role of wait time in classroom interactions and the effects on student and teacher interactional behaviours. *Cambridge Journal of Education, 46*(1), 37–53.

Ingram, J., and Elliott, V. (2019). *Research Methods for Classroom Discourse*. London: Bloomsbury.

Ingram, J., Elliott, V., Morin, C., Randhawa, A. and Brown, C. (2018). Playing the system: Incentives to 'game' and educational ethics in school examination entry policies in England. *Oxford Review of Education, 44*(5), 545–62.

Jaekel, N., Schurig, M., Florian, M. and Ritter, M. (2017). From early starters to late finishers? A longitudinal study of early foreign language learning in school. *Language Learning, 67*(3), 631–64.

Janesik, V. J. (1998). The dance of qualitative research design: metaphor, methodolatry, and meaning. In N. K. Denzin and Y. S.Lincoln (eds), *Strategies of Qualitative Inquiry* (pp. 35–55). Thousand Oaks, CA: Sage.

Johnson, R. B. (1997). Examining the validity structure of qualitative research. *Education, 118*(2), 282.

Jones, S. (2006). *Antonio Gramsci*. Abingdon: Routledge.

Jones, P., Bunce, G., Evans, J., Gibbs, H. and Hein, J. R. (2008). Exploring space and place with walking interviews. *Journal of research practice, 4*(2), 1–9.

Kaomea, J. (2001). Dilemmas of an indigenous academic: A Native Hawaiian story. *Contemporary Issues in Early Childhood, 2*(1), 67–82.

Keipi, T. (2018). Relatedness online: An analysis of youth narratives concerning the effects of internet anonymity. *Young, 26*(2), 91–107.

Kendi, I. X. (2019). *How to Be an Anti-racist*. London: Bodley Head.

Kerlinger, F. N. (1986). *Foundations of Behavioural Research* (3rd edn). New York: Hold, Rinehart and Winston.

Kettley, N. (2010). *Theory Building in Educational Research*. London: Continuum.

Khazragui, H., and Hudson, J. (2015). Measuring the benefits of university research: Impact and the REF in the UK. *Research Evaluation, 24*(1), 51–62.

Kim, H., and Kim, S. K. (2019). Global convergence or national identity making?: The history textbook controversy in South Korea, 2004–2018. *Asia Pacific Journal of Education, 39*(2), 252–63.

Kincheloe, J. L., and Tobin, K. (2009). The much exaggerated death of positivism. *Cultural Studies of Science Education, 4*, 513–28.

Klapp, A. (2015). Does grading affect educational attainment? A longitudinal study. *Assessment in Education: Principles, Policy and Practice, 22*(3), 302–23.

Koh, A. (2016). On 'Gods' and 'Kings' in the tutorial industry: A 'media spectacle' analysis of the shadow education in Hong Kong. In J. Moss and B. Pini (eds), *Visual Research Methods in Educational Research* (pp. 189–208). London: Palgrave Macmillan.

Krathwohl, D. R. (2002). A revision of Bloom's taxonomy: An overview. *Theory Into Practice, 41*(4), 212–18.

Kuhn, T. (1962). *The Structure of Scientific Revolutions*. Chicago: University of Chicago Press.

Ladson-Billings, G. (2006). From the achievement gap to the education debt: Understanding achievement in US schools. *Educational Researcher, 35*(7), 3–12.

Laing, K., Mazzoli Smith, L. and Todd, L. (2018). The impact agenda and critical social research in education: Hitting the target but missing the spot? *Policy Futures in Education*, *16*(2), 169–84.

Lather, P. (1986). Issues of validity in openly ideological research: Between a rock and a soft place. *Interchange*, *17*(4), 63–84.

Lave, J. (1988). *Cognition in Practice: Mind, Mathematics and Culture in Everyday Life*. Cambridge: Cambridge University Press.

Lave, J., and Wenger, E. (1991). *Situated Learning: Legitimate Peripheral Participation*. Cambridge: Cambridge University Press.

Leonard, M., and McKnight, M. (2015). Look and tell: Using photo-elicitation methods with teenagers. *Children's Geographies*, *13*(6), 629–42.

Lewins, F. (1992). *Social Science Methodology: A Brief but Critical Introduction*. South Melbourne: Macmillan.

Litz, B. T., Stein, N., Delaney, E., Lebowitz, L., Nash, W. P., Silva, C. and Maguen, S. (2009). Moral injury and moral repair in war veterans: A preliminary model and intervention strategy. *Clinical Psychology Review*, *29*(8), 695–706.

Louis, R. P. (2007). Can you hear us now? Voices from the margin: Using indigenous methodologies in geographic research. *Geographical Research*, *45*(2), 130–9.

Lynch, J., and Mannion, G. (2016). Enacting a place-responsive research methodology: Walking interviews with educators. *Journal of Adventure Education and Outdoor Learning*, *16*(4), 330–45.

Makel, M. C., and Plucker, J. A. (2014). Facts are more important than novelty: Replication in the education sciences. *Educational Researcher*, *43*(6), 304–16.

Mann, S. (2016). The research interview. *Reflective Practice and Reflexivity in Research Processes*. London: Palgrave Macmillan.

Mannay, D., and Turney, C. (2020). Sandboxing: A creative approach to qualitative research in education. In M. R. M. Ward and S. Delamont (eds), *Handbook of Qualitative Research in Education* (pp. 233–44). 2nd edn. Cheltenham: Edward Elgar.

Markham, A. (2012). Fabrication as ethical practice: Qualitative inquiry in ambiguous internet contexts. *Information, Communication and Society*, *15*(3), 334–53.

Maslow, A. H. (1943). A theory of human motivation. *Psychological Review*, *50*(4), 370.

McConway, K. (2016). Statistics and the media: A statistician's view. *Journalism*, *17*(1), 49–65.

McDowell, L. (2014). 'A delicate balance …': Language as a tool of identity expression for incarcerated men pursuing higher education. *Changing English*, *21*(2), 131–8.

McGranahan, C. (2020). Introduction. In C. McGranahan (ed.), *Writing Anthropology* (pp. 1–19). Durham, NC: Duke University Press.

McIntyre, D. (1993). Theory, theorizing and reflection in initial teacher education. In J. Calderhead and P. Gates (eds), *Conceptualising Reflection in Teacher Development* (pp. 39–52), London: Palgrave Macmillan.

McIntyre, J., and Hobson, A. J. (2016). Supporting beginner teacher identity development: External mentors and the third space. *Research Papers in Education*, 31(2), 133–58.

McKie, A. (2021). Global metrics experts attack Liverpool redundancy criteria. *Times Higher Education Online*, 26 February 2021. Available from https://www.timeshighereducation.com/news/global-metrics-experts-attack-liverpool-redundancy-criteria. Accessed 10 March 2021.

McLeod, J., Goad, P., Willis, J. and Darian-Smith, K. (2016). Reading images of school buildings and spaces: An interdisciplinary dialogue on visual research in histories of progressive education. In J. Moss and B. Pini (eds), *Visual Research Methods in Educational Research* (pp. 15–35). London: Palgrave Macmillan.

McPherson, D., and Rabb, J. D. (2011). *Indian from the Inside: Native American Philosophy and Cultural Renewal*. Jefferson: McFarland.

Medawar, P. B. (1979). *Advice to a Young Scientist*. New York: Harper and Row.

Mengel, F., Sauermann, J. and Zölitz, U. (2019). Gender bias in teaching evaluations. *Journal of the European Economic Association*, 17(2), 535–66.

Menter, I. (2020). Foreword. In D. Mayer and I. Menter (eds), *Becoming a Teacher Education Researcher*. St Albans: Critical Publishing.

Merga, M. K., Mat Roni, S. and Mason, S. (2020). Should Google Scholar be used for benchmarking against the professoriate in education? *Scientometrics*, 125, 2505–22.

Merriam, S. B. (2001). *Qualitative Research and Case Study Applications in Education* (2nd edn). San Francisco, CA: Jossey-Bass.

Merton, R. K. (1968). *Social Theory and Social Structure*. New York: Simon and Schuster.

Merton, Robert K. (1967). *On Theoretical Sociology*. New York: Free Press.

Miles, M. B., Huberman, A. M. and Saldaña, J. (2014). *Qualitative Data Analysis: A Methods Sourcebook* (3rd edn). London: Sage.

Milgram, S. (1974). *Obedience to Authority: An Experimental View*. New York: Harper and Row.

Mills, C. W. (1959). *The Sociological Imagination*. New York: Oxford University Press.

Mockler, N. (2014). When 'research ethics' become 'everyday ethics': The intersection of inquiry and practice in practitioner research. *Educational Action Research*, 22(2), 146–58.

Mohanty, C. T. (2003). *Feminism without Borders: Decolonizing Theory, Practicing Solidarity*. Durham, NC: Duke University Press.

Morgan, D. L. (2019). Commentary – After triangulation, what next? *Journal of Mixed Methods Research, 13*(1), 6–14.

Morgensen, S. L. (2012). Destabilizing the settler academy: The decolonial effects of Indigenous methodologies. *American Quarterly, 64*(4), 805–8.

Morrison, K. (2001). 'Randomised controlled trials for evidence-based education: Some problems in judging "What Works". *Evaluation and Research in Education, 15*(2): 69–83.

Morse, J. M. (2003). Principles of mixed methods and multimethod research design. In A. Tashakkori and C. Teddlie (eds), *Handbook of Mixed Methods in Social and Behavioral Research* (pp. 189–208). London: Sage.

Morse, J. M., and Niehaus, L. (2009). *Mixed Method Design: Principles and Procedures*. Walnut Creek, CA: Left Coast Press.

Mott, C., and Cockayne, D. (2017). Citation matters: Mobilizing the politics of citation toward a practice of 'conscientious engagement'. *Gender, Place and Culture, 24*(7), 954–73.

Mpinganjira, M. (2009). Comparative analysis of factors influencing the decision to study abroad. *African Journal of Business Management, 3*(8), 358–65.

Natow, R. S. (2020). The use of triangulation in qualitative studies employing elite interviews. *Qualitative Research, 20*(2), 160–73.

Nerlich, B. (2012). Between knotweed and the deep blue sky: Exploring the debate about the value of science. *Impact of Social Sciences Blog*. Available fromhttps://blogs.lse.ac.uk/impactofsocialsciences/2012/06/07/knotweed-rats-debate-value-science/. Accessed 10 March 2021.

Newkirk, T. (1996). Seduction and betrayal in qualitative research. In P. Mortensen and G. Kirsch (eds), *Ethics and Representation in Qualitative Studies of Literacy* (pp. 3–16). Urbana, IL: National Council of Teachers of English.

Newton, P., and Shaw, S. (2014). *Validity in Educational and Psychological Assessment*. London: Sage.

Nicklin, L. L. (2020). *An Ethnographic Exploration of Participant and Practitioner Perceptions of a Shakespeare-Focussed Prison Education Programme*. PhD thesis. University of York. England.

Nisbet, J. (1984). The changing scene. In W. B. Dockrell (ed.), *An Attitude of Mind: 25 Years of Educational Research in Scotland*. Edinburgh: Scottish Council for Research in Education.

Nisbet, J. (2005). What is educational research? Changing perspectives through the 20th century. *Research Papers in Education, 20*(1), 25–44.

O'Donnell, V. L., and Tobbell, J. (2007). The transition of adult students to higher education: Legitimate peripheral participation in a community of practice? *Adult Education Quarterly*, *57*(4), 312–28.

OECD (Organisation for Economic Co-operation and Development) (2009). *PISA Data Analysis Manual* (2nd edn). Paris: OECD.

Ofsted (2019). *Schools' Inspection Update January 2019 Special Edition*. London: HMSO. Available from https://assets.publishing.service.gov.uk/government/uploads/system/uploads/attachment_data/file/772056/School_inspection_update_-_January_2019_Special_Edition_180119.pdf. Accessed 28 May 2020.

O'Leary, Z. (2004). *The Essential Guide to Doing Research*. London: Sage.

Oliver, M. (1992). Changing the social relations of research production? *Disability, Handicap and Society*, *7*(2), 101–14.

Oliver, M. (1997). Emancipatory research: Realistic goal or impossible dream. *Doing Disability Research*, *2*, 15–31.

Open Science Collaboration (2015). Estimating the reproducibility of psychological science. *Science*, *349*(6251), 943–51.

Osborne, S. (2019, 12 February). Bolsonaro regime to remove Brazilian textbook references to feminism and homosexuality. *Independent Online*. Available from https://www.independent.co.uk/news/world/americas/brazil-jair-bolsonaro-school-textbook-feminism-homosexuality-lgbt-violence-women-a8775271.html. Accessed 15 March 2021.

Paat, Y. F. (2013). Working with immigrant children and their families: An application of Bronfenbrenner's ecological systems theory. *Journal of Human Behavior in the Social Environment*, *23*(8), 954–66.

Pacheco-Vega, R., and Parizeau, K. (2018). Doubly engaged ethnography: Opportunities and challenges when working with vulnerable communities. *International Journal of Qualitative Methods*, *17*(1), 1–13. DOI: 1609406918790653.

Padilla Peralta, D. (2020). *Darkness Visible: The Haunted House of Classics*. In 'All This Rising: The Humanities in the Next Ten Years'. Stanford University, 2 November 2020. Available from https://www.youtube.com/watch?v=sqbJl71H1t0.

Patel, L. (2016). *Decolonizing Educational Research*. Abingdon: Routledge.

Peim, N. (2018). *Thinking in Education Research: Applying Philosophy and Theory*. London: Bloomsbury.

Perry, L., and McConney, A. (2010). School socio-economic composition and student outcomes in Australia: Implications for educational policy. *Australian Journal of Education*, *54*(1), 72–85.

Phillips, R., and Kara, H. (2021). *Creative Writing for Social Research: A Practical Guide*. Bristol: Policy Press.

Pittas, E., and Nunes, T. (2017). Does children's dialect awareness support later reading and spelling in the standard language form? *Learning and Instruction 53*(2018), 1–9.

Platt, J. (1992). 'Case study' in American methodological thought. *Current Sociology, 40*(1), 17–48.

Popper, K. ([1963] 2002). *Conjectures and Refutations: The Growth of Scientific Knowledge*. Abingdon: Routledge.

Pratt, M. G. (2008). Fitting oval pegs into round holes: Tensions in evaluating and publishing qualitative research in top-tier North American journals. *Organizational Research Methods, 11*(3), 481–509.

Punch, K. (2014). *Introduction to Social Research* (3rd edn). London: Sage.

Punch, K. F. (1998). *Introduction to Social Research: Quantitative and Qualitative Approaches*. London: Sage.

Rapley, T. (2011). Some pragmatics of qualitative data analysis. In D. Silverman (ed.), *Qualitative Research* (pp. 273–290). London: SAGE.

Rasmussen, Kim (2004). Places for children – children's places. *Childhood, 11*(2): 155–73.

Reay, D. (2004). 'It's all becoming a habitus': Beyond the habitual use of habitus in educational research. *British Journal of Sociology of Education, 25*(4), 431–44.

Reay, D., and Wiliam, D. (1999). 'I'll be a nothing': Structure, agency and the construction of identity through assessment. *British Educational Research Journal, 25*(3), 343–54.

Reilly, P. R. (1987). Involuntary sterilization in the United States: A surgical solution. *Quarterly Review of Biology, 62*(2), 153–70.

Reilly, R. C. (2013). Found poems, member checking and crises of representation. *Qualitative Report, 18*, 30.

Renold, E. (2006). 'They won't let us play ... unless you're going out with one of them': Girls, boys and Butler's 'heterosexual matrix' in the primary years. *British Journal of Sociology of Education, 27*(4), 489–509.

Rice, J. M. (1898). *The Rational Spelling Book*. New York: American Book.

Richards, L. (2015). *Handling Qualitative Data: A Practical Guide* (3rd edn). London: Sage.

Richards, S., Clark, J. and Boggis, A. (2015). *Ethical Research with Children: Untold Narratives and Taboos*. London: Palgrave Macmillan.

Richardson, K. (2002). What IQ tests test. *Theory and Psychology, 12*(3), 283–314.

Robbins, J. H. (2008). *Connoisseurship, coursework and the credibility of teacher assessments, presentation at the Institute of Educational Assessors National Conference*, 3 May 2008. Available online at http://www.ciea.org.uk/news_and_events/events_listing/past_events/iea_national_conference_2008.aspx. Accessed 6 June 2011.

Robinson, K. (2006). *Do schools kill creativity?* TEDx Talk. Available from Do schools kill creativity? | Sir Ken Robinson.

Robson, C. (2002). *Real World Research: A Resource for Social Scientists and Practitioner-Researchers* (2nd edn). Oxford: Blackwell.

Rocco, T. S., and Plakhotnik, M. S. (2009). Literature reviews, conceptual frameworks, and theoretical frameworks: Terms, functions, and distinctions. *Human Resource Development Review*, 8(1), 120–30.

Rodgers, C. (2002). Defining reflection: Another look at John Dewey and reflective thinking. *Teachers College Record*, 104(4), 842–66.

Rodríguez, L. F., and Brown, T. M. (2009). From voice to agency: Guiding principles for participatory action research with youth. *New Directions for Youth Development*, 2009(123), 19–34.

Römer, U. (2004). Comparing real and ideal language learner input: The use of an EFL textbook corpus in corpus linguistics and language teaching. In G. Aston, S. Bernadini and D. Stewart (eds) *Corpora and Language Learners* (pp. 151–68). Amsterdam: John Benjamins.

Rose, H., and McKinley, J. (2018). Japan's English-medium instruction initiatives and the globalization of higher education. *Higher Education*, 75(1), 111–29.

Rossiter, K., Kontos, P., Colantonio, A., Gilbert, J., Gray, J. and Keightley, M. (2008). Staging data: Theatre as a tool for analysis and knowledge transfer in health research. *Social Science and Medicine*, 66(1), 130–46.

Roussel, S., Joulia, D., Tricot, A. and Sweller, J. (2017). Learning subject content through a foreign language should not ignore human cognitive architecture: A cognitive load theory approach. *Learning and Instruction*, 52, 69–79.

Rowe, M. B. (1972). *Wait-time and Rewards as Instructional Variables: Their Influence on Language, Logic and Fate Control.* Paper presented at the National Association for Research in Science Teaching, Chicago, IL, April 1972.

Rowe, M. B. (1974). Wait-time and rewards as instructional variables, their influence on language, logic and fate control. Part one. Wait-time. *Journal of Research in Science Teaching*, 11, 81–94.

Rowe, M. B. (1986). Wait time: Slowing down may be a way of speeding up! *Journal of Teacher Education*, 37, 43–50.

Ruggiero, J. A., and Johnson, K. (2009). Implications of recent research on Eastern European adoptees for social work practice. *Child and Adolescent Social Work Journal*, 26(6), 485–504.

Sackett, D. L. (1979). Bias in analytic research. *Journal of Chronic Diseases*, 32(1–2), 51–63.

Saini, A. (2019). *Superior: The Return of Race Science.* London: 4th Estate.

Saldaña, J. (2016). *The Coding Manual for Qualitative Researchers*. London: Sage.

Sandel, M. J. (2020). *The Tyranny of Merit: What's Become of the Common Good?* London: Allen Lane.

Schraw G., Olafson L. and VanderVeldt M. (2012). Epistemological development and learning. In N. M. Seel (ed.), *Encyclopedia of the Sciences of Learning*. Boston, MA: Springer. https://doi.org/10.1007/978-1-4419-1428-6_355.

Schugurensky, D. (2014). *Paulo Freire*. London: Bloomsbury.

Shadish, W. R., Clark, M. H. and Steiner, P. M. (2008). Can nonrandomized experiments yield accurate answers? A randomized experiment comparing random and nonrandom assignments. *Journal of the American Statistical Association*, *103*(484), 1334–44.

Sharp, J. G., Bowker, R. and Byrne, J. (2008). VAK or VAK-uous? Towards the trivialisation of learning and the death of scholarship. *Research Papers in Education*, *23*(3), 293–314.

Sharra, S. (2009). Towards an African peace epistemology: Teacher autobiography and uMunthu in Malawian education. In D. M. Caracciolo and A. M. Mungai (eds), *In the Spirit of Ubuntu* (pp. 23–38). Rotterdam: Sense.

Shoda, Y., Mischel, W., and Peake, P. K. (1990). Predicting adolescent cognitive and self-regulatory competencies from preschool delay of gratification: Identifying diagnostic conditions. *Developmental psychology*, *26*(6), 978–86.

Sieber, J. E., and Tolich, M. B. (2013). *Planning Ethically Responsible Research* (2nd edn). Sage.

Silberzahn, R., Uhlmann, E. L., Martin, D. P., Anselmi, P., Aust, F., Awtrey, E., ... and Nosek, B. A. (2018). Many analysts, one data set: Making transparent how variations in analytic choices affect results. *Advances in Methods and Practices in Psychological Science*, *1*(3), 337–56.

Simon, G. (2018). Eight criteria for quality in systemic practitioner research. *Murmurations: Journal of Transformative Systemic Practice*, *1*(2), 40–62.

Simpson, L. R. (2004). Anticolonial strategies for the recovery and maintenance of Indigenous knowledge. *American Indian Quarterly*, *28*(3/4) 373–84.

Skocpol, T. (2003). Doubly engaged social science: The promise of comparative historical analysis. In J. Mahoney and D. Rueschemeyer (eds), *Comparative Historical Analysis in the Social Sciences* (pp. 407–28). Cambridge: Cambridge University Press.

Smagorinsky, P. (2008). The method section as conceptual epicenter in constructing social science research reports. *Written Communication*, *25*(3), 389–411.

Smagorinsky, P. (2011). Vygotsky's stage theory: The psychology of art and the actor under the direction of Perezhivanie. *Mind, Culture, and Activity* *18*(4): 319–41.

Smith, C. A., and Garrett-Scott, D. (2021). 'We are not named': Black women and the politics of citation in anthropology. In *Feminist Anthropology*. Online first, pp. 1–20.

Smith, S. U., Hayes, S. and Shea, P. (2017). A critical review of the use of Wenger's Community of Practice (CoP) theoretical framework in online and blended learning research, 2000–2014. *Online Learning*, *21*(1), 209–37.

Snelson, C., Wertz, C. I., Onstott, K. and Bader, J. (2017). Using World of Warcraft to teach research methods in online doctoral education: A student-instructor duoethnography. *The Qualitative Report*, *22*(5), 1–20.

Sparkes, A. C. (2000). Autoethnography and narratives of self: Reflections on criteria in action. *Sociology of Sport Journal*, *17*(1), 21–43.

Spencer, L., Ritchie, J., Ormston, R., O'Connor, W. and Barnard, M. (2014). Analysis: Principles and processes. In J. Ritchie, J. Lewis, C. McNaughton Nicholls and R. Ormston (eds), *Qualitative Research Practice* (2nd edn, pp. 269–93). London: Sage.

Steinhauer, E. (2002). Thoughts on an Indigenous research methodology. *Canadian Journal of Native Education*, *26*(2), 69.

Sterling, T. D., Rosenbaum, W. L. and Weinkam, J. J. (1995). Publication decisions revisited: The effect of the outcome of statistical tests on the decision to publish and vice-versa. *American Statistician*, *49*, 108–12.

Stovall, D., and Delgado, N. (2009). 'Knowing the ledge': Participatory action research as legal studies for urban high school youth. *New Directions for Youth Development*, *2009*(123), 67–81.

Strand, S. (2014). Ethnicity, gender, social class and achievement gaps at age 16: Intersectionality and 'getting it' for the white working class. *Research Papers in Education*, *29*(2), 131–71.

Sukarieh, M., and Tannock, S. (2019). Subcontracting academia: Alienation, exploitation and disillusionment in the UK overseas Syrian refugee research industry. *Antipode*, *51*(2), 664–80.

Sundaram, V., and Sauntson, H. (2016). Discursive silences: Using critical linguistic and qualitative analysis to explore the continued absence of pleasure in sex and relationships education in England. *Sex Education*, *16*(3), 240–54.

Swalwell, K., and Sinclair, K. (2020). The appeal of a controversial text: Who uses a People's history of the United States in the US history classroom and why. *Journal of Social Studies Research*, *45*(2), 84–100.

Sweller, J. (1988). Cognitive load during problem solving: Effects on learning. *Cognitive Science*, *12*(2), 257–85.

Syed, M., and Nelson, S. C. (2015). Guidelines for establishing reliability when coding narrative data. *Emerging Adulthood, 3*(6), 375–87.

Sylva, K., Melhuish, E., Sammons, P., Siraj-Blatchford, I. and Taggart, B. (2004). *The Effective Provision of Pre-School Education (EPPE) Project: Final Report: A Longitudinal Study Funded by the DfES 1997-2004.* Institute of Education, University of London/Department for Education and Skills/Sure Start.

Takayama, K. (2009). Globalizing critical studies of 'official' knowledge: Lessons from the Japanese history textbook controversy over 'comfort women'. *British Journal of Sociology of Education, 30*(5), 577–89.

Takeda, A. (2013). Reflexivity: Unmarried Japanese male interviewing married Japanese women about international marriage. *Qualitative Research, 13*(3), 285–98.

Te Aika, L. H., and Greenwood, J. (2009). Ko tātou te rangahau, ko te rangahau, ko tātou: A Māori approach to participatory action research. In *Education, Participatory Action Research, and Social Change* (pp. 59–72). New York: Palgrave Macmillan.

Teddlie, C., and Sammons, P. (2010). Applications of mixed methods to the field of educational effectiveness research. In B. P. M. Creemers, L. Kyriakides and P. Sammons (eds), *Methodological Advances in Educational Effectiveness Research* (pp. 115–53). London: Routledge.

Teddlie, C., and Tashakkori, A. (2009). *Foundations of Mixed Methods Research: Integrating Quantitative and Qualitative Approaches in the Social and Behavioral Sciences.* London: Sage.

Temple, B., and Edwards, R. (2002). Interpreters/translators and cross-language research: Reflexivity and border crossings. *International Journal of Qualitative Methods, 1*(2), 1–12.

Thein, A. H. (2018). Beyond the personal and the individual: Reconsidering the role of emotion in literature learning. In A. Goodwyn, C. Durrant, L. Reid and L. Scherff (eds), *International Perspectives on the Teaching of Literature in Schools: Global Principles and Practices* (pp. 55–67). London: Routledge/NATE.

Thomas, K., Hardy, R. D., Lazrus, H., Mendez, M., Orlove, B., Rivera-Collazo, I. ... and Winthrop, R. (2019). Explaining differential vulnerability to climate change: A social science review. *Wiley Interdisciplinary Reviews: Climate Change, 10*(2), e565.

Thorndike, E. L. (1920). The constant error in psychological ratings. *Journal of Applied Psychology, 4,* 25–9.

Tuhiwai Smith, L. (1999). *Decolonizing Methodologies: Research and Indigenous Peoples.* London: Zed Books.

Tuhiwai Smith, L. (2005). Building a research agenda for indigenous epistemologies and education. *Anthropology and Education Quarterly*, *36*(1), 93–5.

Tuhiwai Smith, L. (2019). Revisiting 'Insiders' and 'Outsiders' in Indigenous Research. In L., Tuhiwai Smith, E. Tuck and K. W. Yangand (eds), *Indigenous and Decolonizing Studies in Education* (pp. 12–13). Abingdon: Routledge.

Tuhiwai Smith, L., Tuck, E. and Yang, K. W. (eds) (2019). *Indigenous and Decolonizing Studies in Education*. Abingdon: Routledge.

Torres, A. C. (2014). 'Are we architects or construction workers?' Re-examining teacher autonomy and turnover in charter schools. *Education Policy Analysis Archives*, *22*(124), 1–26.

Tuck, E. (2019a). Writing to one another. In L. Tuhiwai Smith, E. Tuck and K. W. Yang (eds), *Indigenous and Decolonizing Studies in Education* (p. 5). Abingdon: Routledge.

Tuck, E. (2019b). Locating our work in education, when it might have had a home in other fields. In L. Tuhiwai Smith, E. Tuck and K. W. Yang (eds), *Indigenous and Decolonizing Studies in Education* (pp. 8–10). Abingdon: Routledge.

Tuck, E. (2019c). Losing patience for the task of convincing settlers to pay attention to indigenous ideas. In Tuhiwai Smith, Tuck and Yang (eds), *Indigenous and Decolonizing Studies in Education* (pp. 13–16). Abingdon: Routledge.

Tuck, E., and Yang, K. W. (2012). Decolonization is not a metaphor. *Decolonization: Indigeneity, Education and Society*, *1*(1), 1–40.

Tuhiwai Smith, L. (1999). *Decolonizing Methodologies: Research and Indigenous. Peoples*. London: Zed Books.

Tuhiwai Smith, L. (2019). Revisiting 'Insiders' and 'Outsiders' in Indigenous Research. In L. Tuhiwai Smith, E. Tuck and K. W. Yang (eds), *Indigenous and Decolonizing Studies in Education* (pp. 12–13). Abingdon: Routledge.

Tuhiwai Smith, L., Tuck, E. and Yang, K. W. (eds) (2019). *Indigenous and Decolonizing Studies in Education*. Abingdon: Routledge.

Tusting, K., McCulloch, S., Bhatt, I., Hamilton, M. and Barton, D. (2019). *Academics Writing: The Dynamics of Knowledge Creation*. Abingdon: Routledge.

Tversky, A., and Kahneman, D. (1974). Judgement under uncertainty: Heuristics and biases. *Science*, *185*, 1124–31.

Vallett, D. B., Lamb, R. and Annetta, L. (2018). After-school and informal STEM projects: The effect of participant self-selection. *Journal of Science Education and Technology*, *27*(3), 248–55.

Venkatesh, S. (2009). *Gang Leader for a Day*. London: Penguin UK.

von der Fehr, A., Sølberg, J. and Bruun, J. (2018). Validation of networks derived from snowball sampling of municipal science education actors. *International Journal of Research and Method in Education*, *41*(1), 38–52.

Vygotsky, L. S. (1976). Play and its role in the mental development of the child. In J. Bruner, A. Jolly and K. Sylva (eds), *Play: Its Role in Development and Evolution* (pp. 537–54). Harmondsworth: Penguin Books.

Vygotsky, L. S. (1978). *Mind in Society*. Cambridge, MA: Harvard University Press.

Wagenmakers, E. J., Wetzels, R., Borsboom, D., van der Maas, H. L. and Kievit, R. A. (2012). An agenda for purely confirmatory research. *Perspectives on Psychological Science*, *7*(6), 632–8.

Wagner, D., and Herbel-Eisenmann, B. (2008). 'Just don't': The suppression and invitation of dialogue in the mathematics classroom. *Educational Studies in Mathematics*, *67*(2), 143–57.

Wahba, M. A., and Bridwell, L. G. (1976). Maslow reconsidered: A review of research on the need hierarchy theory. *Organizational Behavior and Human Performance*, *15*(2): 212–40.

Walford, G. (2001). *Doing Qualitative Educational Research: A Personal Guide to the Research Process*. London: Continuum.

Walford, G. (2012). Researching the powerful in education: A re-assessment of the problems. *International Journal of Research and Method in Education*, *35*(2): 111–18.

Walter, M., and Andersen, C. (2016). *Indigenous statistics: A Quantitative Research Methodology*. Abingdon: Routledge.

Watermeyer, R. (2016). Impact in the REF: Issues and obstacles. *Studies in Higher Education*, *41*(2), 199–214.

Watts, T. W., Duncan, G. J. and Quan, H. (2018). Revisiting the marshmallow test: A conceptual replication investigating links between early delay of gratification and later outcomes. *Psychological Science*, *29*(7), 1159–77.

Welch, Shay (2019). Native epistemology and embodied cognitive theory. In *The Phenomenology of a Performative Knowledge System* (pp. 53–89). Cham: Palgrave Macmillan.

Wenger, E. (1998). *Communities of Practice: Learning, Meaning, and Identity*. New York: Cambridge University Press.

Westbrook, J. H. (1960). Identifying significant research. *Science*, *132*(3435), 1229–34.

Whetung, M., and Wakefield, S. (2019). Colonial convention: Institutionalized research relationships and decolonizing research ethics. In L. Tuhiwai Smith, E. Tuck and K. W. Yang (eds), *Indigenous and Decolonizing Studies in Education* (pp. 146–58). Abingdon: Routledge.

White, J. (2020). *Terraformed: Young Black Lives in the Inner City.* London: Repeater.

White, P. (2013). Who's afraid of research questions? The neglect of research questions in the methods literature and a call for question-led methods teaching. *International Journal of Research and Method in Education,* 36(3), 213–27.

Wiliam, D. (1998). 'The validity of teachers' assessments', paper presented at the 22nd annual conference of the International Group for the Psychology of Mathematics Education, Stellenbosch, South Africa. Available from http://learn.shorelineschools.org/spec/wasl/documents/wiliam_validity_of_teachers_assessments.pdf. Accessed 6 July 2011.

Willis, P. (1978). *Learning to Labour: How Working Class Kids Get Working Class Jobs.* Farnborough: Saxon House.

Wilson, A., and Laing, M. (2019). Queering Indigenous education. In L. Tuhiwai Smith, E. Tuck and K. W. Yang (eds), *Indigenous and Decolonizing Studies in Education* (pp. 131–45). Abingdon: Routledge.

Wilson, S. (2008). *Research Is Ceremony: Indigenous Research Methods.* New York: Fernwood.

Wodak, R. (2014). Critical discourse analysis. In C. Leung, and B. Street (eds), *The Routledge Companion to English Studies* (pp. 302–16). London: Routledge.

Woodcock, S., and Reupert, A. (2012). A cross-sectional study of student teachers' behaviour management strategies throughout their training years. *The Australian Educational Researcher,* 39(2), 159–172.

Woolgar, S. E. (1988). *Knowledge and Reflexivity: New Frontiers in the Sociology of Knowledge.* London: Sage.

Worth, E. (2019). Women, education and social mobility in Britain during the long 1970s. *Cultural and Social History,* 16(1), 6783.

Xerri, D. (2018). Two methodological challenges for teacher-researchers: Reflexivity and trustworthiness. *The Clearing House: A Journal of Educational Strategies, Issues and Ideas,* 91(1), 37–41.

Yanar, Z. M., Fazli, M., Rahman, J. and Farthing, R. (2016). Research ethics committees and participatory action research with young people: The politics of voice. *Journal of Empirical Research on Human Research Ethics,* 11(2), 122–8.

Yin, R. K. (2018). *Case Study Research: Design and Methods* (6th edn). Thousand Oaks: Sage.

Young, M. (2009). Education, globalisation and the 'voice of knowledge'. *Journal of Education and Work,* 22(3), 193–204.

Younge, G. (2020). *Who Are We? How Identity Politics Took over the World.* London: Penguin.

Index

a priori analysis 104–7
Action Research 38
alignment 26–8
anonymity 131–6
anti-racism 146–7
Arts-based research 40–1, 77
assent 130, 139
attainment gap 5, 9, 65, 122
axiology 25–6

behaviourism 4, 7, 50–1
bias 43, 44, 47–9
Biesta, Giert 15, 72, 82
Blackfeet Nation 58–9
Bloom's taxonomy 72
blue skies research 123–4
Bourdieu, Pierre 65, 101–2, 149
bread-eating 3
Bronfenbrenner, Urie 47, 75–6
Bruner, Jerome 41, 61–2, 66–7
Butler, Judith 147–8

capital 65, 102, 149
case study 45–7, 84
causality 15
certainty of knowledge 16, 18
cherry-picking 49
child participants 130–1
citation 148–53
citational ethics 151
climate change 128–9
coding 105–7, 115–16
cognitive dissonance 74, 152
cognitive load theory 78

cohort study 37
colonization 86
Communities of Practice 78, 108–9
concept 70–80
conceptual framework 81
Connell, Raewyn 22, 23
consent 130, 136–9, 139–41
constructivist 10, 14, 27, 59
convenience sampling 44
Conversation Analysis 34, 41, 60
creative approaches 40–1, 117–19
Crenshaw, Kimberlé Williams 76–7, 154–5
Critical Race Theory 77, 154–5
critical realism 14, 16
cross-sectional designs 38
cultural capital 65, 102
cultural hegemony 28–9, 144

data as constructed 59–62
data sources 41–4
deception 136–7
decolonization 23, 85, 90, 129
Decolonizing Methodologies 129
deductive analysis 105
Dewey, John 10–11
disciplines 5–7
disclosure 133–4
documents as data 60
double-consciousness 21
Du Bois, W. E. B. 20–1
Dweck, Carol 8, 64

ecological systems theory 75–6, 78, 83
education debt 5

elite interviews 61, 91, 107, 133, 158
emancipatory research 155-6
embodied knowledge 40
embodiment 87-90
emergent analysis 104-7
epistemic authority 19, 20, 53-4
epistemicide 22
epistemological beliefs 16, 18, 21, 27
epistemology 13, 15-19
- Indigenous epistemologies 23-4
- standpoint epistemology 20
ethnomethodoloy 34
evidence-based practice 62-5
experimental designs 38
extractive reading 159-60

Fanon, Frantz 85-6, 154
Figured Worlds 78
Foucault, Michel 98, 121
found poetry 108, 117
Freire, Paulo 80-1, 142, 153-4

Gardner, Howard 119-20
gatekeepers 139, 159
Gender Trouble 147
generalisability 49-50
Gillick competence 130
Gramsci, Antonio 28-9, 144
Grand Theory 76-8
Grounded Theory 34, 38, 43
growth mindset 8, 64

habitus 101
halo effect 125
hegemony 28-9
hidden curriculum 144
hierarchy of needs 58-9
hooks, bell 96, 142, 157

impact 122-5
implementation research 65
imputation 47-8, 132

incentives 127
indigenous communities 126-9
Indigenous epistemologies *see* epistemology
inductive analysis 105
insider research 96, 111
internet-based research 93-4
interpretivism 16, 24, 115
intersectionality 76-7, 150
intervention studies 38

justification for knowing 16, 19

Kendi, Ibram X. 146-7

Ladson-Billings, Gloria 5
land 14-15, 83, 90
language 111-13, 144
Lave, Jean 78, 108-9, 149
Learning to Labour 7-8
listening 140
longitudinal studies 37

marginalization 96, 150
marshmallow test 56-7
Maslow, Abraham 58-9
McIntyre, Donald 63
member checking 107-8
messy data 84
methodolatry 34
metrics 4, 122
middle-range theory 78
Milgram experiment 136-7
misalignment 26-8
mixed methods 36-7
MMORPG's 9
moral injury 152
multiple intelligences 119-20

narrative research 41, 61-2
natural experiments 38

nerve toxin 3
nested case study 47

objectivist 14, 15, 16
observer effect 89
ontology 13, 14–15
origins of knowledge 16, 19

p hacking 104–5
panopticon 98
paradigm shift 71
paradigm wars 16
Participatory Action Research 38, 40, 50, 99–100, 134–5
Pedagogy of Hope 142
Pedagogy of the Oppressed 80-1, 153–4
Piaget, Jean 39
place 90–4
policy borrowing 49
politicized bodies 100, 147
positionality 94–7
positivism 14, 16, 25, 27, 47, 59, 65, 155
post-positivism 16
power 130–1, 135, 143
power dynamics 91
powerful knowledge 29
practical theorizing 63
practitioner research 7, 98–9, 133, 138
pragmatism 25–6, 27
probability sampling 42
publication bias 49
purposive sampling 42–3

quantification 4
quasi-experimental designs 38

random sampling 42
rapport 89, 139–41
RCT 65–6, 123
reciprocal appropriation 26
reflexivity 94–7
refugees 127–8

registered reports 49
relational 14, 18, 26, 70, 85, 128
reliability 55–6, 109–11
replicability 56–7
representational nature of data 61
research questions 32–4
research design 31, 34–9
research friendship 134
retroductability 57–8
rigour 47, 54

sampling 41–4
saturation 43
scaffolding 66–7
selection 41–2, 47–8
significance (statistical) 59
Siksika 58–9
simplicity of knowledge 16, 18–19
Skinner, B. F. 4, 50–1
smash and grab 149
Smith, Linda Tuhiwai *see* Tuhiwai Smith, Linda
snowball sampling 44
social acceptability bias 48, 140
social reproduction 8
socio-cultural activity theory 44
Southern Theory 22, 23
spiral curriculum 67
Spivak, Gayatri Chakravorty 113–14
Stanford Prison Experiment 137–8
status anxiety 6, 25, 40
Stenhouse, Lawrence 7
stigmatized behaviours 141
stratified sampling 42
subaltern 113–14
surveillance 98
systematic reviews 63–4

taxonomy 72
teacher-researcher 7
Teaching to Transgress 142
Tearoom trade 137

textbooks 144
theoretical framework 81–3
theoretical sampling 42, 43
theory 69–85, 153–4
theory as carpentry 72
transferability 49–50
translation 111–13
triangulation 36, 61
trustworthiness 47
Tuck, E. 23
Tuhiwai Smith, Linda 71, 96, 129

unit of analysis 104

validity 54–5
vignettes 132
visual data 60–1, 92
voice to the voiceless 157–8
vulnerable participants 130
vulnerable populations 126–9
Vygotsky, Lev 8, 44–5, 79

walking interviews 92
Wenger, Etienne 78, 108–9

ZPD 8, 45, 67

www.ingramcontent.com/pod-product-compliance
Ingram Content Group UK Ltd.
Pitfield, Milton Keynes, MK11 3LW, UK
UKHW022203150125
453704UK00003B/39